The Transforma
Rural Scotland

Social Change and the Agrarian Economy, 1660–1815

T. M. DEVINE

JOHN DONALD PUBLISHERS LTD
EDINBURGH

John Donald Publishers Ltd
Unit 8, Canongate Venture, 5 New Street,
Edinburgh, EH8 8BH

Typeset in Lasercomp Times Roman
by ROM-Data Corporation Ltd, Falmouth, and
printed and bound in Great Britain
by Redwood Books, Trowbridge, Wiltshire

A CIP record for this book is available from the British
Library

ISBN 0 85976 507 5

JOHN R. STEPHEN.

Contents

Preface

IN the later decades of the seventeenth century Scotland was a relatively poor and underdeveloped country on the periphery of Europe. Around 100 years later it was in the throes of an extraordinary and remarkable transformation which laid the basis for the nation's world economic pre-eminence in the Victorian era. Two aspects of this 'great leap forward', the Industrial Revolution and the Highland Clearances, have been much studied. But a third and vitally important dimension, the process of transition in the rural lowlands from peasant to capitalist agriculture, has attracted less attention in recent years. In a sense, it was the most fundamental development of all. In the early years of the eighteenth century, at least eight out of ten Scots lived on the land and were employed in agriculture or related activities. The majority of them stayed in the Lowlands. Furthermore, urbanisation and industrialisation could not have developed as rapidly if the agrarian system had not been able to supply the foods and many of the raw materials for the growing manufacturing centres at acceptable prices.

There can be no doubt of the intrinsic importance of the lowland rural economy and society to the overall evolution of Scotland in its great age of material advancement and cultural change. General assessments are available from the pens of J. A. Symon and James Handley, but these can be criticised for an over-reliance on the abundant 'improving' literature of the later eighteenth century and a too easy acceptance of some of its conclusions. In the 1940s and 1950s valuable papers on landscape change were published by such historical geographers as J. H. G. Lebon and Betty Third. More recently, R. A. Dodgshon and Ian Whyte have produced substantial studies from a geographical perspective of agrarian economic and social change in the seventeenth and early eighteenth centuries, while Malcolm Gray has traced some of the social effects of the commercialisation of agriculture in the decades after *c*. 1760 on the basis of contemporary printed sources. Thus far, however, no sustained examination has appeared of the entire process of economic and social change in the rural lowlands which covers the period from the later seventeenth to the early nineteenth centuries.

It is not claimed that this volume is such a comprehensive study. Its aims are much more modest. A fuller understanding of the dynamics and social impact of agrarian development in the Lowlands requires a series of regional and local analyses. The complexity and spatial diversity of eighteenth-century farming systems ensured that generalisations based on one area cannot easily be applied to another. The conclusions of this study derive primarily from a systematic evaluation of landed, legal and government records relating to the counties of Ayr, Lanark, Fife and Angus: for the most part, little reference is made to the Borders, the Lothians or the north-east counties. These four lowland counties varied significantly in agrarian emphasis, farm size, terrain, climate and access to large markets, and it is hoped that they can be regarded as representative of the experience of agrarian change in most of the lowland region, from the south-west to the fringes of the north-east zone. Within each county, the estates examined in depth have been selected with some care to ensure that the lands of aristocratic grandees, medium-sized lairds and lesser gentlemen have all been included. It must be emphasised that the arguments advanced depend for the most part on an examination of sources confined to the study area. Others in due course may wish to determine whether they have any application elsewhere.

This work could not have been carried out without the financial help of the Economic and Social Research Council (R000231506). The Council's generous support enabled me to employ consecutively two excellent research assistants, Willie Orr and Peter Clapham. Both carried out their duties with exemplary patience, care and ingenuity. Peter bore the brunt of the work and I am especially grateful to him for the central contribution he has made to this volume. The award of a British Academy/Leverhulme Trust Senior Research Fellowship to me in 1992–3 expedited the completion of the project and enabled this book to be written. That it has appeared so quickly is mainly due to the efficiency of two first-class typists, Mrs Alison Armour and Mrs Jean Fraser. I am especially grateful to Mrs Fraser for her effective organisation of the tabular material.

TOM DEVINE

Abbreviations

Ayrshire Arch. and Nat. Hist. Colls	*Ayrshire Archaeological and Natural History Collections*
Econ. Hist. Rev.	*Economic History Review*
HPL	Hamilton Public Library
NLS	National Library of Scotland
NRA(S)	National Register of Archives (Scotland)
OSA	*The Statistical Account of Scotland*, familiarly known as the *Old Statistical Account*
Scott. Hist. Rev.	*Scottish Historical Review*
SGM	*Scottish Geographical Magazine*
SRO	Scottish Record Office
TIBG	*Transactions of the Institute of British Geographers*
£	£ sterling

List of Maps Figures and Tables

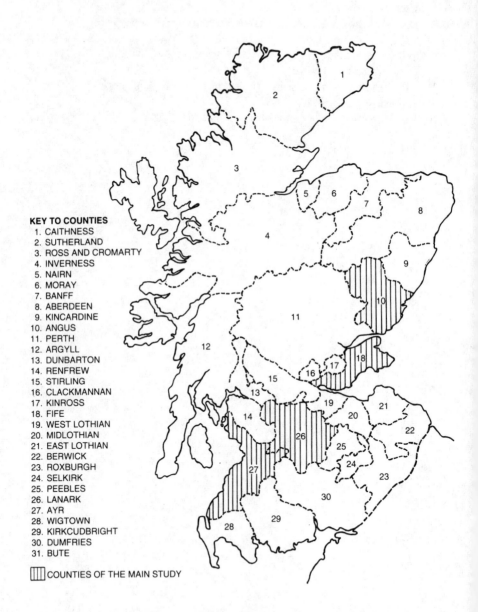

KEY TO COUNTIES
 1. CAITHNESS
 2. SUTHERLAND
 3. ROSS AND CROMARTY
 4. INVERNESS
 5. NAIRN
 6. MORAY
 7. BANFF
 8. ABERDEEN
 9. KINCARDINE
10. ANGUS
11. PERTH
12. ARGYLL
13. DUNBARTON
14. RENFREW
15. STIRLING
16. CLACKMANNAN
17. KINROSS
18. FIFE
19. WEST LOTHIAN
20. MIDLOTHIAN
21. EAST LOTHIAN
22. BERWICK
23. ROXBURGH
24. SELKIRK
25. PEEBLES
26. LANARK
27. AYR
28. WIGTOWN
29. KIRKCUDBRIGHT
30. DUMFRIES
31. BUTE

COUNTIES OF THE MAIN STUDY

MAP A   Counties of the main study

KEY
1. GALSTON
2. CATRINE
3. DALMELLINGTON
4. BLANTYRE
5. HAMILTON
6. LARKHALL
7. LANARK
8. CARSTAIRS
9. BIGGAR
10. DOUGLAS
11. PEEBLES
12. LINLITHGOW
13. CUPAR
14. KIRRIEMUIR

- - - - - FORTH – CLYDE CANAL

MAP B   Some locations and waterways

1

The Old Order

Rural Social Patterns in the Lowlands in the Later Seventeenth Century

I

UNTIL comparatively recently, Scotland, in the period before the Union of Parliaments, was often depicted as a society of feud, poverty, economic backwardness and religious intolerance. Over the last two or three decades, however, this negative interpretation has in large part been replaced by a more sympathetic and positive response by historians. Scotland in the later seventeenth century is no longer defined solely in terms of the Massacre of Glencoe, the failure of the Darien expedition, the 'Ill Years' of the 1690s and the bloody Covenanter wars known as the 'Killing Times'. Instead, much revisionist writing has stressed the economic advances of these decades, the continuities between Scotland before and after the Union, and the social and cultural changes which were developing before 1707 and which established a basis for the more spectacular progress of the eighteenth century.[1]

A number of interrelated forces were at work in rural society. The second half of the seventeenth century saw the death of feudalism in the Lowlands. Military land tenures, such as wardship, were in decay. The houses of the landed élite now demonstrated less of a concern for defence and more an enthusiasm for domestic comfort and aesthetic satisfaction. No fortified dwellings were built in the rural Lowlands after the 1660s. The castle and the tower were giving way to the country house. In the Lowlands this was the time of that momentous change in the attitude and function of the British landed class defined by R. H. Tawney, the period when the lairds started to become less concerned with military power and alliance and more interested in the profit and economy of their estates. Land was increasingly seen by many as an asset to be exploited rather than as simply the basis of personal authority and family power.

There were numerous manifestations of this crucial shift in élite priorities.[2] At the national level, the Scottish Parliament, itself dominated by the landed interest, passed two famous Acts in 1695, facilitating the consolidation of lands lying in runrig and the division of commonties. Little of this revolutionary legislation had an immediate impact. Indeed, the new legal context was not effectively exploited in widespread and systematic fashion until the second half of the eighteenth century.[3] Nevertheless, the fact that such measures could be passed reflected the new concerns of the Scottish governing class in the earlier period. The tendency to provide more written leases of longer duration for tenants and to establish more local marketing centres, such as burghs of barony, were further examples of this developing interest. Cost pressures were increasing for Scottish landowners in these decades. The 'Revolution in Manners' of the eighteenth century was still in the future but domestic accounts for the later seventeenth century indicate growing purchases of clothing, furniture and paintings, and increased spending on building and travel.[4] The new concern with the economic potential of landed estates was in large part a direct result of these rising levels of expenditure. Landed property had to be made to yield more cash income.

The capacity of the rural economy to produce this has also been addressed in recent scholarship. Traditionally, Scottish agriculture before the era of Improvement in the eighteenth century has had a bad press. It was seen as inert in structure, primitive in technique and wasteful both of land and labour.[5] It is now recognised, however, that much of this criticism reflected the views of the 'improving' writers of the later eighteenth century. They had a vested interest in demonstrating the weaknesses of the old order and praising the excellence of the new. They were propagandists for the new agriculture and tended to select their evidence skilfully to advance their case. In addition, they were commenting from the perspective of a time when the entire rural economy was shifting to production for the booming urban and industrial centres of the Lowlands. It was inevitable that the earlier system, in which the market sector was a growing but still relatively small enclave, would suffer by comparison. The improving writers also saw the individual farm under the control of a single master as the prime agency of economic advance. Only thus could ambition and initiative be released. The old order, where communal practice was widespread, was – not surprisingly – perceived as conservative, inflexible and rigid.[6]

Modern scholarship has gone a long way to rehabilitate the rural economy in the era before improvement. There have been two parallel developments. First, the bias in much improving writing has been recognised and an effort made to understand the old system within its own terms rather than by the standards of a later and quite different type of society. Second, most recent work has depended on the sifting of original material from the seventeenth century. A start has been made on the exploration of the many collections of estate archives which survive for that period and the research results have then been combined with records of church and state.

The conclusion which is emerging as a result of the enquiries completed to date is that the older agrarian economy was more successful than previously thought. The disasters of the 'Lean Years' in the last decade of the seventeenth century were unprecedented and untypical. They did not reflect the normal condition. Severe crop failure was not unique to Scotland in the 1690s. On the contrary, almost all countries with the exception of England were badly hit, with France and some neighbouring states experiencing a huge increase in mortality which could be estimated in millions. When weather conditions were more benign, the rural economy functioned relatively well. It satisfied the basic criterion of success by feeding the Scottish people in most years.[7] A century earlier, in the period 1560–1600, harvest failure and high grain prices afflicted Scotland to a greater or lesser extent in about one-third of the years between the Reformation and the Union of the Crowns in 1603.[8] The contrast a century later could not have been more dramatic. Widespread dearth only occurred in 1674–5 and more acutely in 1695–9. Placed in context, therefore, the 'Lean Years' appear as a freak, a natural climatic catastrophe with savage demographic effects which were unusual and ephemeral. Indeed, contemporary comment in the decades before the crisis showed more concern with the problem of glut and oversupply in the grain markets, a difficulty confirmed by the trends in prices which can be traced from local areas.[9] This anxiety quickly affected public regulation. In the years before the Union there was a basic change in the traditional policy of the state to the national supply of grain. Legislation altered from historic protection of the grain consumer to vigorous support for the grain producer. This first became apparent in the prohibition of grain imports in 1671 and was further consolidated in legislation of 1695 providing bounties on corn exports.[10]

The explanation for this growing stability in grain supplies is still imperfectly understood. Weather conditions in the later seventeenth century were probably better in most decades than a century earlier. There could also have been a reduction in demographic pressure as a result of the plague crises of the seventeenth century.[11] In addition, however, the possibility that an increasing supply of grain and stock came about because of changes in agrarian organisation and technique cannot be ignored. Adjustment in cultivation practices have been well documented.[12] The traditional Scottish system involved the division of cultivated acreage into two parts: the infield and the outfield. The infield was the best land, was worked continuously and gained most from such manure and fertiliser as was available. Outside favoured areas, the outfield was normally the more extensive and was cultivated for shorter periods and more intermittently. It was indispensable to the functioning of the infield as its major source of manure. These structures were far from static. On some estates outfields were being brought up to infield standards by the liberal application of lime. Increasingly, outfield as well as infield was manured by the folding or 'tathing' of stock in specific areas sequentially. There is also evidence of an increased marketing of grain and stock. In the Borders, the creation of larger sheep and cattle farms was causing the kind of social displacement characteristic of the Highland Clearances more than 150 years later. In pastoral areas of lowland Scotland principal rents were being converted to money by 1700, though in most arable districts rental paid in kind remained the norm. Similarly, the expansion of single, consolidated tenancies in some regions suggests the desire of landlords to establish more farms on their estates capable of producing regular surpluses for market. These limited changes in technique and organisation were probably enough to stabilise food supply. In this period, Scotland was an economy where at least eight out of ten of the population lived and worked in a rural setting. The overwhelming majority in the society were food producers as well as food consumers. Even modest improvements in efficiency or in marketing could quickly result in increased surplus.

II

The achievement of recent research has, therefore, been to present the old agrarian economy in a more positive light and to demonstrate its flexibility and capacity for change. The structure of rural society, which is the main emphasis of the present volume, has attracted less attention, though inevitably contributions to agricultural history *per se* do cast considerable light on the social framework.[13] The orientation of this book is towards an analysis of the radical social changes which took place in the countryside in the eighteenth century. If those momentous alterations in the fabric of society are to be fully understood, however, they need to be seen against the background of earlier structures. It is especially important to determine, however briefly, the impact of rural economic change on social organisations and relationships in the later seventeenth century.

Fortunately, sources exist for the period which can cast considerable light on these and other topics. Estate records present difficulties for the social historian despite their obvious value for many purposes. They primarily document the activities of the leaseholding tenants who paid rental. Normally, those below that class are absent although the sub-tenants, cottars and servants comprised the majority of the rural population in this period. The main alternative to the estate archive, often providing information on these other groups, were the poll tax returns for the 1690s. In that decade three different taxes were authorised by Parliament: in 1693, 1695 and 1698.[14] The last was confined to those of higher social status but the other two produced returns which cover entire social strata. The material is, of course, far from perfect and the returns are not comprehensive. The poor were almost always omitted from the poll lists as were children over the age of sixteen. Cheating was clearly possible and highly likely as some individuals tried to reduce their poll by claiming to be worth less than they really were. The social categories applied by parish collectors were not consistent. This especially applies to those below the rank of tenant. Above all, however, there is the problem that hardly any poll tax records have actually survived. The only comprehensive return is for Aberdeenshire and it is hardly surprising that it has attracted most scholarly analysis, especially since the data were published in two volumes by the Spalding Club in the 1840s.[15] However, poll tax lists are also available in

the Scottish Record Office for Renfrewshire (also published) and for many
parishes in Midlothian, Berwick and West Lothian, and a few in Selkirkshire.
They represent only a fraction of the original returns for all of Scotland but
are still invaluable. Much of the material is very detailed and quantifiable. In
addition, the territorial coverage is considerable and allows for generalisations
on the contemporary social structure of some representative north-east, south-
east and western counties. Data have been extracted from all 'usable' poll tax
returns for rural parishes and these are presented in processed form in Appendices 2–6. Appendix 1 contains information on problems associated with the
analyses. In all, more than 2,400 'possessions' (mainly tenancies) from six
counties have been examined in the course of the study and the social position
documented of around 25,690 people from sixty parishes. From time to time,
detailed illustrations will be provided in the analysis which follows but confirmation of points can be found mainly in the Appendices. Where appropriate,
information from estate records is combined with poll tax data.

The tenant class was the backbone of the agricultural community in the
later seventeenth century. Owner-occupiers were rare and only existed in any
numbers in some districts of Fife and the south-western counties. The tenant,
in return for an allocated area of land under the terms of a lease or 'tack' from
the proprietor would provide him with rental, predominantly in kind in most
areas, and a range of labour services. Martial relationships had long died out
and the connection between landlord and working farmer had become almost
entirely economic but with some paternalistic overtones. The tenants were the
principal figures in the *ferme touns*, or small settlements of cottages and farm
buildings, where the cottagers, servants and tradesmen – who comprised the
rest of the rural community – lived and worked. As the payers of rent and
employers of labour the tenant class was an élite. Only a minority of the
population were tenants. Nearly 30 per cent of those who paid the poll tax in
Renfrewshire were so classified as were 21 per cent in the coastal strip parishes
of Aberdeenshire.

Yet the essential characteristic of the tenantry was its diversity. First, the
proportion of the rural population who were tenants varied enormously from
area to area. At one extreme, 45 per cent of poll tax payers in Highland
Aberdeenshire were full rent-paying tenants while, at the other extreme, they
comprised only 12 per cent in Midlothian. In general, the south-eastern
counties of West Lothian, Berwick and Midlothian exhibited a social pattern
somewhat different from other areas. Even at this time, farms were apparently
larger there than the Scottish average and tenants much fewer in number.
Land control concentrated in a smaller class and there were very large numbers of dependent cottars and farm servants. In the Midlothian parish of
Carrington, for example, no less than 87 per cent of those recorded were
servants and cottars. Here was a social structure not radically different from
that which was to emerge even more clearly in the later eighteenth century. It
was one which had probably developed because of powerful demand stimuli

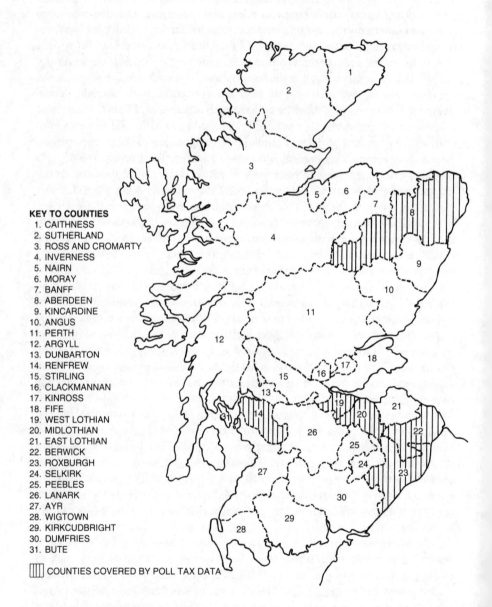

KEY TO COUNTIES
1. CAITHNESS
2. SUTHERLAND
3. ROSS AND CROMARTY
4. INVERNESS
5. NAIRN
6. MORAY
7. BANFF
8. ABERDEEN
9. KINCARDINE
10. ANGUS
11. PERTH
12. ARGYLL
13. DUNBARTON
14. RENFREW
15. STIRLING
16. CLACKMANNAN
17. KINROSS
18. FIFE
19. WEST LOTHIAN
20. MIDLOTHIAN
21. EAST LOTHIAN
22. BERWICK
23. ROXBURGH
24. SELKIRK
25. PEEBLES
26. LANARK
27. AYR
28. WIGTOWN
29. KIRKCUDBRIGHT
30. DUMFRIES
31. BUTE

||||| COUNTIES COVERED BY POLL TAX DATA

MAP 1.1 Counties covered by poll tax data.

from Edinburgh and the geographical potential of the south-eastern zone for intensive grain production for the market. There seems little doubt that subsistence activity had broken down here and commercial pressures were already dominant.

Secondly, there was considerable diversity in the size of holding. The tenant class was far from homogeneous. It was a complex hierarchy which included rich husbandmen employing many dependent workers and poor farmers scratching a living from a few acres of inhospitable land and with little more economic status than cottars. Some precision can be given to this point by converting the rental valuations in the poll tax for each holding to a territorial estimate. When the parish valuations are compared with acreage figures provided for some of the same units in the relevant entries of the *Old Statistical Account*, (*OSA*) 'a rough equivalence' is suggested of about £1 Scots to each arable acre of infield and outfield land.[16] Clearly such a measure can provide only a partial guide to holding size and tenant power because it does not include data on the common grazings which were central to the functioning of the pastoral economy. Nevertheless, the conversion provides a crude estimate of the varying size of units of arable cultivation.

There was a small group of prosperous farmers at the top of the social pyramid. Some styled themselves 'gentlemen' in the poll tax lists, a designation which meant they had to pay a higher rate. But they were a tiny minority: 2 per cent of tenants in the Aberdeenshire sample farmed over 100 acres and 5 per cent did so in Renfrewshire. Once again, the south-east stood out with no less than 36 per cent of all farmers in Midlothian leasing more than 100 acres. A typical example of this élite was George Leith, 'gentleman', a tenant in the parish of Tillinessell, Aberdeenshire. Leith's farm gave employment to seven people in addition to his immediate family: five male and female servants and two herds. Even more impressive was the retinue which surrounded William Nisbet of Crimond parish in the same county. In the 1690s Nisbet was the only tenant in the Kirktoun of Crimond but it still contained a substantial community which was employed mainly by him. Six individuals were recorded as servants or herds. In addition, there were two subtenants, a cottar family and half a dozen tradesmen including a weaver, tailor and shoemaker. It is not difficult to see men like Leith and Nisbet of the upper rank of the tenantry as part of an embryonic farming bourgeoisie whose unusually large consolidated holdings were increasingly committed to servicing the market for grain and stock. Certainly, units of this size generated a surplus above subsistence which would be traded off the land.

But such market-orientated structures were almost certainly still uncommon. The most striking conclusion which emerges from the poll tax analysis is that the vast majority of Lowland farms in the counties examined were very small indeed. In the sample parishes of lowland Aberdeenshire, 45 per cent of tenants possessed less than 20 acres with the proportion of small holdings being significantly higher in the Highland districts of the county. Similar patterns obtained elsewhere. Over half the possessions in Renfrewshire were under 30 acres while even in Midlothian, an 'advanced' county, no less than 37 per cent were in this category. It is hard to imagine that this vast number of small farms, perhaps in large part the result of the continued prevalence of multiple tenancy, could be committed to anything other than subsistence production. Reducing the amount of arable per unit still further was the fact that outfield accounted for a substantial proportion of farm land and only about half at most would be cultivated during any one year.[17] Whyte has argued that yields were improving on the more progressive estates in the eastern Lowlands. Yet returns in the main were still relatively low at around three- to five-fold from infield and with considerable regional diversity.[18] Such yields pushed the smaller tenants, who were in the majority, much closer to the margin of subsistence. A detailed study of the tenantry of the estate of Panmure in Angus in the later seventeenth century confirms that they operated within a very narrow margin between solvency and insufficiency:

> If the debts owing to and by the tenants at their deaths are related to the value of their farming stock, 78 per cent had a net deficit which, had all the debt been called in at once, could only have been met by selling the livestock, implements and grain. In 13 per cent of the testaments the debts owed by the tenants exceeded the combined value of debts owing to them and farming stock, while only 10 per cent had a credit surplus which equalled or exceeded the value of the equipment.[19]

This evidence, if representative, strongly suggests that tenants were very vulnerable to short-term crises such as partial harvest failure. The evolution of a more 'progressive' market-orientated system must have been adversely affected, therefore, by the 'Lean Years' of the 1690s. Not only did these disasters cause mortality to rise sharply in the Highlands and the north-east, they may have also have had a devastating impact on the farm economy of several Lowland counties. The specific effect was a steep rise in rent arrears which had to be paid off in subsequent years from surplus production.[20] On one property which has been examined in detail, arrears from the crises of the 1690s were still being reduced in the 1720s.[21] A disaster of that magnitude must have drained tenant capital and reinforced conservative instincts. As later discussion will demonstrate, the much less severe crises of 1772–3 and 1783–4, during the era of Improvement itself, also had a damaging impact on tenant investment at that time. One can only speculate on the more destructive consequences of the catastrophe of the 1690s on a much poorer farming class.

It was not only the prevalence of small holdings and the debilitating results of harvest failure which mainly locked the rural community into patterns of continuity rather than processes of social change. Essentially, the majority of tenant class was by and large insulated from the grain market because of the structure and nature of rent payment. Commutation of rentals in kind to money rentals were indeed occurring in this period and on pastoral farms conversion was apparently virtually complete.[22] But an examination of nearly 400 tacks from seven estates in the four counties which are the primary focus of this study tends to suggest that the commutation of grain rentals had only taken place in a partial and piecemeal fashion before 1700.[23] For example, on the Earl of Strathmore's estate in Angus in 1695, 76 per cent of the rental was paid in kind. In the Lordship of Melville in Fife in 1715, 65 per cent of the rental was paid in this way.[24] It was in the eighteenth century, as discussed in Chapter 2, that the process of commutation accelerated. Until then, market opportunities had limited direct effect on most tenants. They delivered the oats and bear specified in their rental to the landlord's girnel or to the town or seaport described in the tack. Marketing of the produce and negotiation with prospective purchasers were all managed by the proprietor's factor and agents. Even though, therefore, the market economy was growing, the majority of farmers outside the Lothians area did not participate in it directly. Once again, the forces of conservatism and stability were reinforced.

However, one important change within the tenant structure seems to have been underway in the later seventeenth century. This was the changing balance between single and multiple tenancy. Single tenant farms were cultivated by one individual, his servants and his family. It was the type which became predominant in the later eighteenth century and, partly because of this, scholars have seen them as potentially more 'modern' and progressive: 'Single tenant farms were clearly not hampered by the constraints of communal working and were more positively geared towards maximising output. Essentially, in terms of organisation, they were modern farms.'[25] Multiple tenancy, on the other hand, has been depicted as both more archaic and conservative. Within this structure there were two or more tenants but, in general, rental payments were made separately indicating that specific possessions or portions of land were held by each tenant. These tenurial arrangements were related to the runrig system in which holdings were divided into areas of varying size which lay intermingled with others so that ideally lands of equal extent, quality and exposure to sunlight could be distributed.[26] Multiple tenancy seems more obviously to be consistent with a semi-subsistence rather than a market economy. It had a vital social purpose in a society where most lived on the land, and the distribution of roughly equal access of good and bad soil was desirable in order to enhance both economic security and social stability. In addition, the communal arrangements of touns held in multiple tenancy were well suited to a social order where capital was limited but labour supply was abundant. The sharing of labour resources in the busy seasons of ploughing, harvesting and fuel gathering more than made up for contemporary limitations of technology.[27]

By the later seventeenth century, as Table 1.1 indicates, the tenurial pattern of lowland Scotland was complex. The social system was dynamic rather than wholly static. In most counties enumerated, with the exception of Selkirk, the majority of holdings were already possessed in single tenancy and there is some evidence that the movement from multiple tenancy had been underway for some time, though the actual pattern of development for the period before the

TABLE 1.1   Percentage of multiple and single tenancies by county in the 1690s.

County	Total no. possessions	No. multiple tenancies	Percentage	No. single tenancies	Percentage
Renfrewshire	1,123	360	32.1	536	47.7
Aberdeenshire (only lowland and coastal strip parishes)	477	93	17.5	299	62.7
Selkirkshire	62	32	51.6	21	33.9
Berwickshire	106	28	26.4	63	59.4
Midlothian	157	46	29.3	86	54.8
West Lothian	220	85	38.6	116	52.7

SOURCE   Poll tax returns for each county. See Appendices 1–5.

later seventeenth century is unclear.[28] In superficial terms this was a development of major importance if the dichotomy between single tenancy as
'modern' and multiple tenancy as 'backward' is accepted. Certainly, the
accelerating erosion of multiple touns in the early decades of the eighteenth
century helped create a more appropriate context for more radical reorganisation in the era of Improvement. At that time it seemed easier to plan and
manage the new enclosures and field system in tenancies controlled by one
husbandman.[29] Equally, the contraction in multiple tenancy before 1700,
usually through the reduction, over time, in the number of possessors per
holding thinned the ranks of the farming classes, concentrated resources in the
hands of the few and further increased the size of that majority in rural society
who had only the most tenuous connection with land as cottars and servants.

Yet one must be careful not to exaggerate the significance of these trends
or to imply that they represent a clear discontinuity in the development of rural
society in the later seventeenth century. For a start, the historical importance
of single tenancy may be overstated because of the misconception of earlier
writers that communal tenancy always represented the norm in the medieval
and early modern countryside. Inevitably, when the existence of large numbers
of single holdings were discovered in poll lists and estate archives it was
tempting to assume that this represented the disintegration of these earlier
structures. In fact, as one authority has suggested, 'there had never been a time
when multiple tenancy was overwhelmingly predominant'.[30] Work on
Ayrshire shows that lands held in common by a number of tenants were
steadily diminishing for over two centuries before 1750.[31] Fifteenth- and
sixteenth-century rentals covering a wider area confirm that single tenancy
was a significant element in the Lowlands in the earlier period.[32]

Secondly, single tenancy may imply individual control of land by one man
but it is hard to see this as a liberating influence in the context of the later
seventeenth century. The very large size of the small farm sector described
earlier and the fact that single tenancies may have been in the majority across

lowland Scotland suggest that the host of individual holdings were geared primarily to satisfying subsistence rather than market needs. At the same time, they were just as likely to be insulated from direct market influence by the prevailing rental structure of payment in kind as multiple tenants. Thirdly, the scale of the multiple tenant sector was still very considerable. Even in 'advanced' Lothian counties, the proportions were still relatively high. In Midlothian almost 30 per cent of holdings were in this category, a quarter in Berwickshire and 38 per cent in West Lothian. By 1700, multiple tenancy was a declining but still not a residual or minor feature of the rural social structure. What emerges not only from the analysis of the poll lists but from a consideration of estate papers is of regional and local variety in the incidence of this form of tenure. Evidence from Ayrshire, Renfrewshire and Fife shows properties where it was in retreat, in some in even balance with single tenancy and in others still dominant in numerical terms.[33] In the 1690s, the erosion of multiple tenancy had still some way to go.

III

Analysis of groups below tenant rank is more difficult because documentation for them is much thinner. There is, in addition, confusion and disagreement over terminology. In the literature 'subtenants' and 'cottars' are often different terms for the same class. But in law, as illustrated in sheriff court processes, a specific distinction was often drawn between the two.[34] It would appear that subtenants in the legal sense were those who received subletted land for which they paid a principal tenant for which they paid mainly in rent and some labour services. The main tenant in turn lived on the difference between subletted rental income and the amount he was due to pay his landlord. It was a tenurial system not unlike that which flourished in the Highlands where lands were disposed of by clan chiefs to gentlemen of their kindred or association who in turn sublet to lesser men. The poll tax data confirm that subtenancy was especially common in the Highland fringes of the Lowlands: 41.7 per cent of those recorded in the Highland Aberdeenshire parish of Crathie were classified as subtenants. Elsewhere in that county, however, the average proportion of subtenants in the sampled parishes in the lowland area was 3.7 per cent but individual parishes, such as Peterculter, Crimond, Fraserburgh and Cruden, had much higher figures. It is possible that in other areas poll tax collectors combined subtenants with cottars to produce a composite total and their true numerical significance was thereby concealed.

Invaluable information from the eighteenth century on the nature of subtenancy is available from the Hamilton estate papers for Lanarkshire and enables a fuller appraisal of this shadowy group.[35] On the Hamilton lands, 11 of the 22 farms in Hamilton barony had subtenants in the early eighteenth century. In five cases, subtenants obtained subletted land from multiple tenants. Elsewhere on the estate there were at least another 12 farms with subtenants out of over 140 holdings. The contribution of this group to the total valued rental of these farms was 34 per cent. In the Hamilton case, the subtenants had considerable control over land management and cultivation because most principal tenants were absentees who resided in the towns of Hamilton, Glasgow and Lanark. They included several merchants, a professor of oriental languages at Glasgow College, surgeons, booksellers, goldsmiths and innkeepers who were obviously speculating modestly in the rural land market by obtaining a farm lease rather than aspiring to estate ownership. Because of this, these subtenants were principal tenants in all but name. Not surprisingly, yields from their holdings compared favourably with the mean for Hamilton tenants at this time. A further indication of their status is that it was possible for subtenants to sublet part of their lands and, while several of this group on the Hamilton estate had only verbal tacks, a substantial number had written leases which averaged from 9 to 19 years. When it came to removal, even subtenants with a verbal tack had to be given proper warning and the appropriate legal procedures had to be followed.[36] The Hamilton evidence suggests that subtenants of this type possessed some discretion over management of farms and a considerable degree of legal protection. In that sense, they can be distinguished from cottars, tradesmen and servants.

Cottar families held very small areas of land from tenants or subtenants in return for labour services and sometimes rental payments. There is little doubt

TABLE 1.2   Cottar structure in a Fife fermetoun, 1714.

The Cothouses belonging to the within farm called the Plowlands –

1.	Arch^d Myles in Craigburn possesses a hous yeard and one acre of Land Laboured by the Tennent
2.	Alex^{dr} Miller in Knowhead 2 acres and a half Laboured and payes 3 bolls and 21 lib. of money
3.	James Leslie ane hous yeard and ane acre Laboured
4.	John Robison Sheepherd a hous yeard and ane acre in 2 divisions
5.	David Reekie 2 acres with hous and yeard and land Laboured payes 5 bolls bear 1 shearer and——of money
6.	David Patie ane acre with hous and two years and land Laboured pays 2 shearers and seven lib. of money
7.	Willie Lanceman ane acre without hous or yeard to it 12 lib.
8. & 9.	The Whythons and yeard with 4 acres to it possest by Will: Patrick and Cristian Tullow in 2 Divisions
10.	Thom: Shipherds relict a hous yeard and 2 acres of Land
11.	Wm. Greig a hous and yeard without Land payes 7 lib.
12.	Janet Shipherd ane hous yeard and acre
13.	Andrew Baxter a hous yeard and payes 5 lib it has ane acre of land belonging to it but not possest by him
14.	Alex^{dr} Mackie in hillhead about ane——acre
15.	Alex^{dr} Paterson 3 acres whereof two are on the Westermost march above the highway

---

SOURCE   NRA(S) 874, Berry Papers, Box 12/6, Ane Account of the Rinds and Parcells, Inverdovat, 1714.

that the distinction between them and 'subtenants' of the type described above was blurred. But cottars were often different because their holdings were small, they paid for them in labour rather than rental and they did not possess the same legal rights as subtenants.[37] Cottars lived in holdings of less than a few acres or in rows of cottages known as 'cottowns' within the farm settlement. Main tenants also ploughed their land and usually permitted the use of grazing. A typical set of cottar-tenant obligations is indicated in Table 1.2. Many cottars were also tradesmen, weavers, carpenters, blacksmiths and other artisans who depended on the smallholding for subsistence and who had a house and a yard in the toun.

The most striking and significant feature of cottarage was its widespread extent throughout most of the lowland counties. The poll tax data set out in the Appendices suggest that only in Renfrewshire and highland Aberdeenshire were the number of cottars significantly below the average.[38] These patterns can be mainly explained by the preponderance of small family holdings in these counties which had less need for substantial additional sources of labour. In the 1690s, however, 70 per cent of Midlothian parishes and 58 per cent of Berwickshire parishes had cottars. Equally high proportions were recorded in Aberdeenshire with cottar possessions present in 67 per cent of parishes in the 'lowland' and 'coastal strip' sample.

Cottars were prevalent for a number of other reasons. First, the system of allocating small plots of land in return for periodic service had a basic rationality when much of the work of the farm was concentrated on a few periods of peak demand for labour such as ploughing, harvesting and fuel gathering. This cycle combined phases of maximum need with much slacker periods. The cottar families provided the reserve supply of labour guaranteed to meet requirements in the busy times but they could also easily be laid off for much of the year. Second, by paying labour in land with only additional requirements rewarded at day rates, tenants saved on cash outlay when the money economy in some localities was underdeveloped. In addition, as shown in Table 1.2, cottars sometimes paid rent and provided the farmer with an additional source of income to help fund his own outlay on rental. Third, tenants were burdened with considerable labour services to their landlord of this period.[39] They were required to provide a certain number of days' work on the mains farm, additional labour at harvest and help with the carriage of the landlord's grain, manure and lime and the provision of his fuel. Cottar families represented a pool of labour to assist in these tasks.

Fourth, and more generally, the work routine of the time demanded abundant supplies of labour. Almost all jobs were highly labour-intensive and technology was primitive. As farm size increased, therefore, numbers of cottars and servants inevitably had to rise also. Enclosures were few and far between and much labour had to be employed in herding. The absence of roads and their poor quality ensured that much carriage had to be done by creels or currachs carried on the back. Peat-gathering was a crucial task which endured throughout the summer months. The method of ploughing, using the 'old Scots plough' with large teams of up to twelve animals, required several men as well as creating further labour requirements in maintaining and feeding the animals. Fifth, many but not all tradesmen were cottars. To some extent, the large number of families in this group can be explained by the spread of textile production through the rural communities, with the spinning and weaving of woollens especially significant in the Border countryside and Aberdeenshire, and the manufacture of linens occurring virtually everywhere else.[40]

There may be a temptation to sentimentalise the way of life of the cottar class because, on the face of it, their possession of some land gave them more 'independence' than the landless servants and labourers who worked for wages alone. But their freedom can be exaggerated. They had few rights. The evidence suggests that they had no protected occupancy of the type afforded those subtenants who possessed a verbal or written tack and could be required to move with their masters when a tenancy changed hands, as it often did in this period.[41] Their dependency is also illustrated by the fact that many were required to pay a modest rental for their patch of land as well as provide labour. Poverty must have been endemic because of the limited opportunities for work on the tenant's holding outside the summer and autumn months. References to cottar eviction rarely appear in sheriff court records which suggests that they could be removed at will by the tenant and were regarded as 'labourers' rather than 'possessors'. Contemporary comments on them are few and far between but one graphic description from the Duke of Douglas's estate in Angus supports the view that cottars did indeed endure a life of hard toil and economic insecurity:

> A Tenant here for every plow has Two sometimes 3 or more Familys of Cottars and these have two or three acres of land each which are set so Dear as that they commonly pay the half and sometimes the whole of the Taxman's Rent: if your Graces estate here was set at the same Rate as the Cottars and Subtenants Possessions are, it would be Ten or perhaps twelve times the rent it now is. These cottars uphold their own houses and work all the work, for I hardly have observed a Tennant work here; the Cottars slavery is incredible and what is worse they are liable to be turned out at the Master's pleasure to whom they work ...[42]

Male and female servants were distinguished from cottars in that they were in full-time employment.[43] Married servants, who were common in the south-eastern counties, were not unlike cottars because as well as being paid in kind they had the use of some land and the keep of a cow. But cottars were only obliged to provide a few days' service whereas the married servant was entirely at his master's disposal. The married man, however, had some land. Single male and female servants, who comprised the vast majority of this class outside Fife and the south-east, had no such partial independence. They were landless, were paid partly in money and kind, lived within the farmer's household and ate with his family in the kitchen. The poll tax lists suggest that the number of servants in some counties was greater than the total of cottars, a pattern common in Berwick, Midlothian and Renfrewshire. The growing preponderance of such a large landless class in some districts seems on the face of it to be in conflict with the view that land and its possession was the basis of the Scottish rural social structure before 1700. But the inconsistency was only apparent not real. As one scholar has commented:

> Often they [the servants] came of cottar families and on marriage might set up as had their parents. Sub-tenants, cottars and servants formed a seamless group, in which, through life, the child of a cottar bound to give service for some days in the year, yet with that precious if insecure title to land, would move into full-time service for a period before marrying and returning finally to the cottar position.[44]

IV

In every social system there exists a tension between the forces of change and continuity. Rural Scotland in the later seventeenth century was no exception. Some landowners were giving even more priority to the economic return from their estates. The marketing of stock and grain increased at both local and national level. At the same time, producers in both the Highlands and Borders were exploiting rising demand for Scottish cattle and sheep in England. The tenant class, already a minority in the rural population, albeit a substantial one in certain regions, seems to have contracted even further. The legal right to land, as guaranteed by a verbal or written lease, was probably confined to fewer individuals in 1700 than in 1600. By corollary, the majority of the country population, while having for the most part access to land at some time in their lives, had only a tenuous connection with it and could relatively easily be displaced through the decision of proprietors or principal tenants. Everywhere there was an intricate hierarchy connecting the various gradations of the social structure. However, in the south-east counties, social stratification had already gone particularly far. In Berwick, Midlothian and East Lothian, the farming class consisted for the most part of a small élite working holdings of 100 acres and above and employing large numbers of servants and cottars. This was a type of social formation which was eventually to become the norm in many parts of lowland Scotland by the end of the period covered by this book. However, the south-east region was clearly exceptional with a social structure fashioned by distinctive market forces and a favourable combination of benign climate and suitable land endowment. But most areas had consolidated farms under the control of one master, worked by several cottars and servants and producing enough for market sales as well as for subsistence consumption. The most dramatic example of this trend was in the Border counties where English demand for cattle and sheep resulted in the emergence of large-scale pastoral holdings.[45]

Yet, the evidence presented in this chapter suggests that it would be an exaggeration to conclude that the rural Lowlands in general were on the move by 1700. Movement occurred but it was essentially *within* rather than *of* the prevailing structure. It would appear that the forces of continuity were still more powerful than the forces of change. There were several indicators of this. First, the vast majority of the population were heavily dependent on land and land-related employment. Hardly any groups were entirely landless outside the larger towns and even tradesmen and textile workers were normally integrated into the way of life of the touns. Second, recognition of the existence and growing importance of a market sector cannot obscure the continuing significance of subsistence relationships. This is most strikingly illustrated in the evidence presented above of a host of small single tenancies and the continued existence of multiple tenancy touns, many of whose occupants possessed minute holdings. When low crop yields and rental payments are taken into account, such small farmers must have had precious little left over for market sales. Teodor Shanin has defined a peasant society as one in which production was dominated by farmers dependent largely on family labour and giving the main priority to the cultivation of the subsistence food crop but perhaps with a subsidiary cash crop for the market.[46] On this definition, a peasant social structure still prevailed in many regions of the Lowlands. Even where landed estates had a stronger market orientation, the continuation of rentals in kind in grain-producing areas ensured that many cultivators had little direct connection with the external structure of demand. In an important sense, this book is about the triumph of commercial forces and relationships in Scottish rural society in the eighteenth century. In 1700 that process, in so far as it was to affect and mould the social structure below landlord level, was only in its early stages.

It is not surprising that commercialisation was still immature in most lowland regions. Urban growth was occurring but *urbanisation*, the basic change in the structure of society triggered by massive town expansion, only happened in the later eighteenth century. The potential market for rural producers until then was relatively limited outside those districts catering for the needs of such large centres as Edinburgh and, increasingly, Glasgow. In 1700, however, fewer than 20 per cent of the population lived in urban surroundings and, *pace* the 'Lean Years', they were usually adequately supplied with food.[47] The relative stability of grain prices in most years was a clear proof that the 'unimproved' system, despite its obvious inefficiencies, was meeting the needs of the time. The market stimulus for more basic change still lay in the future.

REFERENCES

1. See, *inter alia*, R. A. Dodgshon, *Land and Society in Early Scotland* (Oxford, 1981); I. D. Whyte, *Agriculture and Society in Seventeenth Century Scotland* (Edinburgh, 1979); R. H. Campbell and A. S. Skinner, eds, *The Origin and Nature of the Scottish Enlightenment* (Edinburgh, 1982); R. A. Houston and I. D. Whyte, eds, *Scottish Society, 1500–1800* (Cambridge, 1989); T. M. Devine, 'The Union of 1707 and Scottish Development', *Scottish Economic and Social History*, 5 (1985), pp. 23–40.
2. Much of the current evidence is collected in Whyte, *Agriculture and Society*.

3. See Chapter 3.
4. R. Mitchison, *A History of Scotland* (London, 1970), pp. 291–302.
5. Older views are summarised and evaluated in T. C. Smout and A. Fenton, 'Scottish Agriculture before the Improvers – an Exploration', *Agricultural History Review*, 13 (1965), pp. 73–93.
6. There is a classic exposition of these views in Sir John Sinclair, *Analysis of the Statistical Account of Scotland* (Edinburgh, 1825), I, pp. 229–33.
7. R. Mitchison, 'The Movements of Scottish Corn Prices in the Seventeenth and Eighteenth Centuries', *Econ. Hist. Rev.*, 2nd ser., XVIII (1965), pp. 278–91.
8. S. G. E. Lythe, *The Economy of Scotland in its European Setting, 1550–1625* (Edinburgh, 1960), ch. 1.
9. Mitchison, 'Scottish Corn Prices', pp. 278–91.
10. Smout and Fenton, 'Scottish Agriculture', pp. 73–93.
11. M. W. Flinn, ed., *Scottish Population History from the Seventeenth Century to the 1930s* (Cambridge, 1977), pp. 133–49.
12. The principal studies are Dodgshon, *Land and Society, passim*; 'The Nature and Development of Infield Outfield in Scotland', *TIBG*, 59 (1973), pp. 1–23; 'The Removal of Runrig in Roxburghshire and Berwickshire, 1680–1766', *Scottish Studies*, 16 (1972), pp. 121–37; 'Farming in Roxburghshire and Berwickshire on the Eve of Improvement', *Scott. Hist. Rev.*, LIV, pp. 140–54; 'Agricultural Change and its Social Consequences in the Southern Uplands of Scotland, 1660–1780' in T. M. Devine and D. Dickson, eds, *Ireland and Scotland, 1600–1850* (Edinburgh, 1983); Whyte, *Agriculture and Society, passim*.
13. But see I. D. Whyte and K. A. Whyte, 'Some Aspects of the Social Structure of Rural Society in Seventeenth Century Lowland Scotland' in Devine and Dickson, eds, *Ireland and Scotland*.
14. For the background to the poll taxes and their historical value see Flinn, ed., *Scottish Population History*, pp. 51–2, 55–7.
15. J. Stuart, ed., *List of Pollable Persons within the Shire of Aberdeen, 1696* (Aberdeen, 1844), 2 vols.
16. M. Gray, 'Scottish Emigration: The Social Impact of Agrarian Change in the Rural Lowlands, 1775–1875', *Perspectives of American History*, VII (1974), p. 109 fn. 11.
17. Dodgshon, *Land and Society*, p. 243.
18. Whyte, *Agriculture and Society*, pp. 74–9.
19. I. D. Whyte and K. A. Whyte, 'Continuity and Change in a Seventeenth Century Scottish Farming Community', *Agricultural History Review*, 32 (1984), pp. 159–69.
20. The evidence of crisis can be picked up in the following sample of Lanarkshire and Fife estates: NRA(S) 2177, Hamilton Rentals, E1.32–3, 53; NLS, Acc. 4322, Lockhart of Lee Papers, Box 9/11–14, Estate Rentals, 1670–1774; SRO, GD26/5/251–81, Leven and Melville Rentals, 1675–1720; SRO, GD150/2061, Morton Papers, Rentals, Barony of Aberdour, 1661–1820.
21. Whyte and Whyte, 'Continuity and Change', pp. 159–69.
22. Dodgshon, *Land and Society*, p. 244.
23. These tacks have been extracted from the estate papers listed in n. 20 and, in addition, NRA(S) 859/174/11, Douglas-Home Papers, Rentals, Douglas and Roberton; NRA(S) 9904, Earl of Glasgow, Box 2, Tacks 1698–1749; SRO, GD45/506, 420, Dalhousie Muniments, Rentals and Tacks.
24. NRA(S) 885, Earl of Strathmore Papers, Box 65/2, Rental Books Glamis; SRO, GD26/5/288, Rental Crop 1715, Lordship of Melville.
25. Whyte, *Agriculture and Society*, p. 141.
26. R. A. Dodgshon, 'Runrig and the Communal Origins of Property in Land', *Juridical Review* (1975), pp. 189–208.
27. M. Gray, 'North East Agriculture and the Labour Force, 1790–1875' in A. A. Maclaren, ed., *Social Class in Scotland: Past and Present* (Edinburgh, 1976), pp. 86–104.
28. Whyte, *Agriculture and Society*, pp. 137–72.
29. See below, p. 96.
30. Dodgshon, *Land and Society*, p. 212.

31. J. H. G. Lebon, 'The Process of Enclosure in the Western Lowlands', SGM, 62 (1946), p. 105.

32. Dodgshon, *Land and Society*, p. 212.

33. See sources enumerated in n. 23 and n. 24 above.

34. This point comes through frequently in court records. See, for example, SRO, Sheriff Court Processes (Lanark), SC38/22/14–15; Sheriff Court Processes (Hamilton), SC37/8/7–20.

35. What follows is based on NRA(S) 2177, Hamilton Papers, Bundles 778, 1134–6; HPL 631/1, John Burrell's Journal, vol. 2.

36. SRO, Sheriff Court Processes (Lanark), SC38/22/14, Lybell of Removing by James Mevross.

37. This discussion of the cottar class has been developed from scattered references in estate and legal papers. See NRA(S) 874, Berry Papers, 12/6; SRO, GD26/12/7,14 Leven and Melville Papers, Social Structures of Monimail, Fife, 1640, 1694 and 1719; NRA(S) 859/55/3, Douglas-Home Papers, Sir Robert Pollock to Duke of Douglas, 7 Dec. 1759; SRO, Wiston Kirk Session Records, CH2/376/3 (1747); SRO Sheriff Court Records (Lanark), SC38/22/14.

38. See Appendices 2 and 3.

39. This is revealed in the tacks examined in the sources listed in n. 23 above.

40. I. Carter, *Farm Life in Northeast Scotland* (Edinburgh, 1979), pp. 16–17.

41. SRO, Sheriff Court Processes (Lanark), SC38/22/14, Lybell of Removing of Sir Archibald Denholm and below

42. NRA(S) 859, Douglas-Home Papers, 55/3, Sir Robert Pollock to the Duke of Douglas anent his Grace's estate in Dundee, 7 Dec. 1759.

43. T. M. Devine, ed., *Farm Servants and Labour in Lowland Scotland, 1770–1914* (Edinburgh, 1984), pp. 1–96, *passim*.

44. M. Gray, 'The Social Impact of Agrarian Change in the Rural Lowlands' in T. M. Devine and R. Mitchison, eds, *People and Society in Scotland, I, 1760–1830* (Edinburgh, 1988), p. 54.

45. Dodgshon, 'Agricultural Change'.

46. T. Shanin, *Peasants and Peasant Society* (London, 1971), p. 15.

47. On these points see M. Lynch, ed., *The Early Modern Town in Scotland* (London, 1987); T. M. Devine, 'Urbanisation' in Devine and Mitchison, eds, *People and Society in Scotland*, pp. 27–52.

2

Before Improvement

Rural Society and Economy, c. 1700–1750

I

THE period from the Union of the Parliaments in 1707 to the middle decades of the eighteenth century is one of the most enigmatic in modern Scottish social and economic history. It is wedged between the later seventeenth century – which has attracted considerable attention, largely because of the importance of the Union – and the phase of economic 'take-off' and rapid growth after *c.* 1780. Yet an understanding of this middle period is of crucial importance to one of the questions addressed in this book: whether rural social change in the Lowlands can be seen as an elongated process of evolution stretching back into the early modern era and accelerating in later times or as much more disruptive and revolutionary with the social order being altered fundamentally over just a few decades in the later eighteenth century. The issue of 'Agricultural Revolution' or evolution has indeed attracted attention in recent years from Scottish historical geographers but the debate petered out without any satisfactory or convincing resolution of the issues.[1] In large part, this was because of the acknowledged ignorance of trends in the decades between 1707 and 1760. The evolutionary school gained support from Whyte's work on the seventeenth century which identified significant alterations in tenancy structure, leasing and cultivation practices.[2] On the other hand, specialists on the later eighteenth century emphasised the basic discontinuities in trend which occurred in farm organisation, rural social structure and cropping regimes which concentrated in those decades.[3] All this seemed to add up to revolutionary change. The missing link, the essential bridge between the two phases, was the period 1707–60 and the extent to which the seventeenth-century advances were maintained, intensified or slowed down.

The issue of the Union further complicated matters because one of the key themes of post-Union historiography was the perceived impact of enlarged markets and English technical example on Scottish agriculture. Historians have speculated that the Union fashioned a more intimate political and social relationship between Scottish and English élites.[4] The Scottish aristocracy, it is argued, became familiar with advanced English agricultural methods as they travelled to London and became more involved in the fashionable life of the capital. According to this thesis, the union relationship became a conduit through which ideas and methods could flow from one rural economy to another. This stimulating effect was then consolidated by the additional advantage of English markets. The Scots had sent grain, cattle and sheep to the south in great volume before 1700 but the new common market, in theory at least, ought to have created vast new opportunities for agricultural producers. The limited information currently available on Scottish agrarian development in the decades immediately after the Act of Union makes it very difficult to determine the validity of these suggestions. The most significant recent contribution is that of R. A. Dodgshon on Roxburgh and Berwick between 1680 and 1766.[5] Dodgshon examined a series of rentals, demonstrated that multiple tenancy was still widespread in a majority of touns and showed a decline in multiple tenancy over the period of study. Dodgshon's conclusions are tantalising and suggestive, indicating a possible continuation of the trends identified by Whyte for the later seventeenth century. Yet Roxburgh and Berwick may not necessarily be representative of the Lowland pattern. Because of their proximity to English markets and Roxburgh's emphasis on stock-rearing they could have been exceptionally influenced by demand forces from the south. Moreover, Dodgshon concentrated mainly on the organisation of tenancies, using rental data as the main basis of the investigation. The pattern of tenancy development is a crucial indicator of rural social change but in itself is not enough. Evidence is also necessary on agricultural technique, the layout of farms, cropping arrangements and the broader elements in rural social structure. The Dodgshon study terminated in the 1760s but a knowledge of developments thereafter gives perspective to investigation of earlier decades by placing them in context. The long-run, quantitative and systematic approach adopted by Dodgshon in his pioneering work is a model for future researchers. However, the Roxburgh – Berwick study has to be extended to other geographical areas and additional indices of rural social and economic activity need to be examined if more light is to be cast on the first half of the eighteenth century.

The sources for such an investigation do exist. Twenty-three landed estates in the four study counties of Lanarkshire, Ayrshire, Fife and Angus were considered.[6] For ten of these properties the rental data were sufficiently rich and coherent to allow the construction of time series from the later seventeenth to the early nineteenth centuries. These indicated, *inter alia*, trends in tenant numbers and single/multiple tenancy. In all, over 800 separate tenancies were analysed. Examination of three other sources in estate papers was also undertaken. First, landlord correspondence provided information on estate strategy. Second, the compilation of a sample of 306 tacks from the 23 sets of estate papers for the period 1680–1760 enabled conclusions to be drawn about the balance of money and victual rents, cropping structures and the presence or absence of improving clauses. Third, a spatial dimension to the study was added by a scrutiny of estate plans. They exist in great quantity for the eighteenth century.[7] Their chronological incidence is itself a guide to land improvement as estates were normally surveyed in precise detail before schemes of large-scale reorganisation were launched. Often such plans provide a remarkably clear impression of the estate structure before and after improvement.

The voluminous records of the great landed families are the staple sources of rural social and economic history. But other material can be included to give a further perspective on what actually happened in this period. By the middle decades of the eighteenth century, it had become common for landlords to advertise farms in the press as a national market grew for improved tenancies and estates tried to attract farmers skilled in the new husbandry from other districts. These advertisements can constitute an invaluable guide to the development of farming practice because of the amount of detailed information often included in them. In addition, sheriff court records contain – among the vast documentation of small debts, petty assaults and the like – legal processes relating to removal of tenants. If used with care, such summonses of removal can form the basis of a long-term index which could be employed as a rough guide to the chronology of estate reorganisation. It was common for landowners to issue writs of removal to ensure tenants vacated their holding at the end of a lease. But cross-checking between the legal processes and estate papers seems to suggest that the expense of going to law was most often incurred when substantial changes, such as enclosure development, were being contemplated or when the lands were being prepared for substantial numbers of new tenants. The sheriff court records of Cupar, Peebles, Dunblane and Linlithgow were examined on a sample basis of one year per decade for the period between the 1670s and 1800.

II

The period from 1700 to the 1750s can be regarded as one of ongoing change in tenure and tenant structure. On all the estates examined, written leases were virtually universal with verbal agreements between landlord and tenant confined on the whole to very small possessions or to cases where tenancies were being let on an annual basis prior to reorganisation. Equally indicative of a secure tenant structure was the proliferation of long leases. The agreement for nineteen years, often thought to be characteristic only of the later eighteenth century, was common in earlier decades. On the extensive Leven and Melville estates in Fife, 11 per cent of tacks in the years 1675–99 were for nineteen years; by 1700–24, the proportion had risen substantially to 40 per cent.[8] Of the seventy extant tacks for the Hamilton estate in Lanarkshire for the years 1710–50 all but two were for nineteen years.[9] Similarly, of the 139 extant tacks for six other Lanarkshire properties before 1750 all but six were for terms of fifteen to nineteen years or more.[10] This pattern was repeated on the Earl of Glasgow's estate in Ayrshire where all extant pre-1750 tacks were for nineteen years.[11] Even on these properties where nineteen-year leases were still unusual, long lease periods were still the norm. This was the pattern on the Earl of Panmure's Angus lands where the mean tack length in the 1700s and 1710s was fifteen years.[12] This tendency towards written and longer leases was a continuation of later seventeenth-century trends.[13]

In other respects, however, the first half of the eighteenth century saw more distinctive and significant developments in tenant structure. Of major importance in this regard was the changing relationship of tenant farmers to the market. Before 1700 more grain and stock were being sold off the land. The increase in the population of large towns such as Edinburgh and Glasgow, the foundation of more smaller marketing centres such as burghs of barony, the expansion of a vigorous commerce in cattle and sheep to England and the rise of a trade in grain to Scandinavia were all factors in this development. Yet, it has been argued in Chapter 1 that such apparent commercialisation did not significantly erode customary or subsistence relationships on the land. This was partly because mainly rural areas close to large towns or seaports, or districts able to become involved in the long-distance trafficking of stock were influenced by significant market expansion. But the causes went much deeper than this. The vast majority of tenants remained locked within a broadly subsistence system because they were insulated from the market as a result of their traditional tenurial relationships with their landlords.

The nature of this relationship can be traced in contemporary tacks. In addition to the customary feudal obligations of thirlage, carriage and labour services, the majority of seventeenth-century Lowland farmers, as shown in Chapter 1, paid their rentals mainly in kind. One example of the key clauses in a typical tack of the 1680s from the Earl of Morton's estate will suffice as illustration:

> For the whilke cause The saids William and James Kaims Binds and obliedges them conjuntly and severally ... to pay to the said Master Robert Douglas his airs and executors and assignees all and haill the number of Twentie four bolls of bear yerd and sufficient stuff growing upon the said lands ... and the soume of Fourtein pound Scots for the house maill at the said terme of Martinmas and the eight cappons Eight Henns and Eight loads of Coalls to be payed when it pleases The said Master Robert Douglas.[14]

The general custom of payment in kind with only modest money contributions ensured that most tenants did not have direct contact with the market. They were required to deliver their victual rents either to the landlord's girnel or, if the estate was within distance of a town or seaport, to a local merchant. Prices, delivery and transportation were negotiated by estate factors who dealt with the traders in the neighbourhood. Such a structure was an obvious disincentive to enterprise and progressive farm management. Even significant increases in demand for grain and stock could hardly stimulate major changes in social attitudes or farming practices if tenants were excluded from much of the direct monetary gain. The system was one in which customary structures and obligations were predominant and money relationships below élite level underdeveloped.

It is now reasonably clear that this system experienced a fundamental alteration in the first few decades of the eighteenth century, the importance of which cannot be exaggerated. In less than forty years, the historic connection between landlords, tenants and the market disappeared to be replaced by one where farmers, in virtually all the estates studied, faced the market directly. In simple terms, a rental system where most paid the bulk of their payments in kind was replaced by one where money was decisive. Inevitably, the process of change varied significantly between estates and areas but the trend can be identified almost everywhere. Of the twenty-three properties examined, full-scale conversion to money rentals began first on the Douglas estate in Lanarkshire in the early 1730s.[15] This, however, was unusually early. The vast majority of full-scale rental conversions occurred between the later 1740s and 1760s with only a few estates, such as Bertram of Nisbet, again in Lanarkshire, experiencing full conversion in the 1760s itself. The evidence surveyed here leaves little doubt that this crucial change in tenure had already come about by the middle decades of the eighteenth century.

But full conversion to money rentals presents too simple a picture and conceals the real nature of the process of change. Scrutiny of extant tacks suggests that there was an extended erosion of victual rents with full conversion to money representing the climax rather than the beginning of the transition. The metamorphosis took place subtly. On the face of it, early eighteenth-century tacks show little significant change from those of earlier periods. There are the same customary clauses setting out labour services, carriage and thirlage, all suggestive of the continuation of an older era. Similarly, tacks of this period are full of detailed lists of 'in kind' rental related to the economic specialisation of the individual farm or district. These payments could include butter, eggs, poultry, cheese or linen. Even when some of these items disappeared, poultry usually continued to feature in rentals. Yet these forms of 'in kind' payment, despite their lengthy description in tacks, were normally only a relatively small fraction of the total rent. The principal payments were made in oats and bear. What we see is a definite trend towards conversion of this 'boll rent' in the decades before the 1750s.

In the 1670s less than 10 per cent of rentals on the Leven and Melville estate were paid in money with the majority of tacks for that period showing cash values of between 3–5 per cent. By the 1710s, the mean money value was 46 per cent and 56 per cent by the 1750s.[16] On the Hamilton estate almost half the rental was paid in kind in the 1680s but by the early eighteenth century an obvious acceleration in the speed of conversion can be identified. As early as 1712 only 8 per cent of the rental of the barony of Lesmahagow was paid in kind, while, by 1754, 88 per cent of rental in all five Hamilton baronies was paid in cash.[17] On the Duke's east-coast estate of Kinneil, 86 per cent of the rental was in money in 1753.[18] Similar patterns can be detected elsewhere.

There were hardly any victual payments on the Douglas estate in Lanarkshire by the later 1730s; 94 per cent of the Earl of Glasgow's rental was in cash by 1748; a major part of rent was paid in money on the Tayfield estate in Fife by the early 1740s.[19]

What is especially striking about these trends is their widespread nature. Despite significant differences in agricultural regime, landlord strategy and access to markets, most properties studied in the four counties under examination were moving rapidly towards cash rentals and so drawing the tenant farming class of these areas further into contact with the market. It was a key social change which suggests the creation of a more commercial and competitive environment and the broader development of money relationships in the countryside. The responsibility for servicing the market was shifting more towards the tenant. But why this should have taken place in these decades is unclear. The long-run stagnation of grain prices which set in over the period, only broken in occasional years of poor harvests, may, however, have been influential.[20] In such a context it would have been attractive to landowners to

TABLE 2.1 Tenant structure: estate of Douglas (Lanarkshire), 1737–1815.

	Year	Total no. tenants	No. tenants in multiple tenancies	Percentage multiple tenancies
Douglas	1737	68	39	57.4
	1754	31	6	19.4
	1784	29	6	20.7
	1795	31	8	25.8
	1805	31	8	25.8
	1815	27	6	22.2
Carmichael	1737	30	23	76.7
	1754	41	6	14.6
	1784	34	6	17.7
	1795	39	6	15.4
	1805	39	6	15.4
	1815	20	0	0
Roberton	1737	22	13	59.1
	1754	27	4	14.8
	1784	26	2	7.6
	1795	26	2	7.6
	1805	28	6	21.4
	1815	25	6	24.0

NOTES Total number of tenants includes all tenant names on the rent roll, even counting the same individual separately where he or she held two or more possessions on the assumption that separate leases would have been given for these.

The few examples of multiple tenancies in Roberton after 1737 are all those with two individuals with the same surname. This may have been simply a method to preserve a family's hold on the possession rather than true multiple tenure.

SOURCE NRA(S) 859 Douglas-Home Papers, Boxes, 62, 174; vols 217–19.

Before Improvement

25

shift the burden of responsibility for maintaining returns to the tenantry. This was especially the case because of the relentless cash increase in the consumer expenditure, building costs and social expenses of the élite.[21]

Changes in rental structure were paralleled by another remarkable development before 1750 which is again indicative of an erosion in subsistence activity. On the estates studied for this period the balance between single and multiple tenancy seems to have been decisively altered. Chapter 1 demonstrated that, in the later seventeenth century, multiple and single tenancies were common everywhere, though there was some evidence that the latter were already advancing at the expense of the former. The data presented in Tables 2.1–2.7 suggest that on the estates surveyed this process accelerated in the early eighteenth century.

All seven tabulations reveal dynamic development with, in several cases, a dramatic reduction in multiple tenancy. On the Morton estate, which had 40 per cent of its holdings in this tenure in the 1710s, only 3 per cent were so described in the 1740s. On the Douglas property in Lanarkshire the proportion of multiple tenant possessions fell from 64 per cent as late as the 1730s, to 16 per cent by the 1750s. Other estates experienced less drastic depletion but only in the Strathmore lands in Angus was the trend towards reduction not as striking and this may have been because the data do not allow for easy separation and identification of agricultural and village communities on that

TABLE 2.2   Tenant structure: estate of Hamilton (Lanarkshire), 1738–78.

Barony	1738/40		1753/58		1778	
	Single	Multiple	Single	Multiple	Single	Multiple
Hamilton	24	9	22	6	21	4
Cambuslang	6	4	3	4	3	2
Bothwell Muir	5	5	4	6	10	4
Lesmahagow	26	6	27	5	26	1
Arendale	29	7	33	7	28	4
Dalserf	15	5	17	2	17	1
Coats	2	2	4	2	0	2
	107	38	110	32	105	18

SOURCE   NRA(S) 2177 Hamilton Papers, 2177, Bundles, 778, E1/32, 59, 73, 78, 89.

TABLE 2.3   Tenant structure: estate of Earl of Glasgow, Polkelly barony (Ayrshire), 1720–63 (in %).

1720		1746		1763	
Single tenants	Multiple tenants	Single tenants	Multiple tenants	Single tenants	Multiple tenants
15	3	15	3	16	1

SOURCE   NRA(S) 0094, Kelburn Castle, Earl of Glasgow Papers, Box 5, rentals.

TABLE 2.4   Tenant structure: estate of Lord Melville (Fife), 1675–1780.

	Year	Total no. tenants	No. tenants in multiple tenancies	Percentage in multiple tenancies
Barony of Balgonie	1675	18	2	11
	1720	39	6	15
	1730	72	?	?
	1740	85	3	3.5
	1750	74	4	5
	1760	81	4	5
	1770	77	3	4
	1780	76	4	5
Lordship of Melville	1715	45	5/6	11/13
	1730	50	6	12
	1740	43	3	7
	1750	40	1	5
	1760	66	0	0
	1770	63	2	3*
	1780	55	3	4.5*

NOTES   *These were all examples of smallholders, most of them tradesmen, who were sharing possessions.

The post-1780 rentals were not specific enough on smallholders numbers to allow multiple tenancy percentages to be calculated.

SOURCE   Extracted from SRO, GD26/5/251–95 Leven and Melville Muniments, *passim*.

TABLE 2.5   Tenant structure: Panmure estate (Angus), 1728–1824.

	Year	Total no. tenants	No. tenants in multiple tenancies	Percentage in multiple tenancies
Lethnot and Navar	1728	37	11	29.7
	1736	38	10	26.3
	1758	33	6	18.2
	1775	31	2	6.5
	1785	31	2	6.5
	1824	25	2	8.0
Edzel	1728	79	14	17.7
	1736	75	16	21.3
	1758	68	7	10.3
	1764	65	6	9.2
	1775	65	6	9.2
	1785	65	6	9.2
	1824	63	6	9.5

SOURCE   SRO, Dalhousie Muniments, GD45/18/506–2091, *passim*.

TABLE 2.6   Tenant structure: Strathmore estate (Angus), 1690–1721.

A. *Narrow and wider circles of Glamis, 1690*	
No. of tenants	154
No. of tenants in multiple tenant possessions	126
No. of possessions	42
No. of multiple tenant possessions	26
B. *Lordship of Glamis, 1721*	
No. of tenants	132
No. of tenants in multiple tenant possessions	112
No. of possessions	33
No. of multiple tenant possessions	14
Percentage of multiple tenant possessions	42.4

SOURCE   NRA(S) 885, Earl of Strathmore Papers, Boxes 53, 65, 148.

TABLE 2.7   Tenant structure: estate of Earl of Morton (Fife), 1694–1795.

Year	Total no. tenants	No. tenants in multiple tenancies	Percentage in multiple tenancies
1694	31	11	36
1705	35	14	40
1715	32	10	31
1717	34	10	30
1726	39	9	23
1735	50	10	20
1742	65	2	3
1795	75	0	0

SOURCE   SRO, GD150, 2061, Morton Papers, Rentals, 1694, 1705, 1715, 1717, 1726, 1735, 1742, 1795.

estate. Evidence from five other estates, situated as far apart as Kirkcudbright and Fife, seems to confirm that by the 1750s multiple tenancy was not only in retreat but was fast being eradicated (see Table 2.8). According to virtually all of the estate records examined in the course of this study, single tenancy was apparently triumphant by the middle decades of the eighteenth century.

The implications of this development were profound. First, it adds weight to the argument advanced earlier in this chapter that the emphasis of agricultural production in the Lowlands at farm level was shifting towards the market. There was little point in consolidation and the control of more land by fewer tenants if the strategy was not to enhance the capacity to create more surpluses for sale. Second, the history of wholesale reorganisation of estates in the last quarter of the eighteenth century suggests that enclosure and related innovations could be achieved more easily on single tenancies with individual control rather than on multiple tenancies where endless difficulties were sometimes caused by demarcation disputes and the like.[22] These pre-1750

TABLE 2.8   Single and multiple tenancy on selected Scottish estates, 1757–75.

Estate	County	Date	% single tenants	% multiple tenants
Lockhart of Lee	Lanarkshire	1775	88	12
Earl of Glasgow				
(Shewalton Barony)	Ayrshire	1761	96	4
Earl of Eglinton	Ayrshire	1757	88	12
Preston	Kirkcudbright	1761	87	13
Balfour of Babirnie	Fife	1770	95	5

SOURCES   NLS, Lockhart of Lee Papers, Acc. 4322, Box 34, Lee estate rentals, 1784–   ; NRA(S) 0094, Kelburn Castle, Earl of Glasgow Papers, Box 9/74, Box 4/2, Box 8/vol. 1; SRO, Earl of Eglinton Muniments GD3/vols 8361, 8359, 8436; SRO, Oswald of Auchincruive Papers, GD 213/22 and 54, Rental accounts; SRO, Balfour Muniments, GD 288/4/1–2.

alterations in farm structure, therefore, facilitated later improvement. Third, the trend towards single tenancy had significant social implications. As the movement to eradicate multiple tenancy gathered pace, the tenant class, already a minority in most areas, was becoming even smaller in size. Over time, fewer possessed a lease and more were being forced to migrate off the land or fall in status to the position of cottars or servants.

But the evidence does not suggest that before the 1760s at least this new social order was created by draconian means. The process could not have taken place without inflicting social pain, but tenant reduction – when examined in detail – was enforced in a piecemeal fashion over extended periods of time through the familiar mechanism of the leasing system. Two examples give an indication of how this was achieved. According to poll tax and rental data the toun of Letham on the Melville estate in Fife had six tenants in 1694.[24] Two tacks of the Letham lands for the 1670s suggest that the entire toun was originally held in eight parts. The rent of the four lots laid out in the second of these tacks is exactly half the money rent of the first and almost exactly half of the in kind rent. Thus some of the eight parts of the toun were themselves divided. Clearly this single farm supported a large population. No change was apparent by 1715 when six main tenants paid over half the rental. By 1740, however, the number had fallen to three and ten years later to two tenants. Multiple tenancy was almost certainly ended completely a few years later when, according to a tack of 1755, much of the old Letham lands had become part of the newly created farm of Nisbetfield. The entire process of reduction from the eight or more tenants of the 1670s to the single, consolidated tenancy of the 1750s took over eight decades with an obvious acceleration in the 1720s and 1730s. So far as the evidence allows us to judge, the 'removal' of tenants took place at the end of a tack through the normal process of renewing or ending the lease.

Even when the process of reduction was more concentrated in time, as in the later eighteenth century, there was not always dramatic displacement. As late as 1747 the toun of Carngillan on the Eglinton estate in Ayrshire was held by eight tenants. By 1815 it had become a single tenancy. Numbers started to fall by one in 1757, another tenant was lost ten years later in 1777, a further two in 1787 and another two in 1797.[24] The process of displacement took nearly sixty years to complete. The Eglinton rentals also allow us to trace the emergence of the prosperous and successful Morton family in this toun, who eventually controlled a land area possessed in the 1740s by eight tenants. The Mortons were not listed in the original land rental of 1747. They first appeared in 1757 when one John Morton took over a share of the toun. From then until 1815 he and his descendants slowly consolidated and extended their possession as tenant numbers on the adjacent lands fell over time.

This pattern was being repeated all over lowland Scotland, much of it in the decades before 1760, according to the sources consulted in this study. It was a development which helps to explain why market opportunities were seized so vigorously by many tenants in the last quarter of the eighteenth century. The rise of an independent farming class, controlling its own land with the security of a long lease, was already advanced by 1750. The erosion of multiple tenancy implied the steady destruction of communal constraints and controls and allowed greater opportunity for individual initiative and capital accumulation.

III

Whether similar developments in the areas of agricultural technique can be identified for the period 1760 is a more difficult question. Estate papers and other data do provide evidence of some innovation. Examples of the use of clover and sown grasses can be found. Bertram of Nisbet in Lanarkshire included in his estate tacks in the 1740s regulations for rotations, which included red clover and pease.[25] Many tacks of the early eighteenth century in all four counties specified the use of lime, which had been recognised as an effective means of raising yields from the outfield area at least from the early seventeenth century. Some tacks for the 1720s and 1730s directed that trees be planted around houses and yards, others indicated the proportion of land to be rested each year and a few allowed six-course rotations with crops of bear and oats followed by several years in grass.[26]

The period before 1760 was also noteworthy for the improvement of a number of properties by progressive lairds, such as urban merchants and professional gentlemen, especially lawyers and judges, and landowners active in local improving societies. Cockburn of Ormiston and Grant of Monymusk were only the most famous of these. Doubtless because of their activities it is possible to find examples of enclosure development in the first half of the eighteenth century. Thus, Lord Belhaven in the early 1740s 'inclosed the farm of Bielgrange consisting of 200 acres with double ditches, with Hedges and Lists of Forest-Trees. He subdivided it into thirteen fields and laid the whole down in sown grass.' Significantly the legal process from which this reference was taken also stated that Belhaven '*amused* himself with the Cultivation of

the Grounds lyeing adjacent to his Country-seat'.[27] Early evidence of enclosure also comes from Dunbartonshire where tacks of the 1740s on the lands
of John Arbuthnott, merchant in Edinburgh, gave encouragement to tenants
willing to enclose, and promising compensation if they did so at the end of
their term.[28] Similar initiatives took place on the Preston estate in
Kirkcudbright, the Blantyre estate in Lanarkshire and in other properties in
Ayrshire and Fife in this period.[29]

Such examples of innovative cultivation and improved techniques of land
management reveal little, however, about the general pattern. There is good
reason for scepticism about how common such approaches were. One example
of early aristocratic interest in agriculture may suffice to demonstrate this. The
6th Earl of Strathmore, who held considerable lands in Angus, was an early
member of the newly established Society for Improving in the Knowledge of
Agriculture in 1723. Strathmore also fits the classic textbook illustration of an
'Improver' since he was clearly impressed and influenced by English example.
In 1737 he wrote to his factor instructing him in 'the method of Farming in
England' and this advice was then given to other estate officials. The following
year, a decision was taken to enclose the mains farm and to sow part of it with
clover seed to be supplied by the Earl himself.[30] However, this early dawn of
improvement in Angus was entirely a false one. The 1730s experiment was
exceptional, ephemeral and confined to the lands of the estate actually farmed
by the Earl. An advertisement of 1742 for rouping the Mains of Glamis shows
that at that date it was enclosed with stone dykes, ditches and hedges.[31] But
the estate as a whole did not experience the onset of enclosure until the later
1760s and cropping prescriptions in Strathmore tacks remained fairly rudi-
mentary until the following decade when 'improving' clauses became the
norm.[32] More than three decades, therefore, separated the early enthusiasm
of the Earl from the onset of widespread reorganisation of the estate in the
later eighteenth century. The Strathmore example suggests the need for a more
systematic approach to the problem of improvement before 1750. Argument
by example will not suffice.

The evidence of estate correspondence and tack material indicates that in
22 of the 23 properties studied throughout lowland Scotland the infield –
outfield structure of farming was maintained into the 1760s. The exception
was the Hamilton estate of Kinneil, situated in the advanced Lothians, where
enclosure began in the later 1740s.[33] Thereafter, as will be shown in detail in
the next chapter, the process of general enclosure developed virtually simul-
taneously on most properties between the 1760s and early 1770s. Estate plans
make it clear, however, that there was little *structural* change before that time.
The maps of twenty-five farms for the Balfour of Balbirnie estate in Fife
survive for the period 1750–1820. They depict a landscape which hardly
altered before the 1770s, with large, undivided fields, evidence of rig cultivation and systems of infield–outfield.[34] Similarly, the Dalhousie estate archives
for Angus contain thirty-one plans of various farms in the parishes of Edzell,

Lethnot and Navar in that county. All of these were drawn up by the surveyor, William Ranton, in 1766–7 and each one illustrated pre-improvement land-scapes with rig cultivation, scattered, irregular-shaped parcels of infield, outfield, pasture and many with sizeable areas of waste land.[35] Indeed, in a general sense, the dated plans provide one method of tracing the spread of the enclosure movement. It is clear that few plans were drawn up in the first half of the eighteenth century and that the major period of production was not reached until the decade after 1765.[36]

Other sources confirm the limited impact of extensive reorganisation before the 1760s. A memorial for the Duke of Douglas written in 1792 described how, several decades before, all his lands in Angus, Renfrewshire and Lanarkshire were 'mostly run-rigg or rundale amongst the Tenants, who generally occu-pied their pastures amongst them in common'.[37] Surveys in 1763–4 carried out on the Hamilton estate also demonstrate the prevalence of the infield–outfield system and the absence of even minimal enclosure.[38] Perhaps most telling of all are the data which can be gathered from farm advertisements published in the contemporary newspaper, the *Edinburgh Evening Courant*. In one of the sample years, 1755, a total of sixty-three farms were advertised for leasing. These were not all concentrated in the south-east area, which might have been expected given the *Courant*'s base, but included holdings in Stirling, Ayrshire, Renfrewshire and Lanarkshire. The majority were, however, located in the Lothians and Fife. An analysis of the advertisement details reveals that 16 per cent of these farms were wholly, mostly or partly enclosed and that 9 of these 13 were to be found in the 'progressive' counties of East Lothian and Berwick. An examination of ninety-one farms advertised for sale in the *Courant* in 1750 suggests a similar pattern. At that date, 9 per cent of farms were wholly or mostly enclosed with a further 10 per cent experiencing partial enclosure.[39] Almost certainly, however, even these low figures for enclosure activity exag-gerate its significance since it was likely that landowners would tend to expose their most improved farms to public sale through newspaper advertisements.

If there had been evidence of a systematic assault on the old order in this period some trace of it would almost certainly have appeared in sheriff court records. The issue of summonses of removal was often a prelude to estate reorganisation and alterations in farm size and structure.[40] But such legal action was rare in the processes of the courts of Cupar, Peebles, Dunblane and Linlithgow, which were searched for these years.[41] At Cupar, for example, less than 1 per cent of the actions to remove took place before 1760 while almost 80 per cent were concentrated in the period between 1780 and 1800. At Peebles, the figure for the pre-1760 period was 8 per cent, and at Linlithgow 6 per cent. No actions of this type were recorded at Dunblane. The legal evidence is consistent with the rest of the data examined, i.e. that no large-scale reorganisation of landholding took place before 1760.

In the 1750s, therefore, although substantial and deeply significant develop-ments had already taken place within the tenant class, much of the lowland countryside retained its historic pattern of rig cultivation, infield–outfield divisions and areas of common land. The landscape was relatively static while important changes were occurring within rural society. There does not appear to have been radical change in the management of land in the first half of the eighteenth century. Almost certainly this was due in large part to the stability of grain prices for much of the period, which ensured that the incentive for large-scale investment was reduced. The next chapter will demonstrate that the enclosure and reorganisation of an estate was a highly expensive business. It was unlikely to be contemplated by most proprietors until market opportunities were more propitious. Significantly extensive expenditure on land in the pre-1750 period seems to have been mainly confined to the bigger magnates in the Border country who were facing a buoyant market for their sheep and cattle in the new post-Union environment.[42] On the other hand, the energetic programme of improvement carried out by the celebrated Archibald Grant of Monymusk came to grief precisely because the market did not provide adequate return on investment in his Aberdeenshire estate.[43]

Market conditions were, therefore, probably crucial in postponing major change. But the weak position of many tenants may also have been a factor. Bad weather and poor harvests produced higher than average grain prices in some years, as in 1739–40, but even these were sometimes not enough to compensate farmers for lost output as evidenced by the rapid accumulation of rent arrears on some estates when times were difficult. Occasionally, too, there is the suggestion in some estate archives that the financial condition of many tenants was far from robust and indebtedness to the landowner outside crisis years was not unknown. Thus, between 1731 and 1735 on the Earl of Strathmore's lands the number of tenants in arrears rose to 154 and the total value of arrears from £181 Scots to £6,912 Scots, or 17.8 per cent of estate income.[44] The records of other properties also contain references in these decades to 'eases' or 'rests' of rental, abatements provided by the landowner because of tenant difficulties.[45] Perhaps the general trend towards farm consolidation can be seen as the response to this problem, a strategy enforced by the landed classes to create a more powerful tenantry with the resources not only to service the market but to maintain rental payments on a regular basis at a time when élite demands for more revenue were on the increase.

REFERENCES

1. G. Whittington, 'Was there a Scottish Agricultural Revolution?', *Area*, 7 (1975), pp. 204–6 and responses from I. H. Adams, I. D. Whyte and M. L. Parry in *Area*, 10 (1978), pp. 198–205. For a sceptical approach to the concept of 'Agricultural Revolution' see also G. Whittington, 'Agriculture and Society in Lowland Scotland, 1750–1870' in G. Whittington and I. D. Whyte, eds, *An Historical Geography of Scotland* (London, 1983), pp. 141–64.
2. Collected and synthesised in Whyte, *Agriculture and Society, passim*.
3. For example, Gray 'Social Impact of Agrarian Change', pp. 57–62.
4. R. H. Campbell, 'The Scottish Improvers and the Course of Agrarian Change in the Eighteenth Century' in L. M. Cullen and T. C. Smout, eds, *Comparative*

Aspects of Scottish and Irish Economic and Social History, 1600–1900 (Edinburgh, 1977), pp. 204–15.
5. Dodgshon, 'Removal of Runrig', pp. 121–37.
6. The detailed lists are available in the Bibliography in the section on Primary Sources.
7. I. H. Adams, ed., *Descriptive List of Plans in the Scottish Record Office*, vols 1–3 (Edinburgh, 1966, 1970, 1974).
8. SRO, GD26, Leven and Melville Muniments, Inventory.
9. NRA(S) 2177, Hamilton Papers, 1134–6, 1140, Tacks of Lanarkshire lands, 1702–14 and Miscellaneous Tacks.
10. NLS, Acc. 5474, Lockhart of Lee Papers, Box 1, Estate Agreements, 1628–1728; SRO, GD170/3710, Handaxwood Papers, Tacks; NLS, Acc. 8217, Stuart of Castlemilk Papers, Miscellaneous Tacks; SRO, GD5/1/520, 529, Bertram of Nisbet Papers, Miscellaneous Tacks; NRA(S) 859, Douglas-Home Papers, Box 110/4.
11. NRA(S) 0094, Earl of Glasgow Papers, Deedbox 2, Bundle 8.
12. SRO, GD45, Dalhousie Muniments, 18/1143, 1176, 1211, 420, 455, 1502, 1503.
13. Whyte, *Agriculture and Society*, pp. 152–62.
14. SRO, GD150/1021/1, Morton Papers, Tack by Mr Robert Douglas to Wm. and James Kaimes, 1688.
15. NRA(S) 859, Douglas-Home Papers, 174/11, Douglas estate rentals.
16. SRO, GD26, Leven and Melville Muniments, 12/272, 285, 281; 5/247, 204, 280.
17. NRA(S) 2177, Hamilton Papers, Bundle 77–8; E1.32, 53, 59, 73.
18. NRA(S) 2177, Hamilton Papers, E3.70, Abstract of Duke's Rental, 1754.
19. NRA(S) 859, Douglas-Home Papers, 174/11; NRA(S) 9904, Earl of Glasgow Papers, Boxes 4, 8 and 9; NRA(S) 874, Berry Papers, 16/5, Rental of the Lands and Estate of Inverdovat (1748).
20. Mitchison, 'Scottish Corn Prices', pp. 278–91.
21. R. H. Campbell, 'The Landed Classes' in Devine and Mitchison, eds, *People and Society in Scotland*, pp. 99–100.
22. See below, p. 96.
23. The story of tenant depletion in Letham can be followed in SRO, GD26/5/33,35,170, Leven and Melville Muniments.
24. SRO, GD3/8346, 8359, 8361, Eglinton Muniments.
25. SRO, GD5/520, Bertram of Nisbet Papers, Tack of Kersewell Crofts.
26. Generalisations based on examination of tacks described earlier in the text, p. 20 above.
27. NLS, Session Papers, Douglas Collection, vol. 2, Lord Belhaven vs. William Anderson, late tenant of Bailgrange, 1761.
28. Ibid., Douglas Collection, vol. 4, Petition of John and Donald Fraser, 25 June 1762.
29. SRO, GD213/22, Oswald of Auchincruive Papers, Decreet of Valuation of Lands of Preston, 1767; SRO, GD1/732/10, Blantyre Papers, Miscellaneous Tacks; *Edinburgh Evening Courant*, 1750 and 1755, Farm Advertisements.
30. NRA(S) 885, Box 103/2, Earl of Strathmore Papers, Letters to Earl, 6 Dec. 1737; 23 Sept. 1738.
31. Ibid. 148/5, Advertisement of Mains of Glamis; 103/5/22.
32. Ibid. 95/5, Miscellaneous Tacks, 1759–75; 103/4, Correspondence of John Leslie, factor, 1742–8 and vol. 22A, Ledger of Patrick Proctor as Clerk to Improving Works, 1 July 1771 to 7 Mar. 1776.
33. NRA(S) 2177, 408, Hamilton Papers, Cost of dyking at Kinneil Park, Apr.–Oct. 1748; *Edinburgh Evening Courant*, 20 Aug. 1750.
34. SRO, GD288/241, Balsour of Balbirnie Muniments, Remarks on Sundry of Mr Balfour's Farms; SRO, Register House Plans esp. 23503, 23552, 23515, 23516, 23507, 23506, 23593, 23608.
35. SRO, Register House Plans, 1665–7, Dalhousie estate plans, all dated 1766 or 1767.
36. I. H. Adams, 'The Land Surveyor and His Influence on the Scottish Rural Landscape', *SGM*, 84 (1968), pp. 248–55.
37. NRA(S) 859, 139/2, Douglas-Home Papers, Memorial to Lord Douglas from Robert Ainslie.

38. HPL 631/1, John Burrell's Journal, 1763–9, *passim.*
39. *Edinburgh Evening Courant*, 1750 and 1755.
40. See below, pp. 97–8.
41. SRO, Sheriff Court Processes (Cupar) SC20/5/5; (Peebles), SC42/5/1–7; (Dunblane), SC44/22/1; (Linlithgow), SC42/6/1–3.
42. Dodgshon, 'Agricultural Change and its Social Consequences'.
43. H. Hamilton, *Life and Labour on an Aberdeenshire Estate, 1735–50* (Aberdeen, 1946).
44. NRA(S) 885, 150/8, Earl of Strathmore Papers, Rests of the Earl's rents, 1731–5.
45. See, for example, NRA(S) 859, 174/11, Douglas-Home Papers, List of rents, Lordships of Douglas and Roberton, 1733–42.

3

The Transformation of the Rural Economy

IN the last four decades of the eighteenth century the market context of Scottish agriculture changed swiftly and radically. The national population started to rise, at first modestly, in the middle years of the century, and then more rapidly at the end. The increase in population was not in itself new. What was unprecedented was that the rate of growth was not only maintained but accelerated over time. Numbers rose by around 0.6 per cent per annum between Alexander Webster's census in 1755 and the first civil census of 1801. In the following decade the rate of increase doubled to 1.2 per cent per annum. The nation's population was around 1,265,000 in 1755; by 1801 numbers had risen to 1,508,000 despite substantial emigration, and to 2,091,000 in 1821. The actual population of Scotland rose by two-thirds between 1755 and 1820. These dynamic demographic forces helped to destroy the rough equilibrium between demand and supply of food which had constrained structural change in the agrarian system before 1750.

The fact that there were more people to be fed and clothed was, however, but one part of a wider revolution in the market. There was an expansion too in that sector of the population which did not produce all its own food from its own resources. The pace of urban and industrial expansion in late eighteenth-century Scotland has been acknowledged as among the fastest in western Europe. From being one of the least urbanised societies, Scotland by the 1820s was well on the way to becoming an economy dominated by a group of large cities and towns.[1] As late as c.1700 an estimated 5 per cent of the national population lived in urban areas of 10,000 inhabitants or more. This can be compared to 14 per cent, or almost three times the Scottish figure, for England and Wales. In the years before the Union of 1707, Scotland was only tenth in a league table of sixteen European urbanised societies as measured by the proportion of total population inhabiting towns of 10,000 people or more. By the 1750s Scotland had reached seventh position; and it attained fourth place by 1800. It was an extraordinarily dynamic pattern of urban growth which intensified further so that by 1850 more than one in three Scots lived in

TABLE 3.1   Percentage increase in urban populations (% of total population living in towns of 10,000 or more inhabitants) from previous date, Scotland, England and Wales, 1600–1800.

	1600	1650	1700	1750	1800
Scotland	–	17	51	124	132
England & Wales	–	94	45	42	83

SOURCE   T. M. Devine, 'Urbanisation' in T. M. Devine and R. Mitchison, eds, *People and Society in Scotland, 1760–1830* (Edinburgh, 1988), p. 29.

large towns. A century earlier, in 1750, only one in ten had done so. The implications for the agrarian sector, faced with this enormous new market for foods and raw materials, were clearly very considerable.

The full significance of this development for farmers and landlords requires further comment. First, the fact that it was a truly revolutionary development which was likely to stimulate an equally fundamental response from food producers needs to be recognised. Scotland's urbanisation was quite different from England's. Until 1800 the English pattern, as indicated in Table 3.1, was one of a continuous and protracted process of steadily intensifying urban expansion. Town growth after $c.$1750 in Scotland was much more abrupt and fast. It was not a continuation of previous evolution but a basic discontinuity on trend. By 1800, de Vries estimates that Scotland had already become one of the five most urbanised societies in western Europe alongside England and Wales, the Netherlands, Belgium and northern Italy.[2] But this pre-eminent position had been achieved in the space of only a few decades. All the other countries and regions in the group had had a large and important urban sector for centuries.

Second, urban expansion in the eighteenth century was primarily fuelled by industrial growth in textile manufacturing. This ensured that, while national population as a whole was increasing, the proportion which had to buy much of its food in the market was growing faster still. In linen, Scotland's staple early eighteenth-century manufacture, output doubled every twenty or twenty-five years between $c.$1730 and 1800. Average annual yards stamped for sale were almost three million in 1728–31. By 1800 total output by this measure had reached over 30 million yards.[3] The late eighteenth-century growth in cotton was even more spectacular but absence of solid data prevents precise evaluation. Nevertheless, the estimates for numbers of handloom weavers gives an impression of the scale and extent of the increase. They rose from $c.$ 25,000 in 1780 to $c.$78,000 by 1820.[4] In addition, though at a slower pace, non-agricultural activity in a host of other occupations, ranging from iron-making to sugar-boiling and from building to woollen manufacture, further extended the market for food producers as industrialisation gathered momentum.

The impact can best be illustrated through the trend in grain prices. The fiars prices for oats in Fife, not one of the counties most fully exposed to the market pressures of the industrial economy, showed remarkable advances.

The mean price per boll in 1764–71 was £0.56, an increase of around 56 per cent on mean oat prices for 1725–50. The mean price of £1 per boll in the decade 1800–10 represented a 300 per cent increase on 1725–50 levels and a rise of 212 per cent on prices prevailing between 1751–70.

Table 3.2 provides a fuller picture for the period 1700–1814 by presenting the price changes by five-year moving averages for oats. These data for bear are set out in graph form in Figure 3.1. It was not simply the extent of the new urban market which was important, its depth and quality were also significant. The commonly accepted view is that the standards of living of the British working classes remained broadly stationary from the 1750s to the 1790s.[5] The pattern in Scotland was again quite different. The available data suggest a substantial rise in real income for groups as diverse as mechanics, colliers, weavers and cotton spinners from the 1770s down to the last decade of the eighteenth century.[6] The explanation seems to be that population in Scotland was rising more slowly than in England, yet economic advance was more concentrated and intense after *c*.1760 than in the south.[7] The Scottish, and in particular the urban, labour market was very buoyant and this inevitably fed through into a steep rise in money wages, which was not entirely cancelled out by increases in food and housing costs. One consequence was that demand was likely to expand not only for grain-based foods but for dairy products and meat. Urbanisation also stimulated an increase in both the absolute size and the relative population share of the middle classes. The expansion in overseas and domestic trade and the revolutionary growth in industry were the fundamental influences but the concentration of professional, administrative and legal services in the larger towns was also significant. The new middle class mainly comprised merchants, retailers, manufacturers, lawyers, teachers and physicians. One recent estimate suggests that they made up 10–15 per cent of the Scottish urban population in the 1750s and 20–5 per cent by the 1830s.[8] This section of society was an important market for beef and such high-quality items as fruit and vegetables.

Third, the expanding market was not only for human foods. Urban growth and economic diversification vastly increased demand for horsepower. One contemporary was of the opinion that 'the principal cause' of the rise in oatmeal prices between the 1750s and 1790s was 'the very great quantity now consumed in feeding horses'.[9] It has been estimated that there may well have been one-third to one-half more horses in England and Wales in 1850 than in 1770.[10] The pattern in Scotland was unlikely to have been radically different. In addition, the burgeoning economy required a whole range of industrial raw materials and fuels from the land, including coal, iron ore, peat, wool, leather, timber, sour milk and fat, to name but some of the most important. Straw was also in considerable demand for packaging, as litter in urban stables, in brick-making and for thatching.

Fourth, urbanisation in Scotland was notable for its intensity and concentration. English historians have long commented on the significance of

TABLE 3.2 Fife Prices: 5-year moving averages for oats, 1700–1814.

Year	Oats per boll (£)	5-year mean	Year	Oats per boll (£)	5-year mean	Year	Oats per boll (£)	5-year mean	Year	Oats per boll (£)	5-year mean
1700	0.39	0.49	1729	0.42	0.50	1758	0.40	0.45	1787	0.55	0.52
1701	0.29	0.41	1730	0.37	0.39	1759	0.37	0.41	1788	0.47	0.55
1702	0.37	0.34	1731	0.37	0.37	1760	0.36	0.42	1789	0.50	0.55
1703	0.36	0.32	1732	0.33	0.35	1761	0.39	0.44	1790	0.60	0.55
1704	0.29	0.30	1733	0.33	0.36	1762	0.60	0.48	1791	0.64	0.59
1705	0.26	0.26	1734	0.35	0.36	1763	0.49	0.54	1792	0.55	0.63
1706	0.19	0.27	1735	0.39	0.37	1764	0.55	0.59	1793	0.68	0.65
1707	0.19	0.27	1736	0.42	0.36	1765	0.69	0.60	1794	0.70	0.66
1708	0.40	[error]	1737	0.37	0.37	1766	0.64	0.59	1795	0.68	0.67
1709	0.29	[error]	1738	0.28	0.42	1767	0.62	0.58	1796	0.70	0.66
1710	no data	[error]	1739	0.39	[error]	1768	0.44	0.53	1797	0.57	0.74
1711	0.33	[error]	1740	0.64	[error]	1769	0.49	0.52	1798	0.64	0.94
1712	0.29	[error]	1741	no data	[error]	1770	0.47	0.51	1799	1.08	0.96
1713	0.29	0.34	1742	0.33	[error]	1771	0.58	0.54	1800	1.70	0.98
1714	0.40	0.33	1743	0.33	0.38	1772	0.55	0.55	1801	0.80	1.01
1715	0.37	0.34	1744	0.38	0.39	1773	0.58	0.55	1802	0.68	0.97
1716	0.29	0.35	1745	0.46	0.41	1774	0.57	0.53	1803	0.79	0.81
1717	0.32	0.35	1746	0.43	0.41	1775	0.48	0.51	1804	0.87	0.84
1718	0.37	0.34	1747	0.38	0.40	1776	0.44	0.48	1805	0.90	0.95
1719	0.40	0.36	1748	0.39	0.41	1777	0.45	0.45	1806	0.98	1.03
1720	0.33	0.38	1749	0.38	0.44	1778	0.47	0.45	1807	1.23	1.06
1721	0.35	0.41	1750	0.41	0.46	1779	0.42	0.46	1808	1.17	1.08
1722	0.46	0.39	1751	0.47	0.46	1780	0.47	0.50	1809	1.02	1.11
1723	0.49	0.39	1752	0.53	0.46	1781	0.48	0.54	1810	1.00	1.16
1724	0.33	0.40	1753	0.49	0.47	1782	0.69	0.58	1811	1.15	1.14
1725	0.33	0.38	1754	0.39	0.48	1783	0.65	0.59	1812	1.48	1.10
1726	0.37	0.37	1755	0.45	0.49	1784	0.62	0.61	1813	1.02	
1727	0.39	0.39	1756	0.55	0.47	1785	0.50	0.58	1814	0.85	
1728	0.44	0.40	1757	0.55	0.46	1786	0.60	0.55			

SOURCE SRO, GD26/12/34 Leven and Melville Muniments.

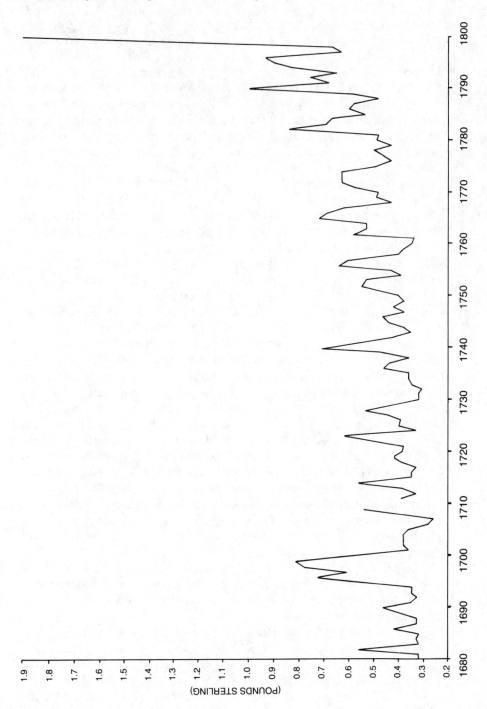

FIGURE 3.1   Fife prices for bear (£), 1630–1800

London in this regard. Scholars point out that the depth and extent of purchasing power in the capital not only helped to promote agricultural changes in neighbouring counties but much further afield as well.[11] In 1801 London accounted for 12 per cent of the total population of England and Wales and for 49 per cent of the urban population of the two countries. This huge market depended on supplies of food and raw materials drawn from all parts of the kingdom. It is arguable that a similarly powerful dynamic for change developed in Scotland in the eighteenth century. Edinburgh had certainly had an energising effect on Lothians' agriculture and on some other parts of the east coast of Scotland from medieval times. After 1750 the city experienced enormous growth, from a population of 57,000 in 1755 to 138,000 in 1821. But its experience was more than matched a short distance away across the valley of the Forth and Clyde by Glasgow, which increased its population more than fourfold between 1755 and 1821. In 1755, the two cities comprised 7 per cent of Scotland's population; in 1801 10 per cent; and, by 1821, 14 per cent. They also lay at each end of a broad land corridor where more and more of the Scottish people lived and worked. It is not difficult to imagine the power and intensity of the market forces which such an urban concentration represented. As early as 1800 no less than 60 per cent of Scottish town dwellers lived in the two cities of Edinburgh and Glasgow.

Fifth, in recognising the profound significance of the Edinburgh/Glasgow axis, we should not neglect the fact that small town and village settlement was also becoming more pronounced in lowland Scotland at this time. This meant that markets for foods and raw materials were being brought closer to many farmers, a vital development in an activity where transport costs were considerable for the carriage of produce which was often small in value but great in bulk. Those who specialised in perishable goods such as milk, fruit and vegetables were likely to be especially favoured by these settlement changes. They came about for a variety of reasons. The increase in textile production encouraged the development of rural weaving communities and spinning mills. Mining and iron-making villages also became more prevalent. To a significant extent, Scottish industrialisation to 1815 was primarily a rural phenomenon and this was reflected in the spread of industrial settlements. In the early 1830s, around two-thirds of handloom weavers lived and worked in villages and country towns and not in great cities.[12] Such settlements also grew as country craftsmen withdrew from the farming communities and landowners developed alternatives for small tenants and cottars who lost land in the process of estate improvement.[13]

The fact of village and small town development has long been known but perhaps its full significance has not always been recognised. The creation of 'planned' settlements was, for example, overwhelmingly concentrated in the period 1760–1815. No less than 85 (or 82 per cent) of those planned villages established in the Lowlands between 1700 and 1840 were founded between 1760 and 1815.[14] Even more significantly, settlement development was not often 'planned' in the literal sense.[15] It was common for proprietors to encourage the erection of a dozen or so houses for weavers and tradesmen beside a main road or a river-crossing. Equally, larger settlements were allowed to grow from existing towns while others were decaying as holdings were consolidated. If the definition of a 'planned village' is employed, only three of those settlements were established in Lanarkshire in the eighteenth century.[16] However, if a looser definition is used, the number rises to sixteen. Data in the *Old Statistical Account* confirm the fundamental local importance of the expansion of small towns and villages in this county. Glasgow remained the dominant market. But the farmers of some districts were relying also on more localised demand because of the mill villages at New Lanark and Blantyre, the lead mines at Wanlockhead, the weaving communities in Hamilton and the expansion of the market towns of Biggar and Douglas.[17]

Sixth, the market was also being brought closer by transport developments. The best-known initiatives took place through the turnpike trusts. Between 1790 and 1815 they spent, according to one estimate, between £2 and £3 million 'to facilitate the internal communication of the country', especially through the construction of bridges and long-distance roads.[18] But they were but part of a general revolution in transportation which combined the development of turnpikes with commutation roads and the less publicised but vital building by landowners of private roads, both within estates and between them and major routes. The construction of the Forth and Clyde Canal was also crucial, enabling, for example, the booming conurbation of Glasgow to be fed by farms as far away as Fife and beyond and completing the link between the two great urban centres of Scotland. It was the new roads, however, that were of more general significance. The proliferation of level surfaces and smoother gradients was basic to the spread of wheeled traffic. As a result, huge savings were made in the costs of both human and animal labour as the cart became the normal means of transporting produce, stores and manures.[19] The *OSA* Reports leave the reader in little doubt that in the 1790s road and bridge construction was widespread and was successfully facilitating the penetration of market forces into all parts of the region under study. The impact of these demand pressures on the rural economy of the four counties will now be considered.

II

There is a good deal of scholarly controversy about the timing, scale and effect of agrarian change in eighteenth-century lowland Scotland. Some see the process as essentially evolutionary in nature with acceleration in the later decades, while others view the movement towards an improved agriculture as more cataclysmic and dramatic.[20] The evolutionist case depends in part on the English analogy where the simple notion of an 'agricultural revolution' has long been questioned as inappropriate to an economy which had been undergoing substantial change long before the second half of the eighteenth century.[21] As Mingay has recently concluded:

This concept (i.e. 'agricultural revolution'), however, has long been abandoned in favour of a much larger time span, stretching back to at least the middle seventeenth and going forward to near the close of the nineteenth; or, alternatively, the process of agrarian modernisation is viewed as recurring through a series of partial revolutions or stages within the longer time span, each with its own characteristics and making its own particular contribution towards increasing the output from the land. Perhaps, however, the whole idea of 'agricultural revolution' is inadmissable in a branch of the economy noted neither for the speed nor for the completeness of change in the past.[22]

It would, however, be unwise to uncritically impose historical patterns derived from the English experience on Scottish development. The argument advanced thus far in this study was that there existed substantial differences between the two rural economies in the seventeenth century and, in several respects, these continued into the decades immediately after 1700. The subsistence sector in Scotland was much more significant, as illustrated by the prevalence of rental in kind, the proliferation of very small tenancies, the perpetuation of multiple-tenant structures and the relatively limited size of the non-agricultural sector. Again, in the early eighteenth century, Scottish agrarian productivity was low by English standards, with average oat yields in the western and central lowlands estimated at between one-third to half of English values.[23] The differences in social systems were even more dramatic. There was little evidence in most parts of England of the cottar structures and multiple tenancies which ensured that most lowland rural Scots still had some access to land, even if only in mere patches. By the 1750s, the classic three-tier system of landlords, single tenants and servants/labourers was already in place in the majority of English counties.[24] The Scottish rural social structure was 'archaic' by comparison.

At the same time, the evidence of movement in Scotland before the 1750s has to be acknowledged. This study has illustrated increases in marketing, small productivity gains and important alterations within the social composition of the tenancy class. The old economy and society were not rigid. But these developments did not result in structural change or radical improvement in productivity. The landscape, agrarian practices and social order of the 1750s in much of the Lowlands would have been familiar to an observer from earlier times. In the final few decades of the eighteenth century, however, this agricultural system was exposed to unprecedented and extraordinary market pressures emanating from an urban and industrial structure in the first throes of economic revolution. How it responded is the subject of the remainder of this chapter and the rest of this book.

Chronology

One significant source on the timing of agrarian change are the comments of the parish ministers in the *OSA* in which they often describe and date the onset of 'improvements' in their own localities. Not all reports contain such information but a simple outline of the chronology of change is available for sixty parishes in the four counties. They suggest a clear pattern. The sluggish and patchy nature of advance before 1750, described in Chapter 2, is confirmed. Only 10 per cent of parishes in the sample indicated that agricultural innovation could be traced to the early decades of the eighteenth century. Significantly, much of the activity which did occur then concentrated in the 1740s. There was a modest increase in the 1750s, with 15 per cent of parishes reporting that improvement first began at that time. Thereafter, the intensity and scale of change became much more apparent. To these observers, however, the 1760s and 1770s seem to have been the crucial decades, with no less than 68 per cent of parishes describing how agricultural change first became established then, compared to 7 per cent locating it in the 1780s and 1790s. It is interesting to note also that this broad chronology was similar in all four counties. Indeed, the key decade throughout the study area for the initiation of improvement was the 1760s with no less than 47 per cent of reporting parishes tracing the origins of improvement to these years and, in particular, the period after the end of the Seven Years War in 1763.

Two other measures suggest a decisive change of direction in the 1760s and 1770s. Information was extracted from estate papers on the chronology of enclosure on thirty-five estates of varying size in the four counties of special interest and also in West Lothian, Stirling, Renfrew and Kirkcudbright. The results demonstrate that enclosure was only established on about five properties before 1750, again confirming the pattern of tentative development described in Chapter 2. Enclosing rapidly accelerated thereafter, however, with six estates in the 1760s and a further sixteen in the following decade involved in this activity. Also, 63 per cent of the sample of thirty-five landed properties started to enclose between 1763 and 1780.[25]

Another major index of improvement which can be utilised was the adoption of leases which prescribed new cropping regulations governing more effective fallowing and the use of sown grasses in the cultivation regime. These leases were usually lengthy, very detailed and prescriptive. They represented a quite different approach to land use to that of the traditional tack which tended to base the contract between farmer and landowner on the custom of the locality and the country. A typical example is reproduced in Appendix 8. The improving lease, as will be shown in more detail in Chapter 4, was designed to encourage innovation and the dissemination of improved agricultural practice. A survey of extant tack material in estate archives can therefore provide a quantitative guide to changing landlord priorities, even if we cannot assume that the terms of such agreements were always enforced in reality. A total of 320 leases were examined for eleven estates for the period 1760–1810. Again, a clear pattern emerged. 'Non-improving' leases were found. But only 27 per cent of all agreements were of this type and most of these dated from the 1760s and from smaller properties. By the 1790s, if not earlier, the improving lease had become the norm on all the estates examined. This was a radical departure from past practice since only a very small number of tacks contained such detailed cropping restrictions in the first half of the eighteenth century.

This short survey of some quantitative measures of the origins of improvement suggests that there was a decisive change of direction. This was recognised by many of the parish ministers of the 1790s who were fully aware that they had witnessed revolutionary advances in their own lifetimes. What is also remarkable is the rapid dissemination of improvement in the four counties. Despite diversity in natural endowment, access to markets and landlord attitudes, there was a general and almost simultaneous movement across the four counties towards the adoption of the new practices. Fife was relatively laggard but not in all respects and was catching up fast in the 1790s.

Commercialisation

Earlier chapters in this book have shown a steady increase in the impact of the market on lowland rural society. The most notable development in the first half of the eighteenth century was the erosion of 'in kind' elements in rentals suggesting that increasing numbers of tenant farmers were facing the market directly rather than through landlord intermediaries. After c.1760 the forces of commercialisation, released by the new demands of the growing cities and developing industries, began to dominate the countryside as never before. The subsistence economy which still prevailed to a significant extent in the later seventeenth century was subject to further erosion in the decades after 1707. But in the period after 1750 the market penetrated all aspects of the social and economic structure.

One indicator was that in most estates which have been studied, the final commutation of rentals in kind to rentals in money took place in the 1760s and 1770s. Even properties where the 'in kind' element was significant in the 1740s had mainly moved to money rentals by the 1780s. Thus the Balfour of Balbirnie estate in Fife, which had a rental of which 59 per cent was still paid in kind in 1748, had commuted entirely to cash by the 1770s.[26] The 320 tacks examined from several estate archives for the decades after 1750 also indicate rapid commutation of in kind rentals in the later eighteenth century. By 1790, payment in kind was unusual. But it did still exist in some areas. For instance, the rentals of the estates of the Earl of Airlie in Angus show payment of meal by tenants as late as the 1800s. Indeed the 'in kind' element in some parishes on the Airlie lands actually increased in the final decade of the eighteenth century. Ironically enough, however, even this probably reflected the new buoyancy of the market for grain which the landowner was attempting to exploit more effectively by absorbing more of the produce of the estate into his own possession.[27]

The OSA data also allow insight into the scale and extent of market penetration, a crucial measure in this analysis. This was evaluated by scrutinising the parish reports for the four counties and noting evidence of the export of agricultural produce. If this was not indicated, other information was sought, such as the existence of a market or trading place within the parish, the presence of dealers or a significant industrial activity which would be likely to be supplied by local farms. The detailed evidence is presented in Appendix 9. By these criteria 78 per cent of parishes in Ayr, 73 per cent of those in Fife and 72 per cent of those in Angus had a significant market orientation. Indeed, these figures suggest that market influence was virtually universal by the 1790s. This is because the percentages were calculated by using the *total* number of parishes in the three counties. Those parishes which gave no information on the relevant topics were not excluded from the denominator. Moreover, these aggregate data conceal local variation and the extent to which some localities had developed almost a special function in the servicing of urban markets. Thus, it was reckoned that half the annual produce of Lunan in Angus was exported from the parish.[28] St Vigeans in the same county sent grain to Leith and Glasgow and cattle to Arbroath.[29] Tealing in Angus had a market for its meal, livestock, dairy produce, linen and whisky in the city of Dundee.[30] The minister of the parish of Cambuslang in Lanarkshire sent almost all butter and cheese to Glasgow, situated about ten miles away.[31] Over a quarter of the farm produce of Covington in the hill country of southern Lanarkshire was exported, while that of the parish of Dalziell was 'mostly sold to Glasgow'.[32] But despite the significance of the big cities with their enormous and rapidly expanding appetite for meal, meat and dairy produce, the impact of more localised market stimuli should not be underestimated. As noted earlier, the presence of industrial workers in the countryside was increasing. The *OSA* data give an impression of its scale. Parishes were enumerated where an 'industrial presence' existed, providing a real alternative to agricultural employment in mill work, weaving, mining and iron-working. By this criterion, 42 per cent of the 183 parishes examined had such an 'industrial presence,' usually indicated by a small town or village community. The pattern varied between counties, with 48 per cent of parishes in Fife reporting such activity but only 27 per cent in Angus.[33] Nevertheless, the data confirm the widespread nature of industrial penetration of the lowland countryside which must have intensified demand for agricultural produce at the local level.

The process of accelerating commercialisation can also be discerned in the changing nature of estate policy. By the early eighteenth century, most land-owners had come to regard their estates primarily as sources of revenue to support rising levels of consumer expenditure. But the concept of investing in land in order to generate more productive capacity which in turn would yield an even greater rental was not yet widely disseminated. In this regard the strategies of the later eighteenth century also differed from those of earlier decades. Many lowland landowners began to spend massive sums on estate infrastructures, not because they saw 'improvement' as a fashionable hobby, but because they now expected a very handsome profit on their investments within a relatively short time-scale by gearing outlay to rent increase. The following four examples from a very large number of documented cases serve as an illustration. Over a five-year period, from 1771 to 1776, the Earl of Strathmore invested £22,223 in a large-scale programme of improvement on his Angus properties which included enclosure, drainage, road and bridge construction, and house-building.[34] Over a much shorter time-scale and on a smaller estate Richard Oswald's outlay on Auchincruive in Ayrshire between May to December 1803 totalled over £2,600.[35] In the early 1770s the Lanarkshire estate of Crawford absorbed £4,710 solely on the provision of enclosures and liming.[36] The equally lavish expenditure in the same period by the Duke of Hamilton on his Lanarkshire lands is described in detail in Chapter 5.[37] The estate of Bonnytown near St Andrews in Fife attracted investment of £10,000 between 1805–12. As was pointed out in the latter year:

> the lands have been completely drained, enclosed and subdivided, with substantial stone-dykes, an excellent modern farm steading built; the mansion house repaired and additions made to it, so as to render it a comfortable place of residence, and about twenty acres of the lands planted. The whole has been completely limed and dunged, so that the lands are at present in the very best possible order.[38]

Such huge outlays were predicted on the assumption that a combination of buoyant markets and gains in productivity from improved practices would produce returns which would rapidly compensate for outlays on this scale. The scheme, set out in Table 3.3, is one of many which were produced at the time to convince proprietors of the profit to be gained by adopting improved farm structures and rotations. On the farm of Ballumbie, this particular system, if adopted, would raise the rental of the holding by an estimated 128 per cent for the proprietor, the Earl of Panmure, in 1768. Another estimate from Fife, in the 1790s, suggested what appears to have been almost a conventional wisdom of the time: enclosing could be carried out at a cost of £2 per acre and the investment would be repaid in additional returns in four years.[39] That gestation period seems to have also governed the strategy of improvement on the Lanarkshire estate of Crawford in the early 1770s described above. There it was suggested in 1772 that the total costs of enclosing and liming were £4,772. However, it was anticipated that this would then result in a huge rent increase of £1,020 per annum which would recoup the outlay in four to five years.[40]

The main manifestation of the new commercial ethos was the unparalleled increase in rentals which was activated from the 1760s and accelerated from the 1790s. Again, space allows only a few examples of this general trend. On the Douglas estate in Lanarkshire, the rental rose from £1,426 in 1737 to £3,593 in 1774 and to £8,849 by 1815.[41] The return to the proprietor had increased sixfold in just over seventy years. This was a much higher rate of increase than the prices of produce and clearly represented gains accruing also from the enhanced productivity of land. But other owners enjoyed even more spectacular results. The Earl of Morton's rental spiralled from £377 in 1742 to £1,701 in 1795 and £3,987 in 1815, although these figures may also reflect some degree of estate enlargement as well as land-value appreciation.[42] The same caveat does not apply to the huge increases in income realised from the Earl of Eglinton's vast estates in Ayrshire. As elsewhere in the Lowlands, significant rises in rental occurred from the 1760s, increasing the rental to a much higher level by the 1790s. In 1797 the value of the rental of the nine baronies which comprised the Eglinton lands stood at £11,084. However, by the end of the Napoleonic Wars this figure had swollen to £25,992 in 1815.[43]

Gains on this scale inevitably produced a basic change in the whole approach to estate management. First, commercial criteria became supreme and the fashioning of the economic and social fabric to maximise returns from the market developed as a central feature of land administration. As tacks became more regulatory in structure, they increasingly contained clauses reserving rights over coal, stone and minerals to the proprietor. This was deeply significant because it provided unambiguous legal support for the landowner's determination to extract as much return as possible from the natural endowment of his estate. It symbolised land as property, as an asset to be exploited systematically. Second, holdings were enlarged, consolidated, divided and reshaped in order to fashion the most appropriate size in relation to agrarian specialisation, farm technology and local land resources. This whole subject will be considered at greater length in Chapter 6 but the scale of adjustment requires emphasis here. No less than 32 per cent of parishes in Ayrshire and 31 per cent of those in Angus reported the 'monopolising' and 'junction' of farms in the 1790s.[44] The drive to create larger units reflected the vital need to establish more holdings with the capacity to produce greater surpluses for the market.

Third, the paternalistic traditions of the older world came under enormous pressure. It would appear from the slight evidence available that eviction for rent arrears was uncommon in the later seventeenth and early eighteenth centuries.[45] Landlords were less compromising in the Age of Improvement. Commercial criteria were more likely to govern the occupation of land. An examination of sheriff courts processes in different parts of the Lowlands produced illuminating results in this respect.[46] They reveal that by the later eighteenth century arrears of rental and breach of lease conditions had now become significant reasons for tenant removal. In the majority of the 410 summonses of removal examined for Linlithgow, Cupar, Dunblane and Peebles after 1750, reasons for the action were either not provided or were stated as resulting from the expiry of a lease. This was so in 55 per cent of all cases. However, a further 12 per cent of summonses in the sample years from 1760 to 1800 were sought because of arrears or breach of tack. The survey of estate records also suggests a more rigorous policy adopted against those who defaulted on rental. As will be shown below, defaulters were especially at risk in the two crises of 1772–4 and 1783–4 when several estates used the bad times to weed out both poor payers and inadequate farmers.[47] It seems to have become axiomatic that tenants who were in arrears for two consecutive years were likely to be evicted; sheriffs normally accepted this as sufficient cause for granting a decreet of removal. The use of the sheriff courts in this area of land

TABLE 3.3   Schemes for improving a farm, Panmure Estate (Angus), 1768.

'A Scheme for Setting the Farm of Ballumbie, 1768'

The Present Rent of Ballumbie:

8 Bolls Wheat 15/- per Boll	£	6
32 Bolls Bear 10/- per Boll		16
40 Bolls Meal 10/- per Boll		20
Money	£	30.17.9⁴⁄12

There are in the above Farm 90 acres Infield 111 Acres Outfield 39 Acres in Grass and 19 Acres Marshy Ground which may be rentalled as follows viz:

Infield	90 Acres @ 10/- per acre	£	45
Outfield	111 Acres @ 6/- per acre		33. 6
Grass	39 Acres @ 6/- per acre		11.14
Marshy Ground	19 Acres @ 1/6d per acre		1.8.6
	259 Acres	£	91.8.6

Suppose the Farm of Ballumbie to be Sett for two nineteen years and a Lifetime:

The first 19 years to pay as above	£91.8.6
The second 19 years to advance £10	£101.8.6
The first 19 years of the Life advance £10	£111.8.6
The remainder of the Life Advance £10	£121.8.6

'A Scheme of the Present Method of Labouring Ballumbie and what it may produce'

The aftermentioned Acres may produce besides the seed as follows viz:

Infield 90 acres in Three Casts

1st Cast	30 acres Bear may produce 60 Bolls @ 10/-	£	30
2nd Cast	30 acres Oats may produce 60 Bolls @ 10/-		30
½ 3rd Cast	15 acres Wheat may produce 30 Bolls @ 15/-		22.10
½ 3rd Cast	15 acres Pease may produce 15 Bolls @ 10/-		7.10
	90 acres	£	92

Outfield 111 Acres in Eight Casts

Lee Crop	14 Acres may produce 71½ Bolls 10/-		£	8.15
Auitt Crop	14 Acres may produce 24½ Bolls 10/-			12. 5
Third Crop	14 Acres may produce 10½ Bolls 10/-			5. 5
Fourth Crop	14 Acres may produce 10½ Bolls 10/-			5. 5
1,2,3, and 4 years grass 55 Acres		@ 6/- per acre		16.10
Pasture Grass 39 Acres		@ 6/- per acre		11.14
Marshy Ground 19 acres		@ 1/6d per acre		1. 8.6
Outfield etc. 169 acres				61. 2.6
Infield 90 acres				90
	259 acres		£	151.2.6

'A Scheme for Labouring the Farm of Ballumbie when improven and what it may produce'

154 Acres to be divided into Eleven Fourteen Acre Parks:

14 Acres Oat may produce	84 Bolls			
Deduct Seed	14	70 @ 10/-	£	35
14 Lint Neeps etc.		@ £3 per acre		42
14 Barley	98			
Deduct Seed	10½	87½ @ 10/-		43.15

TABLE 3.3   (Continued)

14 Clover and Rye Grass for Hay	@ 50/- per acre	35
14 Clover and Rye Grass for Hay	@ 50/- per acre	35
14 Pasture	@ 15/- per acre	10.10
14 Pasture	@ 15/- per acre	10.10
14 Pasture	@ 15/- per acre	10.10
14 Pasture	@ 10/- per acre	7
14 Pasture	@ 10/- per acre	7
14 Pasture	@ 10/- per acre	7
154		£ 243.5
39 Grass	@ 6/-	11.14
19 Marshy Ground	@ 1/6d	1. 8.6
212 acres		£ 256. 7.6

40 Acres Infield in Five Casts as follows viz.:

8 Acres in Fallow				
8 Wheat may produce	64			
Deduct seed	6	58 @ 15/-		£ 43.10
8 Pease	24			
seed	6	18 @ 10/-		9
8 Bear	56			
seed	6	50 @ 10/-		25
8 Oats	48			
seed	8	40 @ 10/-		20
40 Infield acres				97.10
212 Outfield etc. acres				256. 7.6
7 Fences and roads acres				
259 acres				£ 353.17.6

'Another Scheme for Labouring the within Forty Acres of Infield'

The 40 Acres Infield to be divided into Six Casts viz.:

6⅔ Acres in Fallow			
6⅔ Acres Barley may produce	53⅓ Bolls		
Deduct seed	5	48⅓ @ 10/-	24.3. 4
6⅔ Acres Oats	53⅓		
seed	6⅔	46⅔ @ 10/-	23.6. 8
6⅔ Acres Pease	20		
seed	5	15 @ 10/-	17.10
6⅔ Acres Bear	40		
seed	5	35 @ 10/-	17.10
6⅔ Acres Oats	40		
seed	6⅔	33⅓ @ 10/-	16.13. 4
40 Infield acres			89. 3. 4
212 Outfield acres			256. 7. 6
7 Fences and Roads acres			
259 acres			£ 345.10.10

SOURCE   SRO, Dalhousie Muniments, GD45/18/2277, Scheme for Setting the Farm of Ballumbie, 1768.

management is in itself significant. Several of the old baron courts continued to function after they were abolished in 1747. But their decline and the developing role of the sheriff court in landlord – tenant relations suggests the emergence of a more formal and impersonal system of justice in rural areas.

Fourth, the rapid impact of market forces is made apparent in accelerating the trend towards agrarian specialisation. Lowland farming had been, and remained throughout the era of Improvement, mixed in structure with both crop-growing and stock-rearing combined in most parts. Pockets of pastoral husbandry flourished in the hill country and dairy farming existed close to towns in the western lowlands. What we see, however, in the later eighteenth century is an intensification of these tendencies to local specialisation as different areas were now able to exploit their comparative advantage because of market demand for their surplus.[48] Equally, it suggests that transport developments were sufficiently advanced to allow localities with arable specialisations to draw on the production of pastoral zones and vice versa.

It was at this time that dairy and fruit farming developed more emphatically in Ayrshire, Renfrewshire and Clydesdale to supply the booming industrial centres.[49] But perhaps the most striking example of agrarian specialisation, especially because of its impact on local society, was the increase in sheep and, to a lesser extent, cattle farming in the southern parishes of Lanarkshire, the uplands of central Ayrshire and the highland parishes of Angus. The OSA reports demonstrate that in all these areas large-scale pastoral farming was advancing and that the new agrarian system was displacing large numbers of small tenants and cottars in its wake in a manner very reminiscent of the Highland Clearances.[50]

Landscape

To contemporary observers the most visible and dramatic aspect of the economic revolution in agriculture was the alteration in the physical form of the Lowland countryside. Essentially, the modern rural landscape of trim fields, separated by hedge and ditch, surrounding compact, single farm steadings was in the process of formation in the decades after 1760. Once put in place, it was a structure that remained virtually unaltered until into the twentieth century. As one scholar has remarked, this gave lowland Scotland 'a face lift which was more thorough-going than in any other country of Europe in the course of the eighteenth century'.[51] Over time virtually all traces of the old agriculture and the ancient social structure were removed. The clustered touns and cottouns, the system of infield – outfield cultivation and the rigs of land worked by different possessors were all eliminated, though the pace and nature of removal varied significantly both within and between different regions and the process was only finally completed in the 1830s and 1840s in some areas. The purpose of this section, however, is to demonstrate that it was already well advanced in the area of study before the end of the eighteenth century.

Two fundamental forces in landscape change were division of commonty and enclosure. Commonities were uninhabited lands varying in size from a few acres to several thousand.[52] They provided a source of building materials and fuel for neighbouring settlements. They could also be used for rough grazing and supplied a reserve of arable land. Such areas were not 'commons' in the literal sense because the rights to use them went with the lands adjacent to them. In a sense, therefore, they were a part, though an undivided part, of the private estates which surrounded them. The legal framework for the actual division of commonties among owners was created by Acts of the Scottish Parliament in 1608, 1647 and 1695. The latter was the most important. Not only did it set out the process by which commonties could be divided, it also permitted any one landowner with an interest to pursue division in the Court of Session whether other parties were in agreement or not. Inevitably, however, such legislation produced dispute and controversy about the actual rights to share in the commonty.[53] There was, therefore, often a considerable time-lag between the initiation of a process of division and its successful completion.

Nevertheless, where commonty division can be dated, it offers a rough guide to the timing of landscape improvement, even if the legal process was not always followed by the immediate absorption of the lands into regular cultivation and pasture. Of the commonty divisions which occurred in the four counties of study between 1600 and 1914, fifty-eight can be dated. The 150 years before 1750 are revealed as a period of very low activity, with only seven divisions. Over the 100 years from 1815 to 1914, twenty-five were counted. However, the phase of peak activity, with twenty-six or 45 per cent of all divisions between 1600 and 1914, fell between 1760 and 1815.[54]

Of much greater consequence in changing the face of the landscape was enclosure. One eighteenth-century estate factor described it as 'the principal and lasting improvement of an estate'.[55] Certainly, as will be shown in Chapters 5 and 6, enclosure was regarded as the *sine qua non* of estate reorganisation and, when combined with the new rotations and effective liming of the land, the fastest means of increasing productivity and rental. The main thrust of enclosure in the later eighteenth-century Lowlands was towards the division of the scattered rigs of land into fields separated by hedges, ditches or dykes.[56] The physical structure of these divisions varied over time and space depending in large part upon the prevailing natural resources of particular districts. Many were constructed of earth mounds, topped by thorn hedges, and flanked by ditches. The building of stone dykes was also common, especially since it was complementary to another vital improvement, the clearing of stones from the soil. The potential economic advantages from enclosure were very considerable. The splitting-up of land into separate, convenient units facilitated the introduction of the new crops such as turnips, sown grasses and potatoes, and enabled the more effective planning of the cycle of improved rotations. Enclosure also accelerated the dissolution of the old structure of infield and outfield and hastened the emergence of regular, equal and intensive use of all arable land around the farm. One crucial effect may have been psychological because enclosure represented a dramatic physical break with the past and symbolised that a new order was being established. But there was no necessary connection between it and productivity gains. Enclosure created a context where faster change was possible but could not always be guaranteed. In some cases, new rotations were put in place without it. Moreover, costs were high and enclosure could sometimes only proceed in a piecemeal and gradual fashion. Certainly, some of the large estates examined in this study, even with sustained investment, took a couple of decades to enclose most of their lands and activity came to a complete halt in such crisis years as the early 1770s and early 1780s. What compounded the problem was that enclosure usually took place in parallel with other expensive improvements such as road and bridge construction and the building of farm houses and villages. Perhaps the need to reduce costs helps to explain why some early enclosures were poorly made and had to be reconstructed at a later date.[57]

After all the qualifications have been made, however, it is still the remarkable speed and scale of enclosure development in the later eighteenth-century Lowlands which impress. In England, enclosing of pasture land had been under way on a significant scale from late medieval times. Enclosing for sheep and cattle occurred in south-west Scotland in the seventeenth century. Yet the enclosure of tenants' holdings in lowland Scotland had hardly developed at all outside parts of the south-east region by the 1750s. The OSA data indicate a huge expansion in enclosing activity thereafter with, as Table 3.4 demonstrates, the majority of parishes in all four counties reporting significant advances. Enclosure was still proceeding in the second and third decades of the nineteenth century but the transformation of landscape, even if it was not complete, was already apparent long before then. In the 1790s, 69 per cent of parishes reported some enclosing and 37 per cent indicated that 'most' or 'all' lands were enclosed and divided. This is a remarkable finding when it is remembered that much moor and rough pasture land in Ayr and Lanark were left unenclosed and work was concentrated mainly in the arable districts. In addition, it should be remembered that the data have been derived from the reports of all 197 parishes in the study area. Parishes which gave *no* information on enclosure were not excluded from the denominator. If they had been, the quantitative significance of enclosure would have become even more apparent.

TABLE 3.4   Enclosure in the 1790s: Angus, Ayr, Fife and Lanark (% of parishes).

County	Enclosure			
	Part	Most	All	Unspecified
Angus	20.4	25.9	5.6	27.8
Ayr	4.3	28.3	17.4	15.2
Fife	11.7	25	3.3	28.3
Lanarkshire	10.2	21.6	18.9	5.4
Average	13.15	25.2	11.3	19.1

SOURCE   *OSA* parish reports for the relevant counties.

But in one important respect enclosure did not alter the traditional landscape. The physical formation of the old ridges, on which crops were grown and furrows between them dug to drain surface water, was broadly maintained. Not until the system of underground tile drainage became widespread later in the nineteenth century could this method be dispensed with entirely. Thus, as one observer commented of Ayrshire in 1792, 'the ridges still continue in many places, very high and broad; the furrows being often 20, 30 and 40 feet asunder'.[58] However, even the system of ridges and furrows was not immune from the impact of landscape change. Although the basic structure was preserved, considerable adjustments took place. Ridges were straightened, levelled in part and reduced in height in districts which were naturally well drained. In Angus in the 1790s, 'the ancient, broad, crooked and high-crowned ridges, that yet prevail in the hill district are almost all in the lower part disused. The ridges are now generally straight, much levelled, some in very wet places; and may be about 16 or 18 feet wide.'[59]

One indication of the development of more easily worked ridges was the evolution of ploughing technology. Thirty-three per cent of parishes in Ayrshire, Fife and Angus reported on the ploughs in common use in the 1790s. Their comments are tabulated in Table 3.5. Plainly, the 'old Scots' plough with its large team of oxen and horses was still prevalent. This was not a reflection of conservatism. The traditional plough was preferred for ploughing stiff land, especially where only one ploughing was given. Also, as one improving writer put it, ' ... it sets up the edge of the furrows most properly and furnishes a plentiful mould for the seed'.[60] But the old plough, as Table 3.5 shows, was also subject to adaptation and improvement which were now possible because of landscape changes. In Lanarkshire, by the last decade of the eighteenth century, it had become shorter in the head, stilts and beam than formerly. Less animal and human labour was required to manage it. At the same time, the new, lighter ploughs were also beginning to be adopted alongside the more traditional implement.[61]

Working the Land

Ultimately, one of the main tests of agrarian transformation is whether or not there was a radical increase in the productive capacity of the land and, in particular, whether crop yields improved at a rate which was revolutionary over the levels prevailing in earlier times. There was little contemporary

TABLE 3.5   Ploughing technology in the 1790s (types as % of total in each county).

Type of Plough	Ayrshire	Fife	Angus
'Old Scots'	10.9	6.7	9.3
Modified Scots plough	6.5	3.3	7.4
New, James Small, ploughs	4.3	38.3	13.0

SOURCE *OSA* parish reports for relevant counties.

scientific understanding of the relationship between types of cultivation and output, but through observation, experimentation and trial and error, farmers had evolved a variety of techniques to boost yields. The first and the most familiar was fallowing. This, of course, was commonplace in the old agriculture in which it was customary to allow parts of the outfield to lie uncropped for years at a time. 'Improved' fallowing did not simply rest the land, however, it also manured and renewed it with dung and lime used in vast quantities to refresh the soil. Grass seed was also sown. A short extract from a typical Lanarkshire tack of 1791 gives an impression of the sheer effort which now went into fallowing:

> The division or field that falls yearly to be in fallow, must be equal to a tenth part of the lands to be cultivated; and it must get at least four plowings (*sic*) in the season, and be manured at the rate of sixty cart loads of good dung, or ten cart loads of lime shells to the acre. Turnips may be sown on the fallow field after it has been laboured and manured as aforesaid, and along with the following crop, it must be sown with grass seeds, at the rate of two bushels of rye grass, and twelve pounds of clover seed to the acre. Thereafter it must remain in grass five years, in one of which years only it may be cut for hay.[62]

Dung and lime were also increasingly applied in copious quantities. Scottish urbanisation and the building of better roads enabled more areas to import manure from the towns and cities. But the application of lime remained more common and more important. Liming could be a costly operation, mainly because of the expense of transporting such bulky material. Moreover, although some landowners were fortunate to have abundant supplies on their estate, others had to look further afield. Some Angus parishes, for instance, acquired lime from as far away as the Firth of Forth and Sunderland.[63] It was a further reflection of the incentive of rising produce prices that lime could be applied so lavishly. On all the estates studied, enclosure of land was usually followed by liming of the fields at a rate of 400–600 bushels per acre. It was regarded as an especially effective means of absorbing former outfield land and bringing it rapidly to infield standards. As one observer put it, 'first, liming produces visible increases in fertility. If left moderately cropped thereafter and then left several years to rest, the effects of the second liming upon fertility are even more marked.'[64] Contemporaries confidently anticipated that its perceived benefits were such that the outlay on liming could be recouped after three to four crops.[65]

There was also significant acceleration in the diffusion of such sown grasses as rye and clover. These crops had long been cultivated in the Lothians and in some progressive farms elsewhere but the mass of ordinary tenant farmers did not use them to any significant extent. From the 1760s, however, improved rotations incorporating sown grasses spread at an astonishing speed. The OSA reports for the 1790s indicate that they were already grown in at least 40 per cent of parishes in Ayrshire, 46 per cent in Lanarkshire, 62 per cent in Fife and 71 per cent in Angus. Their impact on yields was likely to be dramatic: 'They increased the supply of fodder, allowed a greater carry of animals, and, just as important, allowed a production of dung half as much again as that arising from white-crops even when both ear and straw were fed to the animals.'[66]

Historians have suggested that the adoption of turnip husbandry with its capacity to support more and better stock lagged somewhat behind the cultivation of sown grasses.[67] It would indeed appear that in some areas the diffusion of this crop was more protracted. For instance, only 19 per cent of Ayrshire parishes and 27 per cent of Lanarkshire parishes reported its use in the 1790s. But even turnips, and the more sophisticated and productive rotations of which they were an integral part, were spreading more rapidly in the later eighteenth century than some accounts suggest. In Fife, 65 per cent of parishes and in Angus, 82 per cent of parishes noted the cultivation of turnips by the 1790s and, in the majority of cases scrutinised, the crop was well consolidated into the prevailing systems of rotation.

The revolutionary effect of fallowing, liming, sown grasses and, to a lesser extent, turnips can be measured from contemporary data on crop yields. Whyte estimated seed-yield ratios for several seventeenth-century Scottish estates, most of which were situated in the more favoured east coast.[68] The progressive nature of East Lothian agriculture already stood out with some estates in that county producing oat yields of 6–9. Elsewhere the pattern was less impressive with the average maximum for the seventeenth century being 6 and the average minimum just over 4. Returns were even lower in the west. One run of oat-yield figures for the estate of the Earl of Cassillis in Wigtownshire for the period 1655–61, years of good harvests, suggests a mean of 2.4.[69] Despite the limited evidence and the bias towards east coast properties with a better climate for grain-growing in the sample, it would appear that oat-yield ratios in the seventeenth century were normally around 3–4 but that slightly lower and higher returns were also recorded. Data for the first half of the eighteenth century are even more elusive. However, information extracted from the Hamilton estate papers in Lanarkshire, the Tayfield property in Fife for 1714 and the Morton lands in the same county for 1745 indicates that there had been no substantial improvement on seventeenth-century levels.[70] In one example, the oat yield was estimated at 2.55 while in the other two instances the return hovered around 3–4. In 1771, the 'unimproved' estate of Crawford in Lanarkshire, the 'average return' (*sic*) was 'almost 6 bolls on their croft (infield) land and about 3 bolls in their field (outfield) land'.[71] This suggests an overall average of around 4–5. Significantly, these were considerably below contemporary English yields for oats which by the 1740s were averaging 6.5–8.5.[72]

The Scottish pattern of the later eighteenth century can be reconstructed from evidence in the *OSA* and the Agricultural Reports of the 1790s. In some cases ratios of seed return are provided. More often, however, the information is given as 'bolls per acre'. Fortunately, a single *OSA* account for the parish of Brechin suggests that between 3 firlots and 14 pecks of seed were normally

TABLE 3.6   Oat yields in 18 parishes, 1790s.

| | | Return ratios sowing per acre | |
		At 3 firlots	At 14 pecks
Parish	County		
Airly	Angus	6.7	5.7
Auchterhouse	Angus	16.0	13.7
Brechin	Angus	9.3	8.0
Edzell	Angus	16 (seed-yield ratio given)	
Essie & Nevay	Angus	13.3	11.4
Kinettles	Angus	16.0	13.7
Liff & Bervie	Angus	13.3	11.4
Maryton	Angus	10.7	9.1
Denino	Fife	6.7	5.7
Dunfermline	Fife	9.3	8.0
Kirkcaldy	Fife	10.7	9.1
Dysart	Fife	6 (seed-yield ratio given)	
Colmonell	Ayr	3–4 (seed-yield ratio given)	
		7–9 (after ley, dung & lime)	
Sorn	Ayr	7 (seed-yield ratio given)	
Straiton	Ayr	6–7 (seed-yield ratio given)	
Cadder	Lanark	16.0	13.7
Pettinain	Lanark	13.3	11.4
Shotts	Lanark	8.0	6.9

SOURCE *OSA*, Angus, Fife, Ayr and Lanark.

sown per acre.[73] On the assumption that this was general practice it is possible to produce conversion to sowing to reaping ratios: 3 firlots equal 0.75 of one boll, whereas 14 pecks (4 pecks to the firlot) represent 0.875 of one boll. Using this information, return ratios have been calculated for eighteen parishes in the study area (see Table 3.6).

These data suggest two main conclusions. First, and not surprisingly, the considerable variation between counties in yields suggests the varied pace of the dissemination of improved practices, the influence of local climatic patterns and diversity in soil quality. Second, even these complexities cannot conceal the remarkable increase in yields over seventeenth- and early eighteenth-century levels. The mean Angus yield on the basis of these figures was 12.46, in Fife it was 7.68, in Ayr 7.3 and in Lanark 11.55. It is unlikely that these data give a wholly accurate impression of the precise pattern within each county because of the relatively small sample of parishes provided. Yet the overall impression is that oat yields in Angus and Lanark in the 1790s were triple seventeenth-century averages and in Ayr and Fife approximately double earlier returns. These results are consistent with the remarks of Col. William Fullarton in his survey of the agriculture of Ayrshire in 1793 when he asserted that 'the third of the farms in crop supplied double or triple the yield which had formerly been taken from the whole'.[74] Indeed, his own estimates suggest that the *OSA* figures understate the yield gains in Ayrshire. In Fullarton's view, the farms of the county could not 'uncommonly produce' yields of between

10 and 12 or results closer to the Lanarkshire and Angus averages given above. The *OSA* estimates for Ayrshire are almost certainly affected by the small size of the sample and the fact that at least two of the parishes were located in upland pastoral districts where returns were likely to be lower for climatic reasons. However, elsewhere, the scale of the revolution in grain output, which had taken place in the space of only a few decades, is undeniable. Its origin was graphically demonstrated in the account of the parish of Colmonell in Ayrshire where the minister estimated that the traditional yield from oats was 3–4 but after ley and the sustained application of dung and lime it virtually trebled to 7–9.[75]

If these results are representative, many farmers in these counties had effectively caught up on the output levels of their English counterparts by 1800. B. A. Holderness estimates that English oats ratios were 7–9 about 1800 and had risen to 11–12 by 1850.[76] The mean for all the Scottish parishes tabulated above was 9.7 in the 1790s. Equally, in England there was an average yield increase of about 50 per cent between 1750 and 1800 whereas the Scottish figures suggest an average rise of between 200 and 300 per cent over the same period. This was indeed a transformation which marks out the decades after the 1750s as a period of remarkable change.

REFERENCES

1. Details on urbanisation are derived from Devine, 'Urbanisation', pp. 27–41 and J. de Vries, *European Urbanisation, 1500–1800* (London, 1987), pp. 39–48.
2. de Vries, *European Urbanisation*, pp. 39–48.
3. H. Hamilton, *An Economic History of Scotland in the Eighteenth Century* (Oxford, 1963), pp. 404–5.
4. N. Murray, *The Scottish Handloom Weavers: A Social History, 1790–1850* (Edinburgh, 1978), p. 18.
5. See M. W. Flinn, 'Trends in Real Wages, 1750–1850', *Econ. Hist. Rev.*, 2nd ser., XXVII (1974), pp. 395–413 and E. H. Hunt and F. W. Botham, 'Wages in Britain during the Industrial Revolution', *Econ. Hist. Rev.*, 2nd. ser., XL (1987), pp. 380–99.
6. J. H. Treble, 'The Standard of Living of the Working Class' in Devine and Mitchison, eds, *People and Society in Scotland*, pp. 194–200.
7. T. M. Devine, 'Introduction' in Devine and Mitchison, eds, *People and Society in Scotland*, pp. 2–6.
8. S. Nenadic, 'The Rise of the Urban Middle Classes' in Devine and Mitchison, eds, *People and Society in Scotland*, pp. 109–26.
9. *OSA* (Lanarkshire), VII, p. 149.
10. R. Perren, 'Markets and Marketing' in G. E. Mingay, ed., *The Agrarian History of England and Wales, vol. VI, 1750–1850* (Cambridge, 1989), pp. 263–7.
11. There have been several studies since E. A. Wrigley's seminal article, 'A Simple Model of London's Importance in Changing English Society and Economy, 1650–1750', *Past and Present*, 37 (1967), pp. 44–70.
12. Murray, *Scottish Handloom Weavers*, pp. 22–5.
13. See below, pp. 151–4.
14. T. C. Smout, 'The Landowner and the Planned Village in Scotland, 1730–1830' in N. T. Phillipson and R. Mitchison, eds, *Scotland in the Age of Improvement* (Edinburgh, 1970), pp. 73–106.
15. This topic is explored in detail below, pp. 151–4.
16. *OSA* (Lanarkshire), VII, *passim*.

17. Ibid., pp. 16–17, 21–7, 378–92.
18. Sir John Sinclair, *General Report of the Agricultural State and Political Circumstances of Scotland* (Edinburgh, 1814), III, p. 339.
19. G. Robertson, *Rural Recollections* (Irvine, 1829), p. 145.
20. See, for example, Whittington, 'Scottish Agricultural Revolution', pp. 204–6; I. H. Adams and I. D. Whyte, 'The Agricultural Revolution in Scotland: Contributions to the Debate', *Area*, 9 (1977), pp. 198–205.
21. M. Overton, 'Agricultural Revolution? Development of the Agrarian Economy in Early Modern England' in A. R. H. Baker and D. Gregory, eds, *Explorations in Historical Geography* (Cambridge, 1984), pp. 118–39.
22. G. E. Mingay, 'Introduction' in Mingay, ed., *Agrarian History*, p. 1.
23. See below, p. 42.
24. W. A. Armstrong, 'Labour' and J. H. Porter, 'Rural Society' in Mingay, ed., *Agrarian History*, pp. 671–88, 848–65.
25. The extent of enclosing did, however, vary enormously.
26. SRO, GD288/272/8, Balfour of Balbirnie Muniments; GD288/22/1, Tack of Finglassie, 773; GD288/4/122, Backfield of Pitcairn, 1804; Balbirnie Rentals, 1770–1810.
27. SRO, Airlie Muniments, GD16/16 (Tacks), 30A (Estate Rentals).
28. See Appendix 9.
29. Ibid.
30. Ibid.
31. Ibid.
32. Ibid.
33. Ibid.
34. NRA(S) 885, Earl of Strathmore Papers, vol. 22A, Ledger of P. Proctor's Accounts as Clerk to the Works, 1771–6.
35. SRO, SC6/72/1, Sheriff Court Records (Ayr), Register of Improvements on Entailed Estates (1803).
36. HPL 631/1, John Burrell's Journals, June 1772.
37. See below, p. 000.
38. SRO, GD288/98/47, Balsour of Balbirnie Muniments, Particulars regarding the estate of Bonnytown, 1817.
39. *OSA* (Fife), p. 43.
40. HPL 631/1, John Burrell's Journals, June 1772.
41. NRA(S) 859, Douglas-Home Papers, Rentals, 174/11, 62/1.
42. SRO, GD150/2061/12–14, Morton Papers, Morton Rentals.
43. SRO, GD3/vols 8361, 8346, 8559, Eglinton Muniments, Eglinton Rentals, 1779–1815.
44. See Appendix 9.
45. Whyte, 'Continuity and Change', pp. 160–6. This is also the impression gained from a scrutiny of the Sheriff Court Processes of Cupar, Dunblane, Peebles, Hamilton, Lanark and Linlithgow for this earlier period. See SRO: SC38/7/8, SC38/22/10, SC37/8/6, SC20/5/1, SC42/5/1, SC44/22/1, SC41/6/1.
46. See the courts listed in n. 45 above.
47. See below, p. 73.
48. *OSA* reports for Ayrshire, Lanarkshire and Angus.
49. Ibid.
50. See below, p. 126.
51. A. Fenton, *Scottish Country Life* (Edinburgh, 1976), p. 16.
52. I. H. Adams, *Directory of Commonties* (Edinburgh, 1971).
53. The estate papers considered in this study are full of references to such cases.
54. Calculated from Adams, *Directory of Commonties, passim.*
55. NRA(S) 859, Douglas-Home Papers, 182/6, Memorial for Douglas, 1769.
56. The points mentioned briefly below are explored further in the case studies in Chapters 5 and 6.
57. See, for example, J. Thomson, *General View of the Agriculture of the County of Fife* (Edinburgh, 1800), p. 134.

58. W. Fullarton, *General View of the Agriculture of the County of Ayr* (Edinburgh, 1793), p. 32.
59. Revd Mr Roger, *General View of the Agriculture of Angus or Forfar* (Edinburgh, 1794), p. 19.
60. J. Naismith, *General View of the Agriculture of the County of Clydesdale* (Edinburgh, 1794), p. 58.
61. Ibid.
62. SRO, GD5/546, Lockhart of Lee Papers, Articles and Regulations of Tutors, 1791.
63. *OSA* (Angus), p. 13.
64. Naismith, *General View of Clydesdale*, p. 61.
65. Roger, *General View of Angus*, p. 2. See also John Burrell's emphasis on the merits of liming in HPL 631/1, Burrell's Journals, 1764–1772, *passim*.
66. Gray, 'Scottish Emigration', p. 116.
67. Ibid., p. 120.
68. Whyte, *Agriculture and Society*, pp. 73–9.
69. Ibid., p. 74.
70. HPL 631/1, John Burrell's Journals, 2 Apr. 1774 and 5 Sept. 1774; NRA(S) 874, Berry Papers, 12/6, Rental of the Lands and Estate of Inverdovat (1714); SRO, GD150/2061, Account of Victual Sown on the Strip of Ground call'd the Sankiedeals, Crop 1745. The reader should note that the Tayfield example has been estimated by the following method. A note at the bottom of the manuscript suggests infield (croft) land was divided with four breaks, implying a 4-year rotation of oats/oats/bear/pease. In order to make a rough calculation of crop return, I have assumed, as Whyte did, that the crop yield = rent × 3 = 112 bolls × 3 = 336 bolls.
    By the above calculation the approximate area of cultivated land on the ferme toun is:

Infield	= 47.33 acres
Outfield	= 40.5 acres
Total arable	= 87.83 @ 1½ bolls sown per acre
Total no. of bolls sown	= 131.75
Thus, average yield	= 336/131.75 = 2.55 to 1

    It should be noted, however:
    1. No account has been taken of the money rent (£66 Scots) in the above calculation. This tends to underplay the rent and thus the estimated return of crop.
    2. It is possible that rents may have been reduced following the bad harvests of the late 1690s (though there was no evidence for this) in which case the rental may well have been set below potential returns and would have reduced the estimated value of the yield.

71. HPL 531/1, John Burrell's Journals, 8 July 1771.
72. B. A. Holderness, 'Prices, Productivity and Output' in Mingay, ed., *Agrarian History*, pp. 143–4.
73. *OSA* (Angus), p. 98.
74. Fullarton, *General View of Ayr*, p. 21.
75. *OSA* (Ayr), parish of Colmonell.
76. Holderness, 'Prices, Productivity and Output', pp. 143–5.

4

The Process of Improvement

The Dynamics of Change

I

THERE has been much debate over the years about the role of the landed classes in improving British agriculture in the eighteenth century. In England, the current historical opinion is that, though relevant, the contribution of the great proprietors was not decisive. A recent writer has argued, for instance, that 'the real practical work of experimentation and innovation was the province of lesser country gentlemen, enlightened tenants and forward-looking agents'.[1] English historians, in particular point to the greater tenant farmers as the main contributors to agricultural progress in the eighteenth century, and this almost certainly reflects the relatively advanced and mature condition of the English rural economy at that time.[2] The pattern in lowland Scotland seems to have been strikingly different. Landowners, through their factors, played a very prominent role, especially in the initial phases of agrarian improvement in the later eighteenth century. All the estates examined in the course of this study confirm their leading contribution. As will be seen below, tenant farmers were important. After all, they and not the proprietors actually worked the land. Furthermore, their significance became even greater over time when the first period of structural change had been completed. By the early nineteenth century there was more evidence of a proactive tenantry than in the 1760s and 1770s. But the initiation of widespread improvement, as the detailed case-studies in Chapters 5 and 6 in particular will demonstrate, often came from above.

One illustration of the different Scottish pattern was that in England detailed improving leases were not only less common but were going out of fashion by the early nineteenth century.[3] In Scotland, on the other hand, the improving lease with its comprehensive and intricate cropping prescriptions, buttressed by monetary fines and penalties for non-compliance, was only coming into widespread use in the 1760s. It rapidly became a key mechanism for the dissemination of improved practices. In Scotland, apparently, agrarian change had often to be encouraged from above. It did not simply develop autonomously from below. The improving lease was less necessary in many areas of England because agricultural practice was already more advanced than in most Scottish regions outside East Lothian. In addition, there were many more substantial tenants with the resources to invest in more innovative practices in the south. The discussion of comparative crop yields in the previous chapter demonstrated the relative backwardness and poverty of the Scottish rural economy as late as the 1740s. In Scotland, therefore, the landowners had a more important role. Their commitment to improvement was based on the expectation of hugely increased profits from their lands which would cover the cost of their investment in a relatively short time. In the 1760s and 1770s the conventional wisdom was that judicious outlay in enclosing, roads and farmhouses, and encouragement to improved rotations would triple the rental of an estate. One contemporary observer noted in 1782 that lands in Fife were being sold at double or treble their estimated value because of this extraordinary faith in improvement. As he indicated, 'It is astonishing to what length people will go in these speculative purchases, and to what extent they will carry these expectations on the supposed Capability and Effect of Improvements. Yet these estates are all in a state of nature: no houses, no inclosures, no wood, no lime or coal and so everything to do upon them.'[4] Sometimes the confidence was misplaced, especially during the economic crises of 1772–3 and 1783–4 when the improving movement temporarily foundered amid mounting tenant arrears and farm bankruptcies.[5] But it was this belief in the efficacy of improvement which drove forward the whole movement of agrarian reform and which rapidly overcame custom and traditional inertia in many parts of the Lowlands.

The speed of Scottish rural transformation is one of its most remarkable characteristics. Arguably, nowhere else in western Europe was agrarian economy and society altered so quickly and rapidly in the eighteenth century.[6] In large part this was due to the market influences already considered in Chapter 3. But another major factor was the strongly interventionist role of many landowners and their determination to break with past practice and impose a new economic and social order. Only rarely, however, did individual proprietors become actually involved in the detailed business of planning and implementation. This was normally delegated to factors and agents, especially when an owner was absentee or possessed several properties. Such men had often very wide powers, as the studies of such factors as Robert Ainslie, John Maxwell and John Burrell in Chapters 5 and 6 indicate. However, the landowner was still responsible for the initiation of improvement and its financing. In addition, landlord correspondence demonstrates that they were usually kept fully informed by their factors on the progress of plans and consulted on such issues as the leasing of farms, the use of the law against indebted tenants and the like. The broad powers delegated to factors were in fact another reflection of the extent of intervention by the landlords. They now required larger estate bureaucracies than before with the bigger properties in particular recruiting sub-factors, inspectors and supervisors to monitor the progress of improvement.[7]

In promoting the new structures, Scottish landowners had several distinctive advantages, some traditional and others recently acquired. By any standards, they were a most powerful social class. Historically, most of the Scottish land had been held by a few large-scale proprietors. By the early nineteenth century there were about 7,500 landowners and throughout the eighteenth century the greater landlords were consolidating their position at the expense of lesser lairds.[8] By the 1870s, for instance, 90 per cent of Scotland's land was owned by less than 1,500 proprietors.[9] Inevitably, there were regional variations, with the largest estates located in the Borders, south-east, Highlands and north-east. In the counties under focus in this book there was considerable diversity. In 1771, the proportion of land possessed by 'great' proprietors, i.e. over £2,000 Scots valued rent, was around 50 per cent in Angus, 34 per cent in Ayr, 44 per cent in Fife and 28 per cent in Lanark. The south-west in particular was the heartland of the smaller proprietors.[10] Nevertheless, in general, Scotland had probably the most concentrated pattern of landownership in Europe. This had two implications for improvement. It facilitated capital accumulation in a relatively poor country by concentrating the basic unit of resource in a few hands. In addition, large-scale agrarian change was made possible more quickly because of the extent of territorial control possessed by such a small élite. Two examples illustrate the point: when the Douglas family initiated a programme of improvement in 1769–71, its strategy included lands in Renfrewshire, Lanarkshire, Fife and Angus; the Duke of Hamilton's improvements spread across part of the Lothians, much of Lanarkshire and into Ayrshire.[11]

Considerable social and political authority derived from the territorial ascendancy of the landed class. They virtually monopolised all the levels of power at both local, national and regional level. From their ranks were drawn the Commissioners of Supply, Justices of the Peace, and after 1797, Lords Lieutenant. As heritors, literally the owners of heritable property, they controlled education and poor-relief at the parish level in partnership with ministers and kirk sessions. The right to vote in the county parliamentary seats was confined to those who possessed land or superiorities held directly from the crown and valued at '40 shillings old extent' or £400 valued rent. The manipulative control of the landowners over Scottish politics was increased through the tiny franchise with only 1,337 'real' voters registered in the later eighteenth century.[12]

It was at the estate level, however, that the hegemony of the landed class came through most clearly. Of first and fundamental importance was the virtual absence of peasant proprietorship in Scotland and the fact that most land was worked through tenancies governed by leases granted by proprietors. It is difficult to overestimate the significance of this pattern of landholding and how it facilitated improvement. In most parts of Europe, landlords were often constricted by the prevalence of peasant ownership and the legal traditions which buttressed rights to land. Their room for manœuvre was very limited.[13] In Scotland, landowners could not act as absolute monarchs, but they possessed full legal rights of eviction at the end of a lease and they could build into these contracts mandatory improving clauses which were enforceable at law. These were major advantages for a social class intent on radical change. But in addition they had considerable seigneurial authority. Their feudal rights and privileges were maintained until well into the eighteenth century, long after they had been abandoned elsewhere in Britain. This was ironic in one sense because of the scathing criticism of 'feudalism' by improving writers. Yet many proprietors continued to exact ancient rights of service in leases alongside clauses prescribing the most advanced rotation systems. Feudal traditions lingered longer in the Lowlands than in England because it was only in the later seventeenth century that the old military order finally crumbled. But it was not until 1747 that most 'heritable jurisdictions' were formally abandoned. Even then, some baron courts survived on an informal basis for much longer.[14]

So too did the 'remains of feudal servitude', as one observer put it.[15] Thirlage, in particular, was still common in many leases until well into the first decade of the nineteenth century. By this, the proprietor of an estate bound his tenants to have their grain ground at a particular mill.[16] Arriages, or the ploughing and cultivating of the landlord's farm, Bonnages, or the shearing of his crop, and Carriages, the transporting of the proprietor's fuel and manure, were in decline in the later eighteenth century but can still be found in some leases in the early 1800s. The survival of these services again suggests the speed of the rural transformation. A longer and more evolutionary process would have removed them earlier. The abruptness of the Scottish revolution ensured that the very old coexisted for some time alongside the very new. Equally, the traditional heavy obligations of the tenantry to their landlords may have meant that the new demands of improving lairds were not as oppressive or burdensome as they otherwise might have been. Scottish farmers had long been accustomed to the firm hand of proprietorial authority.

The landlords' legal authority did not simply rest on feudal tradition. By the second half of the eighteenth century, decisions of the pre-1707 Scottish Parliament and United Kingdom Parliament had consolidated their advantages. The legal means by which tenants could be removed from their land had been clarified and procedures set out in detail. The basic legislation was an Act of the Scottish Parliament, 'Anent the Warning of Tenants', passed as early as 1555. This was amplified by an Act of Sederunt of the Lords of Council and Session of 1756. Consent to a removal could be given by a sheriff if the proprietor applied to him at least forty days before Whitsun. Such an action, ' ... shall be held as equal to a warning executed in terms of the Act of Parliament'. It was a simple and speedy procedure and it was also comprehensive. While served against a single tenant, the summons of removal referred not simply to the named individual but also to his family, servants, cottars, subtenants and dependents. If those mentioned in the summons failed to remove they would be 'held as violent possessors and compelled to pay the violent profits of the same, conform to law in all rigour'. Other legislation dealt directly with the management of land, much of it concentrating in the later seventeenth century. The 'Act anent lands lying Run-Rig' and a second statute relating to the division of commonties were both passed in 1695. They helped provide a suitable legal context which facilitated improvement in the eighteenth century. They both shared one key feature. Individual landlords could take the initiative in the exchange and consolidation of lands held by different proprietors under the 'Act anent Run-Rig'. Similarly, the commonty legislation allowed one landowner to force division through rather than requiring a majority to be in agreement. These Acts were manifestly intended to assist those lairds in the van of agrarian reform.

By the eighteenth century the rights and privileges of Scottish landowners had been buttressed further by the development of entail. An Act of the Scottish Parliament of 1685 laid out the general principles: 'The succession to an entailed estate could be confined to a definite series of heirs; a succeeding proprietor had no power to break the line; he could not sell and he was prohibited from contracting debts that might imperil the estate.'[17] One estimate suggested that in 1825 at least half of the landed property of the country was entailed and, significantly, more than half the number of deeds of entail had been registered within the previous four decades.[18] Entail gave protection and security. But the drawback of the system was its rigidity. That was partially alleviated by the famous Act of 1770 which allowed an improving landlord to invest in his estate and become a creditor to his heirs up to the value of four years' rental. On the other hand, the legislation granted only limited freedom as the restrictions were considerable. More important was the fact that entail itself was becoming increasingly popular. It helped to consolidate the security and authority of the old landed élite in a period of rapid economic and social change. They had always held the levers of power and these were being strengthened in the era of Improvement.

II

The remarkable enthusiasm for improvement of many members of that class in the decades after c.1760 was itself due to a set of influences which developed in the course of the eighteenth century. The costs of landownership were rising steeply. The aristocratic world of the period was one of competitive display where social standing was increasingly defined by material status. Larger rent rolls became essential to service the conspicuous consumption of the élite.[19] More elaborate housing, interior decoration and the adornment of estate policies were very fashionable. It is noteworthy how many of the great houses of Scotland were either built or renovated in this period: Inveraray, Culzean and Mellerstain were only the most famous. This was the era when the remarkable Adam family of architects and builders did their best work. But the new costs of élite living extended also to town houses, larger dowries, travel, education and a host of other things. For the highest in the land, the political and social life of London imposed even more financial strains, which meant that rents had to be raised by hook or by crook.[20] One indication of the pressures on the upper class was the insolvency of smaller landed families in the west of Scotland. In the 1790s, it was noted of Ayrshire that 'a great proportion of the landed estates have changed their owners in consequence of individual extravagance, expensive engagements'. The observer described that this had come about because of 'the prevailing course of electioneering, show, equipage and the concomitant attacks upon the purse'.[21]

But the historical processes at work were not simply material in origin. They were also intellectual. The Scottish philosophical revolution of the eighteenth century fed through into the sphere of agrarian reform. The rationalism of the Enlightenment helped to change man's relationship to his environment. No longer was nature accepted as given and pre-ordained; instead it could be altered for the better by rational, systematic and planned intervention. In a sense, Enlightenment thought gave a new intellectual legitimacy to the traditional interventionist role of the landed classes in Scotland by clarifying the objectives of agrarian reform. Not surprisingly in a country where it dominated the economy, the theorists and intellectuals were very interested in agriculture.[22] Adam Smith, for example, showed much more awareness of the rural economy than of the incipient industrial structure. Writers such as Lord Kames, James Anderson and Sir John Sinclair, and many of the contributors to the *Old Statistical Account* and *General Views of Agriculture* of the 1790s formulated ideas about the meaning of improvement, which provided a systematic critique of the old system and a coherent approach to the imposition of the new. When factors and proprietors evolved plans for improvement they were in most instances simply putting into practice this new intellectual orthodoxy which was disseminated widely in books, pamphlets and journals. There was remarkable unanimity about what was bad and had to be changed. Lands 'in a state of nature' were no longer acceptable. They had to be enclosed and brought into regular cultivation. Farms held by more than one tenant and common lands should be consolidated. The rationale behind the old practices and structures was rarely explored. Instead, the emphatic condemnation of the prevailing agrarian regime as archaic, wasteful and ruinous helped to give the improvers an extraordinary moral and intellectual confidence as they vigorously went about the crusade of thorough reformation. Theirs was not simply a narrowly materialistic undertaking, though profit and its increase were the prime movers. It was also a more broadly ideological mission to 'improve' and modernise Scottish society.[23]

The landed classes, however, could not function in a vacuum, whatever their legal powers and the widespread intellectual support which existed for their strategies. And, as will become patently clear later, there were profound obstacles to the successful enforcement of some of their strategies.[24] Of crucial importance also was the response of the tenant farmers who actually worked the land. One estate factor in Ayrshire in 1805 pointed out how, from his experience, 'much depends on the knowledge and ability of the tenant how far he succeeds in the improvements recommended'.[25] By and large, however, improving writers were scathing about the technical and commercial limitations of the farming classes on the eve of improvement and usually asserted that their innate conservatism was a major obstacle to the progress of the new agriculture.[26] Equally, some tenants were critical of the new methods on the grounds that they reflected the theoretical thinking of gentlemen amateurs rather than the practical approach of experienced farmers.[27] This conflict of ideas seemed to crystallise the clash between 'progressive' and 'conservative' forces. In addition, it is clear that there were profound tensions in some areas between the tenantry and the gentry, which diminished the easy and speedy acceptance of improving ideas. This is hardly surprising given the speed of change and the dramatic rate of rent increases. One historian has suggested that many lowland farmers worked with the grain of the improving movement and this pattern of social acceptance was in stark contrast with the vigorous opposition which characterised reactions in the western Highlands and Islands.[28] But this comment partly overlooks the truculent hostility of some tenants on southern estates. The ideology of improvement did not have easy passage or acceptance in all areas.

Thus the Earl of Strathmore's factor in Angus wrote with some concern to his master in 1754 that 'he had enough to do for some time past to keep proper order in the [Baron] Court', which was still functioning at that date. The disputed issue was the reclamation of the mosses in one part of the estate which had disturbed traditional rights of access.[29] In Ayrshire, apparently, tensions were quite widespread. The agricultural reporter for the county commented in 1793 that 'Near some towns where the notions of manufacturers predominate' farmers had formed associations. In these, tenants went so far as to 'find themselves, under severe penalties, never to offer any mark of civility to any person in the character of a gentleman'. The reporter considered these organisations so threatening that he advised proprietors to retaliate by forming counter-associations to prevent their members obtaining leases or providing them on an annual basis or at will.[30] On the Hamilton estates in Lanarkshire in the later eighteenth century it was common for the tenantry of a particular neighbourhood to form a combination to try to ensure that the sitting tenants would triumph when farms were put up for public bidding at the termination of a lease.[31]So effective were these that the Duke's factor counselled against 'public roups' (auctions) where collective action could develop and argued in favour of letting land, wherever possible, through private bargain:

> it is my opinion [sic] that roups for farms in this country are the same with all the other places I have yet the experience of. That is, whatever the private offerer may intend by a private bargain, his mouth is entirely shut up from offering at a publick roup by a Secret Combination which is as Common to them as the Flame of Fire

flies upwards, which establishes that solid oppinnion [*sic*] of mine never to get farms by any other method than private offers ... [32]

A survey of sheriff court and other legal records confirms that the tenant class, and especially that element possessing some means, was wholly capable of taking action to protect vested interests. Proceedings of removal could be and were challenged at law and the pursuers of actions had to be punctilious in following the formal process with great care if they were not to attract objections on technical grounds. [33] The legal representative of the Duke of Gordon in 1770 concluded: 'A Process of Removing which requires the most summary dispatch and from its nature must be extremely simple and plain, has of late years become quite a labyrinth in the law; and an heritor may sooner be dispossessed of his estate by a judicial sale than it is practicable to have a litigious tenant removed from a farm.' [34] In addition, among Court of Session papers, there exists documentation of legal actions taken by tenant farmers against their landlords. These included cases of compensation for building on lands during the tenure of a lease, resisting landlord claims of broken leases, opposing summonses of removal, protesting against the levying of feudal dues and the like. [35]

A perusal of this material suggests that within the tenant class there were some articulate and robust personalities who also had the financial means to challenge their landlords in court and that the idealised partnership between improving laird and enterprising farmer often broke down in practice. This was a time of intense insecurity as well as, in the longer run, material advance. A central bone of contention was rents. In the 1770s and 1780s, especially during and after the crises of 1772–3 and 1783–4, tenant arrears rose dramatically on many estates. The factor of the Lockhart of Lee estate in Lanarkshire recognised in 1780 that the problems were in part the result of estate policy: 'the rents seem to have been raised higher than the value of the lands – so that the tenants are remaining indebted, very incapable to pay, some deserving great deductions or diminutions, others working to give up their leases and others threatening bankruptcy'. [36] This was a comment which could have been echoed by many estate factors in these years. One expert observer roundly criticised landowners for raising rents too quickly. Writing in 1793, James Naismith noted that they deserved credit for improvement but their rental policies merited condemnation. The key mistakes had been made in the 1780s, 'when farmers were making feeble attempts towards improvement, before they had acquired either capital, or experimental knowledge, a sudden and great rise of rent took place'. The consequent stress was apparent not only in tenant insolvency and in families trying to outbid one another in desperate attempts to hold on to land but also in farmers surrendering their leases and emigrating to the colonies. [37]

The process of improvement itself added to the pressures. Consolidation of tenancies and refashioning of farm structures steadily reduced the number of available leases while the rural population was steadily rising. The ability to pay an enhanced rent for fewer holdings in a fluctuating market was now the criterion for entry to farms. Customary possession had become much less important. One contemporary observer noted in 1793 how, 'It was *formerly* [my italics] the custom among the families of the great landholders of Scotland never to remove a farmer as long as any of the same family chose to remain in the farm.'[38] The comment underestimated the extent of tenant mobility before 1750, but in remarking on the customs of a past age the author drew attention to the new era of competition where traditional connection was no longer considered as significant as ability to pay.

These tensions aggravated the difficulties of introducing radically new agrarian practices to a society where custom and tradition were powerful barriers to innovation. Historians argue that improvers circumvented these problems by introducing enlightened and progressive farmers from such centres of contemporary agricultural excellence as East Lothian. Some proprietors certainly tried to attract such tenants but in virtually all of the estates studied they were usually unsuccessful. The evidence, which will be introduced in the next few chapters, will indicate that it was the much-criticised, truculent and 'conservative' indigenous farmers who carried through the revolution of the later eighteenth century. How is this apparent paradox to be resolved?

III

In part, it can be explained by the fact that some of the zealots among the improving writers grossly underestimated the human and economic resources of the old tenantry. The discussion in Chapter 2 suggested that the traditional farming class was already changing significantly before 1750. The erosion of multiple tenancy led to the emergence of more substantial men with bigger holdings and additional resources. Just as importantly, the decline of rentals in kind brought many more farmers than ever before into direct contact with both local, regional and international markets. The majority of tenants may have remained poor but a latent 'bourgeois' element was already present in the rural social structure by the 1740s. Of equal importance may have been the levels of education and literacy which existed among the tenant farming élite in lowland Scotland: 'an educated peasantry more readily turns its back on immemorial tradition because it finds on the printed page an alternative form of authority, and much of the new farming technology was disseminated in books and articles'.[39] The most recent investigation of this topic has concluded that the kirk sessions of the early eighteenth century had done a good job and had made schooling widely available, even below the rank of the farmers.[40] As befitted their status, however, some tenants had received a fuller education than most of the rural population. In the parish of St Ninian's in Stirlingshire, 'Some of our farmers have been favoured with a liberal education. A few of them have been instructed in the rudiments of the Latin tongue. Almost all of them have been taught writing and arithmetic, as well as to read the English language with understanding and ease.'[41]

Many tenants were more capable than some critics allowed. For example, the shape of landlord strategy suggests that the pool of resourceful farmers might have been deeper than sometimes suggested. In the crises of 1772–3 and 1783–4, several proprietors systematically removed tenants for arrears. Throughout the later eighteenth century, sheriff court records also indicate landlord willingness to sequestrate the property of insolvent tenants. These policies could not have been conducted so rigorously if landowners had not been certain of a supply of farmers able and willing to take over vacant holdings. Rents were rising fast because of landlord demands but they could not have done so as generally or as rapidly if demand for leases had not been maintained. The general impressions gained from the estate correspondence examined in the course of this study are also important. There is hardly any evidence that factors were ever seriously concerned with the supply of tenants except in occasional years of acute difficulty when the market for leases became unusually sluggish. For the most part, factors were anxious about *how* leases should be allocated, whether by public sale or private bargain, not *if* there was sufficient demand for them.[42] Looking back from the depressed conditions of 1811, Lord Leven's factor noted that 'in ordinary times we were able to make our own conditions with the tenants but we are obliged to concede a great deal at present'.[43] Similarly, in Angus in the 1790s, where rents had doubled or trebled over the previous few decades, 'tenant farmers pay these increases and even where "adventurers" are sometimes ruined others will step in … '.[44]

However, the most compelling evidence of tenant enterprise is to be found in the activities of individual farmers. An invaluable source in this respect are the formal offers made to proprietors by prospective tenants of vacant holdings. Thus, when one Robert Milne proposed taking a tack on the Earl of Strathmore's Angus estate in 1770, he requested that an adjacent muir be added to the holding and that since 'the houses are presently ruinous' a new dwelling house be built. He himself wished to improve the muir with marl and 'bring it to proper culture'.[45] In the same year, James Adam of Newtoun of Airly also bid for a lease from the Earl of Strathmore and in his proposal asked that the proprietor enclose and lime part of the farm for which he would be willing to pay an additional rent.[46] Similar evidence of initiatives from individual tenants comes from the Earl of Morton's estate in Fife. Farm offers made there in the 1780s contain requests for enclosing, repairs to steadings, drainage of land and construction of roads. Invariably, if the proprietor agreed to fund these improvements, the prospective tenant in his offer consented either to pay interest on the sums invested or accept an increased rental.[47]

In some cases it was apparent that tenants had the financial resources to initiate improvement. When a few consolidated holdings were offered for leasing on the Morton lands in 1762, 'several good tennents' showed interest in them despite the substantially higher rent which they attracted.[48] Again in

Ayrshire a few years later, one tenant of Sir Thomas Wallace-Dunlop of Craigie claimed to have 'laid out every shilling he was possessed of in enclosing and liming' over a period of time. The value of his total investment was around £100 or about five times the annual rental.[49] In Angus, too, reference was made to farmers who were 'substantial enough to be able to afford a good deal of money for improving'.[50] This class was bound to increase in size and significance over time. The process of farm consolidation, surveyed in Chapter 7, was primarily designed to reduce the number of small husbandmen and elevate the power of the greater tenants. This class was also likely to gain most from the dissemination of improving methods and the massive rise in produce prices. Already, therefore, by the 1790s and early 1800s there were signs that the more substantial farmers were adopting an even more proactive role. They funded improvement projects from their own resources and, in their offers for tacks, were quite specific about what they wanted from the proprietor in his part of the contract. Significantly, too, by the final decade of the eighteenth century improving writers were lavishing praise on some farmers. The opprobrium of the past was much less in evidence. Thus, the agricultural reporter for Ayrshire observed in 1793 that the farmers of the county deserved commendation; though they were unwilling to adopt innovations without good reason, they, nevertheless, had shown the capacity to accept those techniques which practice and experience had proven to be beneficial.[51]

IV

It would appear, therefore, that the tenantry of the 1750s were not quite as backward and reactionary as some contemporary observers suggested. There already existed an embryonic leadership class. On the other hand, it would probably be wrong to exaggerate its size or significance. The examination of the rural economy in the early decades of the eighteenth century indicated that the commonplaces of later improvement, enclosure, sown grasses and better cropping techniques were all underdeveloped at that time. Yet, by the 1790s, they had become very widespread. The speed with which this happened was due in large part to the planned and rigorous application of the new structures and methods by a zealous group of estate factors, agents and surveyors in partnership with enterprising tenants. The programme was nothing less than a gigantic strategy of social and economic engineering. It was not simply the way of working the land that had to be altered. The aim was also to change the 'manners' of the people, to render them, as the contemporary phraseology had it, less 'indolent' and more 'industrious'. Land output should rise but so also must human productivity. Historians have documented these developments in industry in this period.[52] But the drive to discipline and to order work and effort in a regulated fashion was also an integral part of the agrarian revolution. The approaches used to achieve this goal will be assessed in the final section of this chapter.

At the heart of the process was the improving lease. Up to the middle decades of the eighteenth century, on the estates studied, written leases were relatively short and simple documents which specified the duration of the tenancy, the rental in both cash and kind, labour services and the need to maintain farm buildings. Instructions on the management of the land, where they were provided, were normally vague and imprecise. Tenants were usually expected to respect the rules of the baron court and ensure that animal manure was retained and used within the farm. For the most part, those entering the lease were simply requested to adhere to the customs of the area or, as a typical tack issued by the Earl of Glasgow in Ayrshire in 1732 had it, ' ... conforme to the law and uses of the tenents of this country'.[53]

The improving lease was radically different and was becoming increasingly common in the last three decades of the eighteenth century. Most of the 'new' leases were for nineteen years. As Table 4.1 indicates, on the Leven and Melville estate in Fife, mean tack length changed significantly over the eighteenth century and the proportion of nineteen-year contracts also became more common. The documents themselves were much longer and more complex. In the early eighteenth century they averaged two to three pages. By 1800, leases of twelve to fifteen pages in length were not unusual. Much of the detail relating to labour services and payment in kind had been removed. In their stead were long clauses outlining how the lands should be managed and the penalties which would be exacted if these rules were not followed to the letter. Often tenants were given little opportunity for initiative or manœuvre. The leases did not simply contain general guidelines to encourage good husbandry. They consisted of mandatory obligations which specified how fallowing should be carried out, the amount of lime to be employed, the precise form of the rotations and how the cropping routine of the farm should vary not simply over time but between the different cultivated areas in the holding. The 'improving lease' brings out clearly the authoritarian nature of the drive towards improvement. A single such document from the Lockhart of Lee estate in Lanarkshire has been reproduced in Appendix 8 in all its considerable detail.

Of course, it is impossible to be entirely sure about the effect of these contracts. There is evidence on the estates of the Earl of Eglinton in Ayrshire and the Earl of Morton of breaches of the cropping agreements by some tenants.[54] But the agreements were not simply formal arrangements with limited practical impact. Factors went to considerable lengths to ensure that the tack did quickly generate improved forms of cultivation. Eviction procedures were sometimes used against the recalcitrant and negligent.[55] The larger estates monitored tenant activity very closely. On the Hamilton lands farms were surveyed twice per annum, deficiencies noted and tenants warned.[56] The extent of detailed supervision is revealed in a letter of the factor of the Duke of Hamilton in 1784 in which he noted the receipt of a report which stated that one farmer was not harrowing his corn in the prescribed manner. An under-factor was dispatched to investigate and the tenant eventually agreed to carry

TABLE 4.1   Leven and Melville estates (Fife), changing mean tack length, 1675–1800.

Period	No. of tacks	Mean tack length (years)
1675–1699	52	10.5
1700–1724	55	14.4
1725–1749	12	14.3
1750–1774	35	20.9
1775–1800	9	17.8

Leven and Melville estates, 19-year and 19-year + leases, 1675–1800

Period	No. of 19-year leases	Percentage of total	No. of 19-year + leases	Percentage of total
1675–1699	5	9.6	6	11.5
1700–1724	21	38.2	22	40
1725–1749	1	8.3	4	33.3
1750–1774	25	71.4	32	91.4
1775–1800	6	66.7	7	77.8

SOURCE   SRO, GD26, Leven and Melville Muniments, Inventory.

out the harrowing properly.[57] On the same estate, the farm of William Robertson was criticised: 'fences and ditches are in very bad order ... house built on the front of the steading without acquainting Mr. Burrell ... '. The building was to be demolished and the stone used to raise the walls of the cattle yard.[58] The Earl of Panmure was advised to establish an inspectorate consisting of three salaried officers to supervise his improvements and their progress. They should also be supplied with assistants: 'with orders to traverse estates several baronies, take Inspection and make report annually as said is: That those who do well may meet with the Applause justly due them; That the Backward may be spurred on, And that the Obstinately Negligent and Deceitfull may be Undone and turned off as an Example *In Terrorem* of others.'[59]

Coercion was used widely and systematically. On the Strathmore estate, in the early 1770s, tenants who dared to vary the cropping restrictions in their tacks were liable to an immediate increase in rental of £3 per acre.[60] In other properties, straightforward monetary fines were favoured.[61] What gave teeth to this policy of sanctions was the determination of landowners not only to remove tenants who fell into rent arrears but to use such difficulties as a way of getting rid of inadequate farmers. In 1782, a Perthshire landowner, Alexander Macdonald, was pursuing a draconian policy of clearance to remove the negligent:

when the respondent [Macdonald] bought these lands they were in a most wretched state of management. They were covered with a swarm of poor tenants ... whose rents were from 10s. to £5 each which had been very ill paid. The cattle upon the lands were inferior in size and value to those of the neighbourhood, and so very execrable was the practice of agriculture upon this estate that, although there were ninety-seven tenants upon it ... yet, as a specimen of their ignorance in this respect, it needs only to be mentioned that, all their harrows for dressing the soil, two excepted, were furnished with wooden teeth ... the respondent was therefore advised to remove them by degrees to let the estate in farms from £20 to £40.[62]

On the Duke of Hamilton's Lanarkshire lands in 1783 about 32 per cent of all tenants were in arrears to a varying extent because of the poor harvests of the time: 33 were in real difficulty but the factor had considerable room for manœuvre in how he responded. Some were given allowances and others time to pay. However, those who were to be 'pushed','struck off' or 'proceeded against' were often also guilty of misdemeanours and of managing their farms improperly.[63] This approach was repeated on other estates. The improving lease possessed muscle partly because it clearly set out what was required of a tenant and outlined criteria by which his performance could be judged. In addition, the series of short-term crises which afflicted lowland agriculture in the later eighteenth century forced temporary increases in rent arrears. These in turn gave landowners the opportunity to select the able for support and the negligent for removal, often by laying vacant arable farms down to grass on a temporary basis. In addition, however, the fact that most estates had little difficulty in attracting replacement tenants, for the reasons described above, was vital. The potency of the lease was surely increased by the knowledge of sitting tenants that there were usually others willing to take their place should they break the terms of agreement.

But most estates also used incentives as well as penalties. Landlords played a direct role in providing investment. On some properties they covered the costs of enclosure, liming and new farm houses from their own resources and secured returns through raising rentals. In most cases, however, the outlay on improvement was given to tenants in the form of a loan repaid over the period of a lease or linked to a percentage of rental. There was also substantial landlord investment in new farm houses because it was recognised that this was an effective way of attracting able tenants and, at the same time, enhancing the status and so the commitment of improving farmers among their peers. In Angus, by the 1790s, 'there was scarcely a parish where farm-houses were not improving and where principal ones are not 2 stories high and slate covered'.[64] There was a similar pattern in Fife. Some steadings continued in the 'barbarous' condition of past years but many others had improved significantly with substantial, two-storey, slate-covered farmhouses, stables, cattle houses, barn, milksheds and strawyards.[65]

Some proprietors may have rack-rented but others understood that the link between improvement and rental should be treated more sensitively. Abatement of rents of varying amounts was often allowed in order to let the result of better cultivation practices filter through into increased output. Some factors counselled the value of modest increases in the initial few years of an improving lease. As the Earl of Morton was advised, the rental should be moderate 'and not so high as to exceed the skill and industry of the tenants ...

as no General can expect good success with a bad disciplined Army'.[66] One method to ensure such an outcome was to provide incentives within the rental structure. On the Bertram of Nisbet estate in Lanarkshire in the early 1760s rents rose over the period of the leases in three stages. But there was also a variant for selected tenants. Over the second period, those who enclosed their farms were allowed a reduction in rental and money grants on completion of improvements.[67]

V

This success of this set of incentives ultimately depended, however, on rising prices of grain, livestock and other farm produce. It was these which allowed rentals to increase, encouraged landlord investment and allowed sufficient return for tenants to encourage them to adopt the new techniques. The trend was for prices to rise and markets to expand but there is a good deal of evidence for the 1770s and 1780s in particular that improvement was running into difficulties and that only in the later 1790s and first few years of the nineteenth century did better times return. The road to successful improvement was much rockier than is sometimes suggested. It would be fair to say that the economic euphoria of the 1760s, which saw the launching of so many schemes, was followed by considerable disappointment, uncertainty and retrenchment in the following two decades. This time of trouble has been obscured because when the abundant printed sources, such as the *OSA* and *General Views of Agriculture*, became available in the 1790s, the crises had passed for the most part and prices for agricultural produce had recovered in dramatic fashion.

The basic problem in the western lowland counties at least seems to have been associated with a climatic cycle. The agricultural reporter for Lanarkshire, on the basis of 'concurring testimony of living individuals and those lately deceased', compiled a weather survey of the western lowlands from the early eighteenth century.[68] The first four decades of the century were broadly favourable, followed by several more difficult seasons between c.1740 and 1757. The period from then until 1772 was mainly benign, with 'several pretty favourable seasons' in the 1760s. Significantly, these years coincided with the first and most dynamic phase of improvement on many estates. But from then on the weather deteriorated dramatically until the early 1790s. The reporter described the incidence of 'many unseasonable frosts in Spring and Autumn'. The years 1779 and 1781 were not as severe as others but in 1772–3 and 1782–3 weather conditions deteriorated sharply and harvests were poor. The impact of these crisis years on improving activity was profound. Arrears rose swiftly on many properties, effectively undermining the vital link between rising rentals, tenant income and landlord investment in further improvement. As the case-studies in Chapters 5 and 6 suggest, only the very wealthiest proprietors, and in particular those with income derived from external sources such as commerce, could afford to maintain the momentum between 1772 and 1784. Some owners of small estates and of more modest means lost their land.

In Ayrshire, ' a great proportion' of the landed properties changed hands as the spectacular failure of the Ayr Bank in 1772 deepened the crisis.[69] In pastoral farming districts of the south-west, the multiple failure of drovers was reported in 1778. Again in Kirkcudbrightshire and Dumfries in 1781 'money continues [to be] very scarce and many people of landed property and tenants are failling'. The same year brought the bankruptcy of John Tait, the greatest cattle dealer in the Stewartry, who left debts of more than £10,000. In 1782, no less than seven estates in this area were put up for sale with three being offered at prices over £72,000.[70]

Tenants were also in acute difficulty in 1772–3 and even more seriously in 1783–4. On the Douglas estate in Lanarkshire, the arrears of 1772 had not been effectively removed before they rose sharply once again in the crisis of 1782.[71] There was a similar pattern on the Bertram property in the same county.[72] In 1783–4, some landowners in the west of Scotland had to distribute seedcorn among the tenantry.[73] That crisis hit hard, not simply because of the deterioration in weather conditions but because farmers were still recovering from the difficulties of the previous decade. In 1780 arrears on the Hamilton estate stood at £3,230 with annual book rental valued at £2,742. Of the 123 tenants, 121 were in arrears to a greater or lesser extent and this on an estate where there had been very substantial landlord investment since the early 1760s.[74] One clear demonstration of the difficulties was that several factors reported that the normally buoyant market for tenancies had become much more sluggish; in Lanarkshire in 1772, 'there was little invitation for people bidding heartily at roups at this present time considering the failures that have happened ... '.[75] These were hard times and in a very real sense the surging demand and price inflation of the Napoleonic Wars from the final decade of the eighteenth century saved the improving movement and allowed the renewal of the momentum of the 1760s and early 1770s. The contemporary agricultural expert, John Naismith, noted in 1798 how the prices of all provisions had experienced a huge increase over the previous five years, 'even to alarm the nation, at one period, with the dread of famine'. As a result, 'the prospects of the husbandman were much elevated'.[76]

REFERENCES

1. J. V. Beckett, 'Landownership and Estate Management' in Mingay, ed., *Agrarian History*, p. 570.
2. Ibid., pp. 570–1.
3. Ibid., pp. 614–17.
4. Thomson, *General View of Fife*, p. 62.
5. See below, pp. 74–5.
6. T. M. Devine, 'Social Responses to Agrarian "Improvement": The Highland and Lowland Clearances in Scotland, 1500–1850' in Houston and Whyte, eds, *Scottish Society*, pp. 148–68; F. Dovring, 'The Transformation of European Agriculture' in *Cambridge Economic History of Europe* (Cambridge, 1965), vol. VI; B. H. Slicher van Bath, *The Agrarian History of Western Europe, 1500–1850* (London, 1963).
7. See below, pp. 71–2.
8. L. Timperley, 'The Pattern of Landholding in Eighteenth Century Scotland' in M.

L. Parry and T. R. Slater, eds, *The Making of the Scottish Countryside* (London, 1980), pp. 137–54.

9. R. Callander, *A Pattern of Landownership in Scotland* (Haughend, 1987), pp. 60–79.

10. Timperley, 'Pattern of Landholding', pp. 137–54.

11. NRA(S) 859, Douglas-Home Papers, vol. 156, Report of Robert Ainslie, 1769; 631/1, John Burrell's Journals, 1764–85, *passim*.

12. A. E. Whetstone, *Scottish County Government in the Eighteenth and Nineteenth Centuries* (Edinburgh, 1981); W. Ferguson, 'The Electoral System in the Scottish Counties before 1832' in Stair Society, *Miscellany II* (Edinburgh, 1984); J. S. Shaw, *The Management of Scottish Society, 1707–1764* (Edinburgh, 1983).

13. J. Blum, *The End of the Old Order in Rural Europe* (New Jersey, 1978), pp. 263–71.

14. See, for example, NRA(S) 885, Earl of Strathmore Papers, 162/4(302), Conditions, Observations and Regulations established by James Menzies, 1772 where reference is made to the Earl of Strathmore's 'Baron Bailie' and his continuing authority.

15. Roger, *General View of Angus*, p. 21.

16. SRO, GD16/5/213, Leven and Melville Muniments, Leven and Melville Tacks, 1808; NRA(S) 874, Berry Papers, 39/3, Tayfield Tacks, 1798; SRO, GD45/18/2010, Dalhousie Muniments, Panmure Tacks, 1795.

17. See, for example, NRA(S) 874, Berry Papers, 39/3, Tack, John Berry to Alexander Meldrum; L. J. Saunders, *Scottish Democracy: The Social and Intellectual Background, 1815–1840* (Edinburgh, 1950), p. 29.

18. Campbell, 'Landed Classes', p. 93; Saunders, *Scottish Democracy*, p. 30.

19. Smout, *Scottish People*, pp. 285–90.

20. Shaw, *Management of Scottish Society*, pp. 1–15.

21. Fullarton, *General View of Ayrshire*, pp. 104–7.

22. E. J. Hobsbawm, 'Scottish Reformers of the Eighteenth Century and Capitalist Agriculture' in E. J. Hobsbawm *et al*, eds, *Peasants in History* (Oxford, 1980), pp. 3–26.

23. Ibid.

24. See below, pp. 89–91.

25. NRA(S) 0094, Earl of Glasgow Papers, 4/8, Remarks by John Dunlop to Col. Bogle, Sept. 1805.

26. Hobsbawm, 'Scottish Reformers', pp. 11–12.

27. For instance, Fullarton, *General View of Ayrshire*, pp. 72–3.

28. Smout, *Scottish People*, p. 310.

29. NRA(S) 855, Earl of Strathmore Papers, 160/3, W. Gammack to A. Burnett, 15 June 1754.

30. Fullarton, *General View of Ayrshire*, pp. 69–70.

31. HPL 631/1, John Burrell's Journals, 18 and 28 Apr. 1772.

32. Ibid., 20 May 1772.

33. There were numerous examples of this in court processes; see, for instance, from one court in Lanarkshire: SC38/22/6, SC38/22/20, SC38/22/14.

34. NLS, Session Papers, Douglas Collection, vol. 9, Answers for his Grace Alexander, Duke of Gordon ... (1770).

35. Ibid., Douglas Collection, vol. 1, Thos. Baillie of Polkemmet vs. Wm. Wardrope (1759); Douglas Collection, vol. 4, Petition of John and Donald Fraser (1762); Douglas Collection, vol. 9, Petition of Marquis of Tweedale and Tutors (1760); Hermand Collection, vol. 1, Petition of John Crediton (1767); Hermand Collection, vol. 1, Petition of Janet Fulton (1770). These are a sample of a much larger number of such cases.

36. NLS, Acc. 5474, Lockhart of Lee Papers, Box 14, Letter accompanying rent roll of 1780 from Mr Waushope, factor.

37. Naismith, *General View of Clydesdale*, pp. 80–1.

38. Ibid., pp. 81–2. All the rentals studied in the course of this project show substantial tenant turnover before 1750. See below, p. 115–18.

39. L. M. Cullen and T. C. Smout, 'Introduction' in Cullen and Smout, eds, *Comparative Aspects of Scottish and Irish Economic and Social History*, pp. 1–18.

40. R. A. Houston, *Scottish Literacy and Scottish Identity* (Cambridge, 1985); D. J. Withrington, 'Schooling, Literacy and Society' in Devine and Mitchison, eds, *People and Society in Scotland*, pp. 171–4.

41. Quoted in Withrington, 'Schooling', p. 172.

42. See below, p. 106.

43. SRO, GD26/5/728, vol. 4, Leven and Melville Muniments, Factor to Lord Leven, 20 Feb. 1811.

44. *OSA* (Angus), p. 589.

45. NRA(S) 885, Earl of Strathmore Papers, 158/6, Proposals by Robert Milne anent taking in tack the Mill and Lands of Holmhill (1770).

46. Ibid., 158/6, Proposals by James Adam of Newtoun of Airly (1770).

47. SRO, GD150/2407/92, Morton Papers, Memorandum as to the Repairing farm houses and Inclosing the Grounds belonging to Lord Morton on his Fife estate (1792); Memorial for Lord Morton concerning his Fife estate, 2 Mar. 1791.

48. Ibid., GD150/3495/84, Memorandum of sundry matters for Lord Morton's Consideration and Orders respecting his Fife estate, Dec. 1762.

49. NLS, Session Papers, Hermand Collection, vol. 6, Petition of Robert Ritchie, tenant in Redrae on lands of Sir Thomas Wallace-Dunlop of Craigie, Dec. 1780.

50. *OSA* (Angus), p. 99.

51. Fullarton, *General View of Ayrshire*, pp. 72–3.

52. See, *inter alia*, S. Pollard, *The Genesis of Modern Management* (London, 1965); M. Berg, *The Age of Manufactures* (London, 1985); C. A. Whatley, 'The Experience of Work' in Devine and Mitchison, eds, *People and Society in Scotland*, pp. 227–51.

53. NRA(S) 0094, Earl of Glasgow Papers, 2/8, Miscellaneous Tacks.

54. SRO, GD150/2388, Morton Papers, Report of the Acre Land of Aberdour and the Farm of Huntly (1801); *OSA* (Ayr), parish of Kilwinning.

55. See, for example, NLS, Session Papers, Douglas Collection, vol. 2, Lord Belhaven vs. Wm. Anderson (1761); Hermand Collection, vol. 1, Petition of John Crichton (1767). There are numerous references in sheriff court records to removals being sought by proprietors for breaches of tack. See, for instance, SRO, SC37/8/20, Summons of Removal by J. Marshall (1782) Sheriff Court Processes (Hamilton); SC37/8/19, Lybell by Wm. Thomson (1780); Summons by David Shaw (1783); SC37/8/18, Petition of Prof. P. Cumin (1779); SC37/8/11 Lybell of Removing by tutors of Duke of Hamilton (1764). Similar examples could be given from the other court records examined in this study.

56. HPL 631/1, John Burrell's Journals, entries esp. for 1772 and 1782–4.

57. Ibid., 12 May 1784.

58. Ibid., 17 June 1783.

59. SRO, GD45/18/2268, Dalhousie Muniments, Memorandum on Edzell Estate, 1767.

60. NRA(S) 885, Earl of Strathmore Papers 162/4 (30a), Conditions, Reservations and Regulations established by James Menzies ... 14 July 1773.

61. SRO, GD26/5/141, Leven and Melville Papers, Tack, George, Lord Balgonie to James Mitchell; NRA(S) 0094, Earl of Glasgow Papers, 8/A, Tack, Patrick Boyle to H. and J. Robertson (1794).

62. NLS, Session Papers, Hermand Collection, vol. 8, Petition of John Maclauchlane, 3 July 1782.

63. HPL 631/1, John Burrell's Journals, 1782–3.

64. Roger, *General View of Angus*, p. 22.

65. Thomson, *General View of Fife*, pp. 75–6.

66. SRO, GD150/2388, Morton Papers, Report of the Acre Land of Aberdour, 1801.

67. SRO, GD5/529, Bertram of Nisbet Papers, Deposition of tenants, tacks and arrears due to the late Archibald Bertram (1768).

68. Naismith, *General View of Lanarkshire*, p. 30.

69. Fullarton, *General View of Ayrshire*, pp. 104, 137.

70. SRO, GD213/54, Oswald of Auchincruive Papers, Maxwell-Oswald Correspondence, 1778–83. See also below, p. 82.

71. NRA(S) 859, Douglas-Home Papers, 142/5 Douglas Rentals, 1775–1812.

72. SRO, GD5/1/498, Bertram of Nisbet Papers, Rentals, 1770–84.

73. HPL 631/1, John Burrell's Journal, 6 Dec. 1784–8, Jan. 1785. Cost of Seed Corn bought over 1783 and 1784.
74. NRA(S) 2177, Hamilton Papers, E.3/74, Abstract Rentals and below, pp. 97–104.
75. HPL 631/1, John Burrell's Journal, 18 Aug. 1772.
76. Naismith, *General View of Clydesdale*, p. 3.

5

The Process of Improvement

Case-Studies

THE MERCHANT LANDOWNER AND IMPROVEMENT

THE estate of Cavens and Preston in Kirkcudbright was acquired by Sir Richard Oswald in 1765. Oswald already owned Auchincruive in Ayrshire. He was a man of immense wealth, with kinfolk among the Glasgow tobacco aristocracy, who had made his large fortune through his merchant house in London and especially as a result of his role as an arms contractor during the Seven Years War.[1] Between his purchase of Cavens and the 1780s the property was subjected to a comprehensive programme of improvement under the supervision of Oswald's energetic factor, John Maxwell. Maxwell's correspondence with his master casts interesting light on how reorganisation was managed in a region with a bias towards pastoral rather than arable husbandry.[2] Examination of the Cavens experience also offers an opportunity to explore the administration of improvement on a property owned by an individual with abundant capital derived from sources outside agriculture, who had perhaps less need to follow the more disciplined cost regime forced upon some other landowners. A significant factor in Scottish agrarian change, especially around the larger towns, was the purchase of small estates by successful members of the urban business class. The most conspicuous example of this process was the movement into landownership of the Glasgow tobacco aristocracy. Between *c.* 1770 and *c.* 1815 around 100 transatlantic traders owned about 145 separate estates in the counties around the city.[3] In some instances this provided a powerful boost to improvement as capital was channelled from commerce to defray the costs of agricultural reorganisation. Richard Oswald's initiation of radical changes at Cavens may be taken as an illustration of this process.

A Decreet of Valuation of the estate in 1767 indicates that Oswald inherited lands which were already in a process of transition.[4] Some enclosure and subdivision had taken place before 1750, lands were dressed with marl and drained, and new houses built. Three years before he took over, a further major reorganisation was underway. The croft of Hillhead was added to the farm of Boreland. The holding of Moat was added to Barleys and Gallyhan

to Lagan. On these two latter enlarged farms, 'there were considerable
improvements made ... by division, dykes and casting a ditch'. The rent rose
from £12.9 to £15.10. One other farm, Lochhill, however, was split into two
with the new joint rental increasing from £36 to £50.[5] In this property, as in
so many others, reorganisation of holdings did not mean simply consolidation. While some farms were united, others were divided. Equally, these early
advances probably helped accommodate many tenants to the new agriculture
and the more radical changes which were to take place when Oswald took
possession of the lands.

The improvements began in 1767 and in that year Maxwell set out his
blueprint for change:

> the first thing to be done in order to fix a rent and method of husbandry is to
> determine the limits of each farm, then cause measure each farm, exactly distinguish-
> ing the quality of each kind of land in each farm, then adopt the most simple and
> proper method of husbandry considering the conveniences and fix a rent. Build farm
> houses and sett by private bargain or by publick roup ...

The scheme was conventional. Indeed, it was the essential improving orthodoxy of the later eighteenth century repeated on countless occasions in those
decades as the lowland landscape was revolutionised. A rigorous examination of existing farm structure, followed by a detailed plan for change, was
especially axiomatic. However, what made the Maxwell formula distinctive
was the comprehensive fashion in which he was able to put it into practical
effect, doubtless because he had the financial resources of Oswald behind
him.

Like most of his counterparts on other estates he placed special emphasis
on enclosure and liming to raise rental and productivity swiftly. A 'draw-kiln'
for lime was constructed. One bushel of coal was required to burn $3-3\frac{1}{2}$
bushels of limestone. But the vast amounts of lime eventually consumed on
the improved farms meant that in one year, 1768, Maxwell had to order an
additional 1,400 bushels from suppliers in Whitehaven. Again, predictably, he
tried to attract an expert farmer from East Lothian who would provide an
example for those in the locality to follow. For two days in September 1766
he entertained a Mr Smart 'from the Louthians [sic]'. Smart had come 'with
good recommendations'. He was enquiring about the possibility of taking a
farm jointly with his brother in law. They were men of means, each with a
stock of over £750. Maxwell tried to tempt him with the farm of Mersehead.
As he wrote to Oswald:

> I proposed that you should build him a dwelling house of 40 ft. long, 15 ft. wide
> within, 8 ft. high, a Barn of the same size, a Stable of 24 ft. a byre of 10 ft. long and
> to build a dyke between the salt merse and arable and bogue lands to defend them
> from the overflow of high tides ... for that and all dykes and ditches the partys shall
> judge needfull for Inclosing, dividing and draining the farm, he to pay 6 per cent
> interest over and above the rent which I proposed should be £150 for the first seven
> years and for the next 14 years £200 ...

Unfortunately, he could not prevail upon Smart to accept. As in virtually all the other estates considered in this study, improvement depended largely on the indigenous tenantry.

Table 5.1 summarises the range of improvements which the tenants carried out under the tacks agreed with Maxwell. His correspondence with Oswald shows how he managed to obtain their agreement and co-operation to the development of the new regime.

It is plain that the Maxwell strategy was to adopt a cautious approach through encouraging participation by discussion and negotiation. There is hardly any evidence of the coercion practised on the Hamilton estate, which is discussed in Chapter 6. This was probably not only a result of Maxwell's personality but because Oswald's wealth may well have insulated the Cavens economy to some extent from the impact of external fluctuations in the prices of both grain and stock. A context of security was first established. There had been a depletion in tenant numbers between 1741 and 1761 of about 22 per cent but only a fall of 3 per cent from 1761 to 1782. Maxwell seems to have been willing to accommodate smaller tenants on the land after division of farms as long as they were willing to pay the increased rental. Moreover, in spite of reorganisation, many families retained possession and were not automatically replaced by others through the lands being offered in public auction. Thus, 8 of the 27 tenants appearing in the Decreet of Valuation in 1767 were still present in 1782. This strategy of preserving small units after reorganisation, which was not confined to this property, was in conflict with the orthodoxy of the time. But it seems to have paid off. In 1778 Maxwell

TABLE 5.1   Improvements on Cavens estate farms, 1761–81.

Farms	Dykes	Inclosed	Houses	Byres etc.	Drains	Lime	Clover	Grass	Turnips
Yellside	1774	1774	1752 1767						1781
Wreaths						1767	1771		
Lochhill	1767 1782		1769			1767			
Glenwaddow	1768	1768	1768	1768					
Newmains	1768				1752 1768			1768	1769
Gateside	1778		1778						
Laggan	1761 1775	1776	1772						
Boreland	1768 1771								
Ardries		1783	1772						
Mersehead	1778		1772		1775				
Barnhourie		1782							
Kyes (Ryes?)		1782 (partly)							

SOURCE SRO, GD213/54, Oswald of Auchincruive Papers, Correspondence of John Maxwell; SRO, GD213/54, Decreet of Valuation, Lands of Cavens, 1767.

noted 'with great satisfaction' the grass, crops and 'culture pursued almost over the whole estate'. He emphasised to Oswald that 'the tenants and their familly's in general are very happy and thankfull to you for the indulgences done them in allowing them a settlement under you *even upon the very small divisions* where they have done much better than expected ... ' (my italics).

During the crisis, which affected both grain and cattle markets in the 1770s and early 1780s, Maxwell did not resort to eviction or sequestration. By Whitsun 1782, arrears had reached £1,566 but he did not take any proceedings. Looking back in November 1784, he commented that the tenants were now doing well and were 'much eased by allowing them time to pay'. Significantly enough, however, he noted that the pressures of the times in 1772–4 had forced some tenants to surrender their leases and emigrate to America. Probably more would have gone if the estate had not acted to protect the remaining tenantry by purchasing cattle from those who were in difficulty.

Doubtless by establishing a context of security and confidence Maxwell helped to ensure the acceptance of his plans. But he still met considerable opposition. At first all went well. The possession of Colvend was set to eighteen families at £66. Maxwell estimated that if let to three tenants it would be worth £90–£100 in rental. He was not willing, however, to countenance the mass clearance involved. Instead, he was prepared to settle for an increase to £80 divided among the existing possessors. This they found acceptable because it allowed them to continue on their holdings: 'to my surprize they all seemed pleased except two small cott crofts which I believe I was mistaken in. However, they all desired to continue and offered to leave the rent to my own naming which shows their confidence in me. This gave me no small pleasure as I did not expect they could have behaved so ... ' Other tenants were more truculent. The possessor of Lochhill was a 'simple, honest man' but 'much prejudiced against any plan of management other than the one he follows'. Maxwell proceeded by discussion, indicating that 'he would be sorie to propose anything that would be prejudiced to him'. The estate wished to divide the farm by stone dykes. This would be to the decided advantage of the tenant as it would 'help much to clear the Ground of the bed of stones with which it was encumbered that would lend to make it easier to work'. Lime, to the value of £20, was also promised and because clearing stones and building dykes would be 'hurtful while in executing' his rental would only rise gradually in compensation, from £43 to £50 in the first three years, £60 for the next and £70 for the final three years. The tenant reluctantly agreed to the new tack, 'if we would agree to free him when he found it would not answer and he would make a tryall'. In this sentence there comes through something of the sense of anxiety and foreboding which must have been felt by many farmers as they contemplated the adoption of radically new ways of working the land.

Even more hostile were the tenants of Wreaths. Maxwell proposed a typical improving regime:

I proposed a rent of £63, that they should have the croft land divided into 3 and with next croft sow ⅓ with grass seeds and let it lay 3 years – the other ⅔ to be cropped, dressed with Dung and with stone marle or with lime at least 3 acres yearly. The outfield brack to be brought into tillage annually to be dressed with Tath and Stone Marle or lime yearly and the oldest break now in tillage left out yearly.

There was little enthusiasm. As Maxwell dryly remarked, 'they did not relish these proposals'. This discussion took place in October 1766. By the middle of November he had still not received an answer from the Wreaths tenants. A further discussion took place in March 1767. Maxwell still showed his determination to proceed by patience. He spent three hours with the tenants 'in reasoning with them ... but to no purpose'. Finally, at about 9 o'clock that night he 'gone done with them'. One of the tenants and the son of another had broken ranks and taken the lease for a short, initial period of three years. In 1771 they agreed to take it for a further three years and, in case they lost possession at the end of term, were to be given compensation for part of their outlay on lime. This policy of patient bargaining, adjustment and cajoling was ultimately successful. In December 1772 Maxwell wrote with some satisfaction to Oswald indicating that 'your tenants of Wreaths are now convinced of the good effects of lime and fallow'. They were also keen to have a lease for nineteen years. The entire process from sullen opposition to enthusiastic commitment to the new system had taken six years.

But the Wreaths tenants were not necessarily representative. Only a minority of farmers showed reluctance and some demonstrated considerable initiative. The composition of the tenant body was complex. The earlier reorganisations on the estate had produced some thrusting individuals who vigorously pursued the new farming and had a predatory interest in absorbing the lands of adjacent farms. In 1782, Robert Newall, a tenant of 46 acres in Lodshill, offered £80 for one of the new divisions of Ardries containing 122 acres. He proposed his own system of crop rotation of which Maxwell approved. A year after being granted the lease Newall had built a new dwelling house, stable and byre and had completed the stone dykes for enclosing and dividing the arable land. He also made a highly favourable impression on the experts. Maxwell had conversed with two colleagues about Newall's system of cropping: 'we are of opinion that the course of husbandry is preferable to any rather yet adopted ... '. Here was striking confirmation of the argument that very quickly after the new structures were put in place some farmers began to play a leading role in the further development of the new agriculture.

ROBERT AINSLIE'S PLAN OF IMPROVEMENT

John Maxwell's supervision of agricultural improvement on the Oswald estate can be described as a success as rents increased and, despite the economic crises of the 1770s and early 1780s, the majority of the tenantry adjusted to the new ways. But Maxwell had two advantages which helped to sustain his programme: the estate had already experienced considerable reorganisation by a previous owner and he was also able to call upon the resources of a wealthy merchant prince. Robert Ainslie, who tried to impose an ambitious plan of improvement on the estates of the Duke of Douglas in Lanarkshire and Renfrewshire in the 1770s and 1780s, was less fortunate. The Douglas family were proprietors of substance with lands in Berwickshire and Angus as well as in the west of Scotland. They were one of the greatest landowners in the southern districts of Lanarkshire, with property stretching across nine parishes.[6] But the process of evolutionary change which characterised many other estates does not seem to have occurred to the same extent before the 1760s on the Douglas lands. In 1769 the Lanarkshire property lay 'mostly run-rigg and Rundale amongst the Tenants who generally occupied their pastures amongst them in common ... no place admitted of more Improvement'.[7] A consideration of Ainslie's 'Plan of Improvement' in Lanarkshire and its limited success over the first two decades of implementation highlights the obstacles which confronted some of the ambitious schemes of this period. In addition, the approach which he laid out in great detail to advance agricultural reform provides an insight into the whole business of improvement and the mind of the improver.

The Douglas estate in Lanarkshire was mainly concentrated in the upland parishes of Roberton, Carmichael and Douglas in the south of the county. It was described in 1769 as consisting of 'great tracts of high moors and sheep pastures intermixed with valleys and arable lands'.[8] Ainslie was scathing in his criticism of the prevailing form of land management when he submitted his report in that year. The area belonging to each farm did not lie contiguous but 'in the most inconvenient runrigg'. The pastoral farms were also 'under the worst management' with sheep and cattle belonging to different tenants being pastured in indiscriminate fashion. The other main weakness was the small size of many farms with the result that there was not enough employment for several tenants throughout the year, a pattern which produced the widespread indolence which Ainslie regarded as a major obstacle to good husbandry.

Given this background, his intention was to raise the estate 'to proper value' through radical changes in farm organisation, land management and the values of the tenantry. Like other improvers, Ainslie recognised that he had to change social attitudes as well as the mode of cultivation. The programme of action was set out in clear terms. The first necessary task, in order to determine the potential value of the property and so transform the rental, was to carry out a detailed and systematic survey of the lands. This was the conventional pattern in the cases considered elsewhere in the book. What is fascinating, however, is Ainslie's emphasis on the depth and thoroughness of the investigation which was a necessary preliminary to a revolutionary change in landscape:

> it will be necessary for a person to perambulate deliberately every field and ridge, with a plan of the ground in his hands so as to make himself acquainted with every house, spring, watering place, morass, rising ground, valley and every other thing

necessary to be attended to in laying out land in farms and inclosures and to have time to deliberate upon the nature of every soil and the conveniences and inconveniences of every situation, with respect to manure, markets, and the other things necessary to be attended in determining the value of land.

Three prime elements were necessary to ensure effective change once a comprehensive scrutiny of the lands had taken place. First, common pasture and runrig were to be eliminated by the division of the estate into 'proper farms'. Even where farms were 'already in a regular situation' they should be partially reorganised and their marches altered. The reason for this was related to the process of encouraging improvement and higher rentals. An 'old' farm would be valued by the local tenants by reference to its customary rent and production. Also, argued Ainslie, 'by getting the farm in its ancient form they too often think themselves obliged to follow the ancient bad husbandry of their predecessors'. The remodelling of farms, therefore, had an important social purpose in influencing attitudes as well as a significant economic rationale. Much of the Douglas estate was out of lease in the later 1760s so the time was ripe for such replanning. But in order to facilitate wholesale change the Duke was advised to purchase the remaining leases or negotiate exchange of land between farms. If this failed, due to the obstinacy of tenants, progress could still be made: 'attach part of the tenant's lands to the new farms designed and sett them so that the part of the refractory man's farm maybe entered to at his removal'.

Secondly, in the division process it was essential that farms be enlarged. Ainslie was not opposed to small units. Indeed, as will become apparent later, he accepted that they had a positive function within the overall plan of estate reorganisation. But such land should be laid out in small lots of a few acres so that 'they should not be reckoned farms' and the possessors instead would rely for their living on other occupations as well as cultivation of the soil. But existing pasture and arable farms had to be extended. Ainslie saw several advantages in this. Sheep farms were, of necessity, extensive:

> It is well known that sheep when kept by a herd never thrive in a confined pasture. The reason is obvious, they are too frequently checked in their motions and disturbed in their feeding. Land therefore that is adapted principally, or for the Sole purpose of Sheep pasture Should be Laid out in pretty Large farms.
>
> There is another Reason for this; the different ages and kinds of Sheep do not agree with the same pasture, the Store Master therefore Divides them into Separate Hirsels each of which must have a herd; a compleat Store or Sheep farm has at least four Separate Hirsels, viz. a live Hirsell an Eald Sheep or Wedder Hirsell, or Drummond Hirsel, and Lamb or Hog Hirsel, each of these Hirsels or flocks must be so Large as to give the Herd proper Employment. To This quantity of Land sufficient to mentain these four Hirsels should be added a proper Quantity for Hay, and if possible to Induce the tennent to raise Turnip for winter feeding, and for Corn for the family, So that the extent of a Compleat Stores farm must appear very Considerable.
>
> If possible every Store farm Should be of this kind, such a quantity of Land is indeed absolutely necessary to Carry on the whole process of breading and feeding

Sheep to the best advantage and a Regard should be paid to this, in the manner of laying out the moor and pasture grounds; sometimes it happens that the differrent pastures proper for the Different kinds of Sheep do not Life so conveniently as to be put into the same farm. Therefore the farmer must often submitt to have only one or two of these kinds of Hirsels, in this Case. The farms may be proportionably less, but Still they ought to be of such an extent as to make the necessary experience of it sit Light upon the profites.

For arable farms, Ainslie recognised that size had to depend to some extent on local land endowment, climate and markets. Nevertheless, he regarded it as axiomatic and 'obvious to every person' that no farm should contain less land than was sufficient for the working of one plough team. He estimated that 50 acres in 'a good climate and middling soil' gave enough work for one plough. However, since in the improved regime about half of all land should be in grass and the other half in cultivation, 100 acres was in reality the optimum size for an average holding. These larger units were not simply designed to more effectively employ the labour of a farmer, his servants and work animals throughout the year and destroy the habits of 'indolence', which Ainslie saw as a chronic weakness of the old order. They also had another purpose:

> In every Business which requires money and skill, there must be an object sufficient to attract the attention of the man possessed of these; very small farms present no such object and therefore where they prevail improvements are not to be expected; it is not necessary that every farm should be a large one, a few of them may perhaps be sufficient to introduce improvements into a country.

Once again he was addressing the need for an attitudinal revolution to enable the economic transformation to take place. Larger holdings would be a catalyst in this process since they would help to lure men of capital with progressive ideas into the neighbourhood.

Thirdly, the success of improvement depended ultimately on the response of the tenantry. Here Ainslie recognised the magnitude of the problem and his language demonstrates the huge gap which existed between the attitudes of the small tenants and the radical ideas of the improvers. He noted contemptuously, 'the adherence of persons of low education to old customs ... and there are no persons in whom this is discovered more than in the low farmers'. To change their practices was very difficult. Equally, however, apparently like many commentators in the later eighteenth-century Lowlands, Ainslie was fundamentally opposed to mass clearance and replacement of the indigenous tenantry by incomers. This was likely to be a 'dangerous and most destructive experiment'. His opposition rested in part on the contemporary assumption that a large population and an expansion in national wealth were inextricably linked. Therefore, he very much regretted the fact that in highland Scotland land improvement was leading to emigration to the colonies. But his opposition also rested on a desire to maintain social harmony in the countryside and on his vision that a rising population was essential to the practical development of agricultural reform: 'improvements cannot be carried on without hands and therefore the present inhabitants of a country instead of being forced from it, should on the contrary be preserved with great care'.

Presented with the problem of the need to change the attitudes of a conservative tenantry and at the same time avoid depopulation, Ainslie suggested several approaches. He recognised first of all that there could be no swift transformation. Reform was impossible 'without a long and patient attention to the cultivation of the manners of the people and soil', a policy with which John Maxwell at Cavens would have concurred. In addition, he accepted that a rent increase above what the tenants could bear would produce the same migration from the estate as large-scale consolidation. Therefore, rent should be raised gradually over the course of the tack, at seven-year intervals. At the same time, those improvements 'the effects of which are soonest discovered', namely enclosure and liming, should be put in place as these would demonstrate quickly and tangibly to the tenants the effect of better methods. Education was also vital. This could be effected by attracting progressive farmers from elsewhere to provide models for native tenants. But such a policy had to be managed with great care since if such incomers failed to prosper the impact on the whole plan of improvement would be disastrous: 'they may not be adventurers but substantial knowing men, for the mischief is if one of these new farmers misgive their fall, tho' by their own mismanagement will strike such a Terrour in the natives that they will dread such improvements and continue to hug themselves in their old practices for many years.' Much better and safer was to send some tenants' sons to improved areas, such as Northumberland and the Lothians, where they would 'shake off that sloth which they have contracted in their youth' and on their return inspire the new generation to better ways.

Despite his opposition to clearance, Ainslie was aware that farm enlargement, which was an essential part of his plan, would result in 'a great many people being turned out'. He gave considerable attention as to how they were to be absorbed and his remarks are intriguing because they articulate what was occurring on many other estates at the time. He was convinced that improvement would not produce depopulation, only a reduction in the number of farmers. Agrarian reform led to a need for more people. Some of the smaller farmers should therefore become servants and labourers. He argued that their work would be more regular and their income higher as a result. He acknowledged that few would be likely to accept work from the remaining farmers in the district but they could find employment on the projects being carried out by the landowner and the 'publick works' which were being established. The key to the policy lay in the creation of villages. These could be built up from some of the touns, such as Aldington and Robertown, and be converted into 'townships'. These would consist

> of a parcel of houses together, where these people might be accomodated with houses and a few acres of land each, barely to maintain a cow and a horse or two, which they will employ in driving carriages and be hired by the proprietor in his works, or

as is common, by the neighbouring farmers in carrying on with rapidity their necessary improvements of inclosing, liming etc.

Ainslie argued that improvement would employ many more than the number who lived on the estate in the 1760s. In addition to demand for labourers, there would be an increased need for wrights, masons, ditchers, hedgers, shoemakers, weavers, tailors and other tradesmen who would all live in the new settlements. All in all, his was a programme of social development as well as economic reformation, as his own summary of his observations on the Douglas estate demonstrates:

This report having Spun out to an unproper Length, I will Sum up the whole Design in the following Generall heads.

By Acquiring a perfect knowledge of the ground, Moddeling the whole into such proper farms as the various Complex Circumstances of the differrent places may Concurr to point out; and to put a proper value upon them.

2dly By Setting the new Moddeled farms to the most Substantial and Intelligent of the old tenents, and with Caution Introducing a few Industrious good farmers from the places which may be got.

3dly By obliging the Tennents in their new Tacks to do what is Right, and to Restrain them from Doing what is wrong on their farms, These Restrictions, with the method of seeing them Executed; will fall under the General and particular Clauses for Managing the farms.

4^{thly} By Giving them the encouragement of inclosing, or planting Stalls on as much of their farms; and even obliging them thereto; as the sum which the new Rent may have Exceeded, the old Rent, yearly will execute, The Tennent paying five p. Cent p. Annum therefore, and mutually with the Landlord being at the expence of weeding, Training up, Scouring, and preserving the fences.

5^{thly} By Granting a proper duration of Tacks, to intelligent men of Substance; and making their Rents no more at first, than the ground in its present natural State will enable them to pay; But Raising the rent progrefsivly every seven or thereby; of a twenty one years Tack and if Longer every ninteen, or twenty one years thereafter; in proportion as the farms may be supposed to Bear By Gradual Improvements.

6^{thly} By Building Convenient farm houses and office houses where needed; and giving additional Buildings when Required; at a Moderate annual rent for the Money expended.

7^{thly} By Preserving the people on the Lands, inducing more to Come thereto; promoting their propagation By encouragement to many, and Giving them Examples of proper Industry.

8^{thly} By introducing into the villages in an easy natural way, some proper manufactory to give Employment to the poor women and their Children, and the Widows and orphans to be Carefully noticed By the Minister and Sefsion.

9^{thly} By Sending Some of the young men of all stations to other places famous for the Branch of Businefs proposed for them to Learn; They will naturally Return home and Carry the Customes along with them, which will be Greedily Swallowed By their friends and neighbours; If they Bring a wife from whence they came, she will keep her husband from falling again into his native habits.

10^{thly} In Short By Defusing honest Industry amongst the people, every thing will prosper; peace; plenty; and Smiling Facility; will run through the whole, with that Blessing, their worthy Patron, will have Joy and Comfort in his permanent profits; But fleeting and Comfortless are the sums squeesed from the Bowels of the Poor.

These foregoing Considerations with many others that occurr in the Execution to a person acquainted with such Businefs, Being properly attended to, and these Last ten propositions being Steadily put in practice with Judgement, are to the best of my knowledge the most proper Steps to be taken to improve that princely fortune, and to obtain as much Best from the grounds, as all things Considered they are able to Bear.

To Attempt to force more will ruin the whole design, and to expect it, and be disappointed is freight with the worst Consequences.

From my Earliest age I have been bred more to the practise than theory of Country Bufinefs, and my Employment in Differrent places has given me greater opportunitys to act then to write on the subject; This I hope will Escuse may Inacuracys in the foregoing; and anything else I may have occasion to say on the subject, It is much more uneasy for me to express, then to perform what I mean, Yet no feeble Attempt of mine shall be wanting to aid the great Design, for the mutuall welfare of The people; and their Beneficial Patron; whose Interest I Shall Study while I have the honour To be Sir

Your Really most obedient serv
Robert Ainslie.

THE IMPACT OF AINSLIE'S REFORMS

Material in the Douglas-Home archives and in the *OSA* enable the effects of Robert Ainslie's reforms to be examined to some extent. It is clear that the programme of improvement was initiated soon after his report was completed in 1769. In 1770, the Douglas estate gave notice of its intention to repair and extend the mansion house of Douglas, carry out enclosures, drain bogs, and mosses, build farm houses and establish plantations. From then until the early 1790s the Register of Probative Writs for Lanark recorded in great detail and in more than 150 pages of text an enormous range of improvements implemented on the Douglas lands in the Lanarkshire parishes of Douglas, Lesmahagow, Carmichael, Wiston, Roberton, Lamington, Crawford and Carluke.[9] Rental was boosted dramatically. A letter of November 1778 indicated that a considerable part of the estate was 'at very great advance'.[10] The lands in Douglas parish were rented at £980 in 1737, at £2,465 in 1774 and £2,988 in 1795. In Roberton, the rental stood at £152 in 1737 and £426 by 1784.[11]

Yet these data give a misleading impression. Closer examination reveals that the entire Ainslie programme was soon plunged into a state of grave crisis in the 1770s and 1780s. As Table 5.2 indicates, throughout the final two decades of the eighteenth century rent arrears were very large in spite of Ainslie's avowed attempt to phase in rent increases over a series of years. The 1780s arrears can perhaps be explained by the harvest difficulties of 1782–3 but rental was still substantially in deficit in 1795. Furthermore, in a retrospective memoir written in 1792, Ainslie himself admitted that his plan had not met with complete success on the Lanarkshire estate, though advances had been dramatic in the Angus and Renfrewshire properties. For 'several years' he was employed by the Douglas family in 'arranging and dividing the runrig and common lands of these extensive properties into as regular farms as the

TABLE 5.2   Rent arrears, Douglas estate, 1782–1805.

	Douglas		Carmichael		Roberton	
	Arrears (£)	Percentage of rent	Arrears (£)	Percentage of rent	Arrears (£)	Percentage of rent
1782	3503.24	137	1398.58	167	649.3	152
1795	3012.04	101	607.94	61	425.24	88
1805	822.98	20	24.41	2	15.74	3

NOTE   Arrears for 1782 are also for preceding years (unspecified in the rentals). Those for the other two years are recorded as for Crop 1795 and Crop 1805. The percentages given are those of the amount of arrears as proportion of the total rent of the parish in the given year, except for 1782 when the rent of 1784 (being the nearest available) was used.
SOURCE   NRA(S) 859, Douglas-Home Papers, 62/1; 174/11.

situation of the houses and ground would admit of'. Despite his assiduous efforts, however, he conceded 'with the highest regret, that Agriculture made slow or indeed little or no progress in Douglas from the time of the sets'. Furthermore, the pressure on many tenants, as a result of the increase in rental, was becoming so acute that several were surrendering their leases.[12] This pattern is consistent with other developments explored in Chapter 4 and with the plight of the tenantry in the Hamilton estate in the same period, discussed in Chapter 6. The success of improvement on many estates hung in the balance in the 1770s and 1780s. The harsh realities of economic life had also compelled Ainslie to lower his horizons. He was not able to attract substantial new tenants from elsewhere and was forced to rely on the indigenous farmers. Because of this the new farms were 'smaller than they might have been'. This was because it was necessary to 'adopt the divisions to their knowledge and ability'.[13] Yet, even though the original idea of wholesale consolidation was amended, the programme failed to halt the flow of people from the district. The population of the parish of Carmichael fell by 13 per cent between 1755 and the 1790s; Douglas declined by 15 per cent; and Roberton by 33 per cent. Those who remained still consisted in large part of small tenants. Lord Douglas's estate factor reported in 1787 that his 'estate in the west country' at that date was 'possessed by a great number of small tenants many of whom are extremely poor'.[14] In the final analysis, the eventual solvency of the estate may have been due as much to the steep increase in farm prices during the Napoleonic Wars as to the plan of improvement. As Table 5.3 demonstrates, it was from the later 1790s that really spectacular rent increases took place. Equally, Table 5.2 confirms that despite this, rent arrears fell equally dramatically in relation to previous levels.

Ainslie blamed the conservatism of the tenantry for the programme's difficulties. He concluded that he had overestimated their capacity to adapt quickly to the new ways. The 'degree of intelligence and industry of the tenantry' was crucial but it was also the most difficult part of the improvement plan to manage. This, he contended, was especially the case in Douglas where

TABLE 5.3   Rental increases on Douglas, Lanarkshire estate, 1737–1815.

Year	Douglas	Carmichael	Roberton
1737	980	294	152
1774	2,465	1,015	473
1784	2,545	835	426
1795	2,988	991	484
1805	4,161	1,117	639
1815	5,771	1,066	1,012

SOURCE   NRA(S) 859, Douglas-Home Papers, 62/1; 174/11.

'the people have long been in a bad Practice of Husbandry, yet are so wedded to their old customs and withal so indolent'.[15] Certainly the *OSA* confirms that changes in practice by the 1790s had not gone very far. In Roberton parish, the mode of farming 'is much the same as has obtained from time immemorial'. Separation of holdings was not yet complete. In Carmichael, the parish minister also concluded that 'Agriculture is for the most part carried on in the old manner'.[16]

But perhaps Ainslie himself underestimated the difficulties of managing improvement in the relatively harsh environment of the hill country of south Lanarkshire. Significantly, his planning came to relatively quick and success-ful fruition on the lowland estates of the Douglas family in Angus and Renfrewshire.[17] The Lanarkshire property was a different proposition, with considerable areas of marginal land and rough terrain set in hostile climatic conditions. This was an environment where the novel must have been greeted with suspicion, especially when imposed from above, and the tried, traditional methods which guaranteed just enough in most years embraced for reasons of basic security. It was said of Douglas that 'the greatest part of this parish seems better adapted for grazing than tillage'. The land was not dry enough for sowing until the end of March and harvest normally took place near the end of September. The district as a whole suffered terribly during the harvest failures of 1782–3 and thereafter.[18] Writing in 1793, the parish minister suggested that with the exception of 1788 and 1791 every crop since 1782 had been defective. The area seemed almost to experience the same level of distress as some Highland parishes in 1782–3. Pease meal was imported from Leith, and oatmeal from Annandale and Nithsdale to the south. Even seed corn for the following year had to be acquired elsewhere.[19] The improvement pro-gramme was therefore more probably halted by tenant poverty and economic crisis than by tenant conservatism. In some areas there was a massive gap between the intentions of the improvers and their practical effect before the end of the eighteenth century. Nor is it surprising, given the tendency towards regional specialisation and the marginal nature of arable agriculture in these parts, that pastoral farming should absorb more and more land. This led in turn to the mass migration and depopulation, documented in Chapter 8, which Ainslie had tried in vain to avoid.[20]

REFERENCES

1. W. P. Robinson jun., 'Richard Oswald the Peacemaker', *Ayrshire Arch. and Nat. Hist. Colls*, 2nd ser., III (1959), pp. 119–35.
2. Unless otherwise indicated this section is based on SRO, GD213/53, Oswald Papers, Maxwell-Oswald Correspondence, 1765–1784.
3. T. M. Devine, 'Glasgow Colonial Merchants and Land, 1770–1815' in R. G. Wilson and J. T. Ward, eds, *Land and Industry* (Newton Abbot, 1971).
4. SRO, GD213/22, Oswald Papers, Decreet of Valuation, 1767.
5. Ibid.
6. NRA(S) 859, Douglas-Home Papers, 139/2, Memorial to the Ft. Hon. Lord Douglas, 8 Feb. 1792.
7. Ibid.
8. Ibid., 256/1, Report of Robert Ainslie, 7 Sept. 1769. Unless otherwise indicated the remainder of this section is based on this source.
9. Ibid. 140/5, Abstract of Register of Probative Writs kept at Lanark.
10. Ibid. 48/5, Letter from Douglensses to Arch. Douglas of Douglas, 27 Nov. 1778.
11. Ibid. 62/1; 174/11; 7/74, Douglas and Roberton rentals, 1737–92.
12. Ibid. 139/2, Memorial to the Rt. Hon. Lord Douglas, 8 Feb. 1792.
13. Ibid.
14. Ibid., 49/2, Letter from Mr. Maconockie, 14 June 1787.
15. Ibid., 139/2, Memorial to the Rt. Hon. Lord Douglas, 8 Feb. 1792.
16. *OSA* (Lanarkshire), pp. 79–80, 307–8.
17. NRA(S) 809, Douglas-Home Papers, 139/2, Memorial ..., 8 Feb. 1792.
18. *OSA* (Lanarkshire), pp. 79–80.
19. Ibid.
20. The extensive out-migration from the district can be illustrated also from a survey of 'testificats' (or testimonials) granted by parish ministers to those entering or leaving parishes. Those for Roberton parish (SRO, CH2/376/3–5) record a substantial increase in departures from the 1750s.

6

The Improvement of a
Great Estate

I

IN the middle decades of the eighteenth century, the Lanarkshire lands of
the Duchy of Hamilton covered much of nine parishes in that county and
formed one of the most substantial aristocratic estates in the western lowlands.
The size and diversity of the Hamilton properties make them suitable for
special study in this examination of the process of agrarian change. In addition, however, the source materials for this particular estate may well be
unequalled in their extent and historical importance. As is apparent from other
chapters, the reshaping of social structure on most properties had to be mainly
reconstructed from rentals, fragments of estate correspondence and legal
records. Such data can provide an understanding of general patterns; they
usually cannot indicate the more subtle and intricate developments which give
a more comprehensive picture of the changes which were taking place.

It is precisely in this area that the Hamilton evidence is especially strong
and rich. Substantial improvements began on the Duke's lands in the early
1760s, led by John Burrell. Burrell styled himself 'superintendent of
improvements' and throughout the two decades of major changes on the
Lanarkshire estate was responsible for both the design, implementation and
supervision of all the major innovations from land consolidation to enclosure
and the introduction of new crop rotations. He was at the very heart of the
improvement process. In addition, throughout his career, he advised a number
of other landed families from the Scottish Borders to the western Highlands
on agrarian reform. Burrell was one of that small group of highly energetic,
influential and knowledgeable surveyors and factors who actually carried
through the great changes in rural social and economic structure in the later
eighteenth century. Unlike others, however, Burrell's personal journals for the
period from 1763 to the early nineteenth century have survived in over three
dozen volumes.[1] Those for the early years are particularly detailed. Burrell
recorded in them his evaluation of the prevailing condition of the estate in the
1760s, his grand strategy for reconstruction, the implementation of these plans
and their economic and social effects. When his notes are combined with the very

full rentals and Hamilton estate correspondence for the period, together with data extracted from the sheriff courts of Lanark and Hamilton, it becomes possible to produce an unusually detailed account of the improvement process on this large property.

II

More than ten years after Burrell began work on the Hamilton estate he looked back and described its condition in the early 1760s as 'long forgotten and neglected'. Neither the prevailing rentals nor agricultural practice bore any realistic relationship to 'the time and intrinsic value of land according to their different soils and situations'.[2] Undoubtedly, as will be seen in more detail below, there was considerable substance in Burrell's claims.[3] Infield–outfield forms of cultivation were general. On several farms, especially on those held under multiple tenancy, runrig prevailed. The tenurial system seems at first glance to be archaic and rigid. For the period between 1690 and 1750, sixty-five tacks were examined. All showed evidence of rental payment in kind with full conversion to money only beginning in 1748, although commutation was already underway before then. The clauses in the tacks were conventional with tenants being advised to maintain the customs of cultivation of the country and 'to eat the fodder upon the ground of the said lands for gooding thereof and not to wear out the said lands but to labour and manure the same orderly … '. Equally, these terms were repeated with little refinement in successive tacks from the later seventeenth to the middle decades of the eighteenth century. References to 'improvement' were notable by their absence with only occasional indications that land should be 'lymmed', suggesting any attempt to enforce increases in productivity. All tacks in these decades also contained clauses referring to thirlage and other feudal services.

Tenancy structure also seemed reminiscent of an earlier age. One characteristic feature of the Hamilton estate before the 1760s was the significant number of subtenants. Eleven of the 28 farms for which tacks have been examined in Hamilton barony had subtenants. They also existed in at least another twelve farms elsewhere on the estate between 1750 and 1768. The clearest indication of the extent and value of subtacks is in the early 1770s. As late as that date, fifteen farms on the entire estate had a total of thirty-four subtenants with an average rent of £8. Their contribution to the total rental paid on the properties amounted to 34 per cent.[4] When it is considered that throughout the estate multiple tenancy was also common with 130 tenants in twenty-eight possessions of this type c. 1715, then Burrell's scathing remarks about the 'neglected' condition of the Hamilton lands, from his perspective, seem convincing and appropriate.

The evidence, which will be examined later in this chapter, indicates that Burrell began a series of radical changes on the Hamilton estate in the 1760s, which represented a turning-point in the development of this part of Lanarkshire in the eighteenth century. As a revolutionary, however, he tended to condemn what had gone before in too dogmatic terms. A scrutiny of that earlier period of apparent stasis suggests that there was a closer connection between the two phases than Burrell allowed and that the relatively smooth transition to a new social order was facilitated by earlier developments whose significance should not be underestimated. Full conversion from rentals in kind to rentals in money did not occur on the Hamilton lands until the 1750s but during the decades before then there was an erosion of victual on many farms which meant that 'in kind' payments were already a residual proportion before total conversion took place. As early as the 1710s, as Table 6.1 confirms, sample analysis of twenty-two tacks indicates that only about one-fifth of rental value was paid in kind. This suggests that many Hamilton tenants were now marketing their crops directly rather than through their landlord. It implies an enhanced commercial ethos. All tenants had written leases and of the sixty-five tacks examined for the period 1690–1750 all except one were for nineteen years.

TABLE 6.1   In kind proportions of Hamilton estate rentals, 1712 and 1714.

Farm	Money	In kind converted	In kind as percentage of 'total'
1712 tacks:			
Mill of Edalwood+	100	47.58	32.2
Lands of Bent	53.6.8	4.25	7.4
Carscallen	40	4.25	9.6
Crookedstone	50	32.94	39.7
1714 tacks:			
½ Thinacres	45	7.13	13.7
Little Bent	48	4.75	9.0
Lands of Quarter	66.13.4	11.88	15.1
Crookedstone	66	48	42.1
Brountod	57.7	9.5	14.2
Carscallen	80	9.5	10.6
Carscallen	40	4.75	10.6
Crookedstone	45	32	41.6
Merryton	125	61.75+31.5 = 93.25	42.7
Merryton	27.4.4	6.75+19 = 25.75	48.6
Quarter	100	19	15.0
Boghead	300	40	11.8
Overwhinbush	105	4.75	4.5
Quarter	166.13.4	19	10.2
Crookedstone	133.6.8	96	41.9
Carscallen	80	9.5	10.6
Airiebog	50	12	19.4
Netherholinbush	48	7.13	12.9
		Mean	21.1

NOTES   'In kind converted' was calculated from the Lanarkshire fiars prices for grain available for 1704, 1712, 1714 and thereafter continuously.
SOURCES   NRA(S) 2177, Hamilton Papers; SRO, SC38/19/1 Sheriff Court Processes.

The tenant class was also in transition. As on other estates, the erosion of multiple tenancy was proceeding before Burrell planned his wide-ranging improvements. A sample of twenty-two multiple tenancies in different parts of the estate was examined for the period 1710–62. In nine of these, substantial reduction in tenant numbers had taken place by the latter date and six had become single-tenant farms (see Appendix 10). Numbers in multiple tenancies had fallen sharply from 130 in 1719 to 84 in 1758. Equally, the existing late seventeenth-century predominance of single tenancy on the estate was reinforced. By 1738–40 no less than 78 per cent of farms were held in this form of tenure. Significantly this trend was not decisively altered thereafter. As late as 1778, 85 per cent of farms were still held in single tenancy.[5]

These conclusions are significant for two reasons. First, in the 1760s Burrell concentrated most of his improvements in single-tenant farms because he regarded them as more progressive and alterations to their cultivation patterns as easier to achieve.[6] Second, there was an intriguing continuity between the 'old' and 'new' structures, not in terms of agrarian practice but in tenant composition. To some extent this can be most easily observed in the evidence of tenant numbers. As noted above, throughout the century there was an ongoing depletion of people on multiple tenancies. However, the reverse was the case among the single-tenant class. In 1745, 108 single tenancies existed on the Lanarkshire estate; by 1778, over a decade after Burrell's changes, there were still 102. The tenant structure of the Age of Improvement on this estate was clearly inherited from an earlier time, a pattern which Chapter 7 will show was also typical of many other estates. Another link with the past was the turnover of tenants. As Table 6.2 indicates, displacement of existing tenants did not start until the later eighteenth century. On the single-tenant farms in the five Lanarkshire baronies of Hamilton, Bothwell Muir, Lesmahagow, Arendale and Dalserf the family names suggest that there were actually more new tenants in the 1750s than in the subsequent three decades. Indeed, in the 1760s and in 1778 the number of tenancies held by the same possessor

TABLE 6.2   Changes in single-tenant farms, Hamilton estate, 1738–79.

Barony	1738			1745			1753–8			1762–9			1778			1779		
	N	S	U	N	S	U	N	S	U	N	S	U	N	S	U	N	S	U
Hamilton	8	9	1	1	12	14	4	14	3	4	14	3	8	12	1	9	6	3
Bothwell Muir	2	1	7	1	3	5	4	–	5	4	–	5	5	1	22	2	6	–
Lesmahagow	–	–	–	8	21	1	4	23	2	4	23	2	8	17	–	15	8	2
Arendale	–	–	–	14	20	8	13	21	4	13	21	4	9	22	2	12	14	–
Dalserf	–	–	–	5	10	–	4	11	–	4	11	–	6	9	–	5	8	–
New tenant	10			24			51			29			36			43		
Same tenant	10			56			57			69			61			42		
Unknown	18			28			13			14			5			5		
Total	38			108			121			112			102			90		

NOTE   N = new tenants; S = same tenants or same name; U = unknown.
SOURCES   NRA(S) 2177, Hamilton Papers, 778, 1134, 1135, 717; El. 32, 33, 59, 73, 78.

considerably exceeded new tenancies. High turnover in the 1740s and early 1750s may have been due to financial failure resulting from the bad harvests of 1740 and 1741.[7] But the rate of change also reveals that long before Burrell's time the farming class on this estate was exposed to the competition of the market for leases. This was not a group cushioned from social crisis by landlord paternalism or customary right of occupation. On the contrary, their access to land depended on ability to pay rental regularly and honour the obligations of the tack.[8] When it lapsed, continued occupation could not be guaranteed. It is not therefore entirely surprising that when he set his improving leases in the 1760s and subsequent decades the vast majority were taken by existing tenants. In 1762–9, only 26 per cent were new possessors and in 1778 only 35 per cent.[9] On this large estate it was the tenants who practised the 'unimproved' husbandry that Burrell so roundly condemned – who, in the main, were responsible for putting his ideas into practice.

III

Enclosure on the Hamilton lands started soon after the 1745 rebellion at the family's east coast estate of Kinneill. An advertisement in the *Edinburgh Evening Courant* of August 1750 offered the property for lease for nineteen years claiming that the farms had been 'surveyed and laid out into proper farms without any Runrig Grounds' and that they also possessed 'New Farmhouses and Officehouses'.[10] Despite these innovations, however, it was not until the following decade that John Burrell's grand design for 'improving' the Lanarkshire estate was accepted by the family. He was encouraged by the high price of grain in the few years after the Peace of Amiens in 1763. He also made reference to the opportunities for selling more produce in the growing city of Glasgow and to the developing textile and market centre of Hamilton.[11] Yet price conditions, though important, were only partially influential. Lanarkshire prices for oats rose steeply between 1764 and 1765. Thereafter, for the subsequent three years, there was an equally dramatic decline. In addition, changes in rental in the early years of the Burrell regime were consistently imposed ahead of grain prices – a more than 50 per cent increase in the Lanarkshire lands was achieved between 1764 and 1769 against a background of relatively stable markets in these years (see Table 6.3). It seems that the advances in rental and the reform in estate structure which supported them were to be imposed regardless of the fluctuations in grain prices. The revolution on the Hamilton estate also occurred almost four decades before the huge rise in agricultural prices during the Napoleonic Wars. It was based on a belief in the efficacy of the improving ideology and the new agriculture as much as on the impact of market forces. Elsewhere in Lanarkshire similar influences were at work. The large estate of the Duke of Douglas was being enclosed in the 1760s.[12] In the same decade, 204 'lybells of removing' were executed between 1763 and 1768, a much higher number than in earlier years: 86 of these were obtained by the Duke of Hamilton; 40 by the Earl of Eglinton;

TABLE 6.3 Rental, Lanarkshire lands, 1764–76 (% changes).

	1765	1766	1767	1768	1769	1770	1771	1772	1773	1774	1775	1776
Hamilton	4	0.4	4	22	3	–	3	8	19	6	11	-5
Bothwell Muir	13	21	29	6	12	2	–	2	-1	–	3	-13
Bothwell	–	–	7	–	19	-2	–	3	9	–	3	29
Kilbryde	–	–	–	–	87	–	–	–	9	–	31	3
Cambuslang	11	51	36	–	6	-20	31	5	0.3	2	1	2
Lord Selkirk's lands	–	–	–	–	2	–	2	-83	–	–	–	223
Arendale	12	24	12	1	3	–	7	2	1	1	1	–
Dalserf	14	14	–	1	1	1	22	8	10	1	–	4
Lesmahagow	–	–	–	–	–	2	86	4	10	3	-4	-7
H'ton Parks	32	9	13	44	0.5	2	1	–	-0.3	–	7	52
Coats.	–	–	–	–	5	48	11	–	–	–	–	–
Average Percentage Changes	14.3	20	16.8	14.8	13.85	5.1	20.3	-6.3	5.8	3	6.3	32
Oat prices	+17.8	-1.2	-3.5	-29	+13.7	+3.0	+19.0	+4.9	-2.9	-3.0	-23.8	-1.6

SOURCE NRA(S) 2177, Hamilton Papers, E.3.74, Abstract Rentals.

33 by Stuart of Coltness; and 16 by Cochrane of Roughsides.[13] These figures suggest that several other county estates were being prepared for improvement.

Burrell was the prime mover and supervisor of the transformation of the Hamilton estate after 1764 although the ducal family had to provide at least tacit consent to his policies, most of which could not be carried through without substantial landlord investment. Nevertheless, it is striking how much freedom of action he was allowed and how his aristocratic employers were often little more than interested but not especially knowledgeable spectators as he energetically went about his work. In October 1767, for instance, in a telling reference, Burrell noted how the Duke himself visited some of the farms and was 'surprised' to see 'corn growing where never anything grew before'.[14] Around the same time, Burrell showed the Duchess a plan of some parks on the estate, 'with some hints of my other improvements which she much approved of'.[15] These were the only significant references to the owners of the estate throughout Burrell's voluminous journals. Similarly, when he discussed his detailed recommendations with the Hamilton tutors, who, in 1764, were legally responsible for the estate, they approved of them in their entirety without demur or qualification.[16]

Initially, Burrell concentrated on those farms which were out of lease, or almost so, and where improvements could be most easily accomplished. From the beginning there was an acknowledgement that the process of change would take a considerable time. At least twelve years would be necessary in order to ensure effective 'inclosing and planting' in the majority of estate farms. But though he favoured a gradual and cautious approach – for the most part being willing to wait until tacks expired before making changes – Burrell was also resolute in the pursuit of his policies. He noted in the early pages of his first extant journal:

> My intention is to construct a particular plan for his whole farms ... all upon sheets of the largest imperial paper. Every farm on one side as they ly, precisely expressing the situation and soill with every mine or mineral that can be found out by a superficiall tryall ... and on the otherside of the same sheet to draw it in ane improved state by inclosing, planting etc. And betwixt every one of these leaves to have blank leaf for giving a compleat history of the farms as they stand and reasons for the alterations, the whole to be bound up in a book representing ane atlas.
>
> This I propose may be done by a month before seed time is ended; a month immediately after harvest for corn countreys and the month of July for the moorland farms.

In spring 1764, he began a tour of the Hamilton lands, noting the activities of the various farmers, the opportunities for enclosure and the plans for improving individual possessions. Occasionally he came across a tenant who was already engaged in enclosing. Such a man was William Porteous in the barony of Lesmahagow who was 'doing more than any of that country'. But for the most part he was caustic in his criticism; the new order would have to be imposed and, for the most part, paid for from above. It was unlikely, in his view, to evolve autonomously. Thus, the tenants of the High and Low Parks were 'hidebound'. The lands of the touns of Allanton and Merryton were 'lying runrig in the most confused manner', while the former, 'by its situation, was locked up from all improvements'.[17]

Yet careful reading of Burrell's journal during this early period of planning and in later years suggests he grossly underestimated the initiative and the contribution of the tenantry of the estate to the implementation of the improvement strategy. Initially he hoped to attract 'substantial tenants from elsewhere and especially from more advanced parts of the country'.[18] In the event he was unsuccessful in this strategy and it proved necessary 'to bring on the native tenantry by degrees',[19] a tactic which may help to explain why single-tenant turnover on the Hamilton estate in the 1760s, as noted above, was curiously limited by comparison with earlier periods. Essentially, therefore, the revolution on the Hamilton lands was carried through for the most part by the indigenous tenant class of the area. In this process there were several examples of tenants taking the initiative by approaching the Duke's factors for assistance with liming, the building of new farm steadings and help with difficult neighbours who were impeding the removal of runrig.[20] There was much more evidence of enterprise than on the Douglas estate, considered in Chapter 5, and that distinction may go a long way to explain the different results of improvement on the two properties. In addition, by 1766–7, Burrell came across several examples of tenants taking responsibility for the subdivision of lands and their enclosure.[21] All this suggests that on this estate in the 1760s there were already men of substance and acumen who were capable of responding to the opportunities of financial assistance from the landowner and the rise in prices for the produce of their farms. It is interesting to note, however, that Burrell offered little overt criticism of those who held single tenancies. Most condemnation was directed at those who practised runrig agriculture on multiple tenancies. In the event, it was these farms which received least investment and where reduction in tenant numbers, during the process of improvement, occurred on a considerable scale.

By the middle of the summer of 1765 Burrell had completed his first detailed survey of part of the Hamilton estate. A total of twenty-seven touns had been investigated, their condition recorded and potential for improved husbandry outlined. This was about a quarter of all farms on the Hamilton lands. Through improvement, their 1765 rental of £1,514 could be boosted to an estimated £2,362, an increase of 64 per cent. However, this would require massive investment in the short-term: a total of over £4,659 would have to be spent on 12,363 acres (or £2.65 per acre) in order to achieve the desired result. From the start, therefore, lavish landlord expenditure was at the heart of the Burrell strategy. There were several additional elements. The most crucial was enclosure: it was axiomatic 'No improvement can be made without inclosing or dividing'.[22] This seems to have been done within the existing layout of farms,

although there was also some straightening of farm boundaries. Most enclosure activity involved the division of farms into several fields separated by
hedges or dykes which would allow the easier adoption of the improved
rotations which would in turn raise land productivity. For example, on
Allanton farm, consisting of 254 acres, twenty-one enclosures were to be built,
none smaller than 6 acres with a mean of 12 acres.[23] In virtually all cases, the
Duke was to pay the costs of division and construction and at the same time
defray the costs of initial liming of enclosed lands.

Burrell did not provide a clear or coherent tabulation of the progress of his
enclosure programme from this first statement of 1765. Nevertheless, both
from his own journals and from the Hamilton estate papers it is possible to
construct a reasonably accurate profile of his activities over the subsequent
two decades. The detailed information is presented in Appendix 11. About 30
per cent of the 170 farms on the estate were tackled between 1765 and 1785.
Over two-thirds of these were enclosed in the period 1765–75 with most
activity concentrated in the first few years after 1765. Clearly, improvement
was not a process which once begun moved forward irresistibly. On the
contrary, there is considerable evidence, which will be examined below, that
the estate experienced a major crisis in the early 1770s and again in 1782–3,
due to poor harvests, which brought virtually all enclosing activity to an
abrupt halt. Between 1781 and 1785, division of lands was only occurring on
2.5 per cent of the Hamilton farms.[24] Moreover, not all tenancies were treated
equally. There also seems to have been special concentration on single-tenant
units. Of those farms enclosed, 63 per cent were of this type, perhaps indicating
that Burrell recognised them to be more 'progressive', or, probably more
likely, because with only a single lease to lapse, improvement could be introduced more easily and rapidly than on multiple tenancies. Whatever the
reason, however, it may suggest that single tenancy facilitated enclosure.

Some of the farms were enclosed with stone dykes but the majority, as
indicated in Table 6.4, were surrounded with a wide ditch or double ditch with
a 'clap' or earth dyke coped with thorns. This type of fence was used extensively in subdivision inside a stone dyke enclosure but also often employed as
a boundary around the improved farm. New structures of this type were
vulnerable, so livestock had to be herded continually or dispensed with
altogether. In one parish, by 1772, sheep had almost disappeared from the
district 'on account of inclosing by ditch and hedge'.[25] Again, in the baronies
of Dalserf and Lesmahagow in 1781, cattle and sheep found in the new
enclosures were to be poinded and the owner fined ½ merk.[26] As the thorns
grew they needed attention and had to be 'plashed', the plashers having to
wear sheep-skin coats, aprons and gloves. The scale of the planting activity
can be indicated by the fact that between 1768 and 1771, 58 farms on the
Hamilton lands were supplied with 796,000 thorns.[27] Once fields were enclosed, it seemed to be the practice to leave them in grass for some years to
rest the ground and possibly to allow the thorns to grow undisturbed. Again,

this represented another cost to the landowner and helps to explain why enclosure on individual farms proceeded slowly and rarely involved all areas at any given time. It also suggests that the impact on employment opportunities of enclosed and improved land may be more complex than is sometimes suggested.

Closely associated with the development of improved farm structures was the elaboration of new regulations for crops and rotations. The Hamilton tacks before Burrell's time did not neglect good husbandry practices. There was considerable emphasis on the need to protect the land from abuse. A common phrase was that the tenant was required to 'consume the fodder on the ground for gooding thereof'. This meant that the dung produced by the fodder should remain on the ground of the farm as fertiliser. Indeed, the Hamilton and Lanark sheriff court records demonstrate that tenants could be and sometimes were taken to court for selling dung from the farm.[28] Some tacks also specified the proportion of land to be rested each year. Yet Burrell's regulations for the new sets in 1764 were much more specific and elaborate:

TABLE 6.4   Type of enclosure on the Hamilton estate, 1765–84.

Farm	Date	
Flemington	1765	Drystone wall 6 ft. high
Skellyton	1765	Dyke with thorns
Cornhills	1769	Ditch, dyke, hedge and cocking
Boghead	1783	Hedges
Airybog	1783	Hedges
Dykehead & Bog	1765	Ditch, dyke and hedges
Cornsulloch	1765	Ditch and hedge
Burnhead	1774	Hedges
Shotlin	1784	' ... base of the dyke to be 8 feet from rut to rut ... the shough to be 6 feet wide at the surface and 4 feet of perpendicular depth ... and to be properly built with fail on coupe ... '
Thinacres	1777	Partly stone dyke
Rodgerton	1780	Stone dykes, earth dykes, hedges and ditches
Motherwell	1781	Ditch, hedge and cocking
Overton	1781	Dykes, thorns and cocking
Achnotrick	1782	Thorns and cocking
W. Greenlees	1783	Hedge and ditch
Raith	1783	Green fail dyke 6 ft. high with hedge on top
Kinniel	1769	Subdivision – hedge and ditch
Mummerch	1770	Drystone dyke
Bonhard	1772	Sunk fence, hedge and ditch 'to be sunk 2 foot and raised 2 foot with a turf copeing and a hedge upon the top of it' March fence to be ditch and hedge
Pielpark	1768	Stone dyke

SOURCE   HPL 631/1, Burrell's Journals, 1763–83.

That the tenants within the Baronys of Hamilton, Cambuslang and Dalserf shall be restricted first from ploughing above one third part of their present possessions; second Never to take up ground without lime or some other manure; third Never to take above three crops running; fourth that all ground shall be richly laid down with clover and ryegrass seeds; three good crops of grain and six good crops of grass alternately.

Any tenant who acts in a contrary way shall be liable in double rent for the ground otherways cropped.[29]

It is noteworthy, in particular, that ryegrass and clover had to be introduced in a nine-year rotation and that failure to respect the requirements of the tacks would invite draconian financial penalties on top of the rent increases which were central to the whole strategy. Supervision, monitoring and regulation, together with the provision of appropriate penalties for non-compliance, were all features of the regime. New ranks of estate officials, including a General Overseer, several subordinates and nurserymen were appointed to survey and report on the improvements. The task of overseer was clearly intended to be onerous. Burrell noted in 1772 that 'the reason we give for the Overseer having half a crown more wages a week than the nurseryman is that he is seldom to be at home in his own bed'. Indeed, the terms of reference for these new officials suggest that improvement was to be run almost like a military operation![30]

Despite this, Burrell had difficulty enforcing the improving leases on some tenants. The possessor of Darngaber farm, despite being supplied with much lime by the Duke, had 'failed in every article binding upon him' over the past five years. Burrell proposed to charge him for the lime provided over that period. Moreover, there were complaints that the old high ridges were often so tough that they could not be sown easily with grass seeds.[31] But in general, progress was good. Burrell's printed regulations of 1780 did not include instructions on the sowing of ryegrass and clover but merely stated that, at the end of a lease, a tenant had to leave one-third of the arable in 4-year old ley, one-third in 2 years' ley and a third in grass.[32] At first sight, this might suggest that some principles of improvement had been abandoned. What is more likely, however, is that already by the 1780s improved rotations were becoming the norm in several parts of the Hamilton estate and such detailed regulations were no longer thought necessary. Two farm surveys tend to support this conclusion and reinforce the argument advanced above that the native tenantry were capable of adjusting to the new farming. An investigation conducted in 1774 into two of the most outlying baronies of the estate, Dalserf and Lesmahagow, revealed that at least 82 per cent of farms were planting beans and pease, although only 54 per cent at that date were fully enclosed.[33] Even more convincing was the result of a detailed assessment of cropping practices conducted on seventy-four farms in 1783. Burrell and his assistants graded each of them on a five-point scale from 'very good' to 'very poor'. No less than 72 per cent were classified as 'very good' or 'good' and only 17 per cent were considered 'poor' or 'very poor'.[34] The demonstration of the achievement is confirmed by yield data on seventy-four farms in 1774. Inevitably, there was considerable variation in seed/yield ratios between holdings because of the transitional condition of the estate at the time. Yet, 24 were expected to produce yields of 9 in oats, 20 yields of 6 and 25 yields of 4. These represent a considerable increase on the yields described by Whyte for western lowland estates in the seventeenth century, which tended to average between 2 and 3.[35]

IV

The evidence seems to suggest that Burrell managed to secure considerable acceptance from the majority of the tenantry for his improving plans. This appears curious because the process of enclosure and land division, accompanied as it was by substantial increases in rental, might be thought to produce significant social dislocation. There is evidence, for instance, of a haemorrhage of people from multiple tenancies during the period of Burrell's improvements. The number of these touns declined from 32 in the 1750s to 18 in 1778 while, as Table 6.5 indicates, multiple tenants fell from a total of 75 in 1758 to 37 in 1795. Multiple tenancies were reduced over the period by 43 per cent and tenant numbers in them by 42 per cent.[36] A search of the sheriff court processes for those years confirms that removals were significantly more frequent in the 1760s. At Hamilton sheriff court, eighty-six lybells of removal were executed in favour of the Duke in the five-year period 1763–8 and these are suggestive of attempts at mass displacement on his estate.[37]

But these statistics probably exaggerate the degree of social dislocation caused by Burrell's reforms. Scrutiny of the wording of the actions of removal reveals that many of the tenants named had reached the end of their tacks and that, unless stated in the tack itself, the issue of an instrument of removal was a legal requirement before tenure of the farm was transferred to another individual. In other words, the execution of these processes may merely indicate a change of tenancy at the expiry of a lease, something which had occurred on a considerable scale long before Burrell commenced his improving regime. It is also important to note that an analysis of the legal processes and rentals shows that 15 of the 86 tenants compelled to quit the Hamilton property continued in their possessions until at least 1778.[38] All this suggests that the clutch of summonses of removal issued in the 1760s did not necessarily mean mass expulsions or wholesale consolidation of land but more probably represented the attempt by the proprietor to clear the way, if necessary, for new tenants or reorganisation of farms. Significantly, the single tenancies, which were central to Burrell's strategy, only declined from 110 in 1758 to 105 two decades later.

Some documentation exists on how he thinned the ranks of the multiple tenants. The toun of Allanton, possessed by three men 'runrig and rundale', was potentially improvable because of its vicinity to the town of Hamilton. Burrell decided to maintain the tenants whose tacks expired before 1767 on

TABLE 6.5 Number of tenants in multiple tenancies, Hamilton estate (Lanarkshire), 1710–1809.

Farm	1710–15	1738	1745	1747–9	1758	1762–9	1774	1778	1795	1801
Allanton	2	3	3	5	1	1	1	1	1	1
Merryton	9	5	5	4	5	4	2	2	2	1
Quarter	4	4	4	7	4	4	2	2	2	2
Thinacres	7	7	7	7	4	7	3	3	1	2
Crookedstone	8	8	8	5	6	6	3	3	4	4
Carscallen	5	5	5	–	6	6	6	1	–	1
Muirhead	3	4	4	–	4	4	3	3	3	2
Dunteelan	4	3	3	–	3	3	3	3	3	3
Mid Bracco	2	2	2	–	2	2	2	2	2	1
Forrest	2	2	2	–	2	2	–	1	–	–
Moffathills	2	2	2	–	2	1	1	1	1	?
Nr. Bracco	3	2	2	–	2	2	1	–	1	1
Draffan	8	8	8	–	4	4	1	1	1	–
Southfield	3	3	3	–	3	3	2	2	2	–
Architygemmel	3	2	2	–	1	–	–	–	2	–
Halhill	2	1	1	–	1	1	–	1	1	–
Boreland	2	1	2	–	2	2	–	1	1	–
Mains Acres	13	13	13	–	14	9	8	8	2	–
Hawkhead	4	4	4	–	4	3	3	3	3	–
Plewlands	2	2	2	–	2	2	–	1	1	–
Drumcloy	3	2	2	–	2	1	1	1	1	–
Over Halkwood	2	1	1	–	1	1	1	1	1	–
22 farms	93	88	87	–	75	79	48	43	37	–
Percentage change (from previous date)	–	5	1	–	–	2	40	12	14	–

SOURCE Appendix 10.

an annual agreement at an 'advanced' rent. Only when all leases had expired
would enclosure take place and the farm be put to public offer. A similar policy
was adopted in Kellyton with four tenants. Three tacks expired before 1770,
and each tenant was to maintain possession until the final lease of Andrew
Hamilton came to an end five years later. There was a possibility of buying
Hamilton out at a 'reasonable bargain' but this was not a pressing requirement.[39] Equally, he did not adopt a dogmatic approach to subtenancy. The
farm of Moffathills was in lease to two men but occupied by about sixteen
subtenants. It was experiencing 'the worst system of husbandry'. Burrell did
not recommend mass removal but the enclosure, drainage and subdivision of
nine enclosures for 'the most substantial subtenants' who were to be maintained in possession within the new order.[40]

These brief examples illustrate various aspects of the Burrell approach. One
element in it was caution and patience. He was usually content to wait until
tacks expired before making changes and then to seek a process of removal to
ensure that any necessary alterations could be made without any legal constraints. But those who lost land did so, not through direct 'coercion', but
through the customary and universally acceptable system of leasing and
releasing of farms. His gradualist approach is illustrated also by the fact that
only rarely did he offer to buy out the remainder of a tack. There were also
sometimes gaps in time between individual farms being surveyed, 'staked out'
and finally fully enclosed. As Appendix 11 reveals, it was unusual for the
planning process to be immediately followed by comprehensive enclosure. For
instance, three of the farms surveyed in 1765 were not fully enclosed until 1783.
The tenantry had to be allowed to adapt to the new ways.

Burrell proceeded also by a combination of carrot and stick. The new order
required more stringent controls and supervision of tenant behaviour.
Throughout his journals, holdings were constantly being inspected and improvements on them monitored. In times of crisis, as in 1772–3 and 1782–3,
when tenants fell into arrears, he used his authority to assist the 'industrious'
and energetic and dismiss the lazy and the inadequate for failure to pay rent.[41]
More generally, the existence of a pool of potential tenants able and willing
to take on improved farms when leases lapsed was vital. As indicated above,
he failed in his attempt to attract progressive tenants from other, more
advanced estates. Yet there is little evidence in his journals that there was ever
a scarcity of potential 'replacement' tenants in Lanarkshire which is hardly
surprising because most estates were squeezing out many tenants as consolidation accelerated. This must have given him considerable bargaining power.

The carrot was also used. The fact that the Duke took financial responsibility for enclosing, liming and the reconstruction of farm houses was clearly
attractive. Burrell argued also that it was not possible 'to make the present
tenants understand what we mean by inclosed ground until they see it'.[42] He
therefore personally spent much time among the tenants, showing and ex-
plaining the divisions and their utility. If tenants wished to carry out enclosure

themselves they would receive an allowance from their rent at a level decided by two arbitrators – one decided by the Duke; the other by them. Burrell was flexible when rental offers were made, in order to defuse any possibility of resistance to the broader strategy of improvement. Of one such offer for the farm of Moffathills in 1765, which was much lower than he had planned, he noted, ' ... though this offer should come somewhat short of what we expect my opinion is to let it go, to prevent concerts or combinations'.[43] Here was further evidence of the point made in Chapter 4 that the tenant class was far from passive in the face of landlord demands and had to be treated with a good deal of circumspection.[44]

Yet as Burrell later made clear, it was not so much his own negotiating skills which helped to ensure the acceptance of the new agrarian system on the Hamilton lands but the combination of high grain prices in 1764–5, together with abundant harvests in 1766 and the following four years. The kirk session records for several Lanarkshire parishes indicate how this stimulus was having an effect on land improvement throughout the county.[45] Burrell himself had no doubt that it was the buoyant market which encouraged tenants to accept higher rentals than before. In a retrospective letter in January 1775 he observed that 'the Tennents at that time being by the High price of Grain and other vivers being nearly impregnated with the Same ideas of improvement ... and in this way they went on from the year 1766 we began to the year 1770 while the seasons were Indulgeing'.[46] He was acknowledging here that whatever the ideological zeal of the improver, the tenant response depended crucially on the very practical matters of markets and harvests. Decisive proof of this came in 1772–3 and again in 1782–4. In 1771 and 1772, 'shakeing winds' were accompanied by 'Rotting Rains' and followed in 1773 by 'parching Drought'. All this had produced a 'General Devastation' and a huge increase in rent arrears. Burrell complained that the 'whole Spirit of Improvement about Hamilton was knocked on the head'. By January 1770, five tenants in the area were bankrupt or had renounced their leases in spite of the high prices which were causing distress in some of the neighbouring smaller towns and villages. In 1774, the tenants' debts almost exceeded the value of their crop and stock and there were vociferous complaints that the rents set in 1765 and 1766 had been pitched at too high a level. The tenants claimed that they were 'so scrimpt that they were hardly able to maintain their families without paying any rent'. The crisis affected the entire programme of improvement, with activity, as indicated by the enclosure index in Appendix 11, declining dramatically in the 1770s.[47]

However, the tenants had scarcely recovered from the bad seasons of 1771–3 when, ten years later, they had to endure another crisis. After two successive bad crops, Burrell had to give eleven tenants allowances on their rent and a further thirty had to be supplied with £319 of seed corn. John Henderson, the tenant of Wellburn, maintained that in 1782 and 1783 he could sow no more than half his crop from his own seed and had to buy 30 bolls of seed costing £30; on a rent of £47 this left no room for investment.[48]

TABLE 6.6 Abstract rental (£) Hamilton lands, including value of victual (feus generally excluded), 1681–1821.

Barony	1681	1712	1722	1738	1745–8	1754	1764	1769	1776	1778	1795	1821
Hamilton	—	—	708	798		968	868	1,183	1,741	1,851	1,990	(780)[+]
Bothwell Muir 275*		—	328	318		325	320	669	595	620	666	(302)[+]
Bothwell			—	122		201	144	183	217	220	167	
Kilbryde			53	53		54	23	43	65	67	67	
Cambuslang			455	455		458	449	1,087	1,213	1,202	1,280	
Lord Selkirk's				—		533	566	575	326	206	246	
Arendale		959	788	665		544	718	1,159	1,288	1,247	1,502	
Dalserf						1,157	431	576	884	876	993	
Lesmahagow		518	—	525		706	623	623	1,220	1,249	1,211	
H'ton Parks							721	1,706	786	101		(1,771)
Coats			72	72			75	86	90	148		350
Lanarkshire			2,404	3,292		5,021	4,951	7,897	8,484	7,640	8,472	28,725

NOTES   * Kain, carriage omitted
       + without feus

SOURCES HPL 631/1, Burrell Journals, 1763–98; NRA(S) 2177, Hamilton Papers, 1146, 1134, 1135, 1136; E.1, 32, 33, 59, 73, 78, 65, 70, 89.

TABLE 6.7   Abstract rental, Hamilton lands, 1720s–1795 (% change).

Barony	1720s	1738	1754	1764	1769	1776	1778	1795
Hamilton	–	12.7	21.3	-10.3	36.3	47.2	6.3	7.5
Bothwell Muir	19	-3.0	2.2	-1.5	109.1	-10.9	4.0	7.4
Bothwell	–	–	64.8	-28.4	27.1	18.6	1.4	-24.1
Kilbryde	–	0	1.9	-57.4	87.0	51.2	3.1	0
Cambuslang	–	-2.2	2.9	-2.0	142.1	11.6	-0.9	6.5
Lord Selkirk's	–	–	–	6.2	1.6	-43.3	-36.8	19.4
Arendale	-17.8	-15.6	-18.2	32.0	61.4	11.1	-3.2	20.4
Dalserf	–	–	293.5	-62.7	33.6	53.5	-0.9	13.2
Lesmahagow	–	1.4	34.5	11.8	0	95.8	2.4	-3.0
H'ton Parks	–	–	–	–	136.6	-53.9	-87.2	–
Coats	–	0	4.2	14.7	4.7	64.4	–	136.5
Lanarkshire	–	–	52.5	-1.4	59.5	7.4	-9.9	10.9

SOURCES   HPL 631/1, Burrell Journals, 1763–98; NRA(S) 2177, Hamilton Papers, 1146, 1134, 1135, 1136; E.1, 32, 33, 59, 73, 78, 65, 70, 89.

Henderson's position was probably typical. The good times of the 1760s had helped to make the improving ethos acceptable to the tenantry. Equally, the difficulties of the 1770s and 1780s rendered it suspect to hard-pressed farmers and their families. As Tables 6.6 and 6.7 demonstrate, the estate also suffered. The spectacular rental increases of the 1760s were reversed in several areas in subsequent decades. Between 1781 and 1785, enclosure activity declined almost to a trickle, with less than 3 per cent of farms enclosed in these years. Burrell's vision of an improved estate had been partially realised but it could not be completed until both market and weather conditions improved again in the 1790s. Ideology and the relentless pursuit of generating more profit from the land were a vital driving force but they were not enough without a favourable economic context.

REFERENCES

1. HPL 631/1, Burrell Journals, 1763–1808. Unless otherwise indicated all references in this chapter are taken from this source.
2. Ibid., 8 Jan. 1774. Copy Letter, John Burrell to Mr Baron Mure, 8 Jan. 1774.
3. The discussion of the 'unimproved' Hamilton estate is based on HPL 631/1, Burrell Journals, entries for 1763–5; NRA(S) 2177, Hamilton Papers, 778 E1.32, E1.53, Rentals and miscellaneous tacks.
4. NRA(S) 2177, Hamilton Papers, E1.73.
5. See Appendix 10.
6. See Appendix 11.
7. For the impact of harvest crisis in 1740–1 see SRO, SC38/22/10, Sheriff court Records (Lanark).
8. See also actions for removal recorded in ibid., SC38/22/10–12.
9. See Appendix 10.
10. NRA(S) 2177, Hamilton Papers, 409, minor payments for mending the park dykes about Kinneil, 1746.
11. HPL 631/1, Burrell Journals, 6 Apr. 1764.
12. See above, p. 89.
13. SRO, SC37/8/6–11, Sheriff Court Processes (Hamilton).
14. HPL 631/1, Burrell Journals, 2 Oct. 1767.
15. Ibid., 14 Oct. 1767.

16. Ibid., Journal for 1763–9, p. 2.
17. Ibid., 17 May 1765.
18. Ibid., 30 Sept. 1767.
19. Ibid.
20. See, for example, ibid., 9 and 11 Mar. 1774; 25 Aug. 1774.
21. Ibid., 13 and 17 Dec. 1766.
22. Ibid., 5 July 1765.
23. Ibid., 14 May 1765.
24. See Appendix 11.
25. HPL 631/1, Burrell Journals, 18 Jan. 1772.
26. Ibid., 21 Dec. 1781.
27. See Appendix 11.
28. See, for example, SRO, SC38/22/20, Sheriff Court Processes (Lanark).
29. HPL 631/1, 27 Sept. 1764.
30. Ibid., 4 Feb. 1772.
31. Ibid., 16 Sept. 1768.
32. Ibid., 21 Aug. 1780.
33. Ibid., 5 Sept. 1774.
34. Ibid., 17 June 1783.
35. Whyte, *Agriculture and Society*, p. 74.
36. See Appendix 10.
37. SRO, SC37/8/7–9, Sheriff Court Processes (Hamilton).
38. See Appendix 10 and Table 6.2.
39. HPL 631/1, Burrell's Journals, 5 July 1765.
40. Ibid., Letter to Baron Mure, 18 Sept. 1765.
41. Ibid., 27 July 1784.
42. Ibid., 16 Sept. 1765.
43. Ibid.
44. See above, pp. 66–7.
45. SRO, CH2/376/3, Kirk Session Records of Wiston and Roberton, Lanarkshire, 30 Nov. 1766; SRO, CH2/378/1, Kirk Session Records of Dolphinton, Lanarkshire, 11 Feb. 1766.
46. HPL 631/1, Burrell's Journals, Copy Letter, Burrell to Mr Baron Mure, 8 Jan. 1774.
47. Ibid.
48. Ibid., 17 and 27 July 1784.

7

Dispossession

The Tenant Experience

I

THE commercialisation of the rural economy seemed likely to have a profound impact on the structure of tenancy. Both economic pressures in the later eighteenth century and the prescriptions of the improvers favoured the extension of farm holdings in consolidated form under the control of single tenants. These trends posed a grave threat to the very existence of the army of small farmers, which, as shown in Chapters 1 and 2, comprised a very substantial proportion of the tenant class as a whole in the counties under study. The compact, enlarged holding had a basic rationale in the minds of the improvers. The removal of multiple tenancies would not only allow more effective management of the land by more substantial farmers, it would also release all the resources of individual initiative, ambition and industry which had supposedly remained sterilised under the communal system. As Sir John Sinclair pointed out: 'In every part of the kingdom, the plan of alternate ridges, cultivated by different farmers ... anciently prevailed. As long as this injurious system prevailed, all attempts at improvement were in vain. The ridges could not be made straight, nor could draining or inclosing be attempted.'[1] There was also a desire to ensure the most effective and continuous use of both human and animal labour power and avoid the presumed waste and 'indolence' of the old social order. No consensus emerged on the idea size of farm. Some regarded about 70 acres as the very minimum which could be worked efficiently by a single plough-team.[2] But others took the view that this was still too small, arguing that since one plough was sufficient for about 50 acres of tilled land, a viable holding, with half its land in grass and the other half in cultivation, needed to be at least 100 acres in overall extent.[3]

Still larger farms than this, however, were seen to possess additional advantages. Substantial units of 200 acres and more could help to reduce the costs of farm house construction and renovation.[4] Since this was an expense covered by the landowner and often involved a very considerable outlay, there were obvious attractions in reducing it to a minimum by consolidating several holdings into one. Improving writers also saw the bigger farm as having positive attractions in enhancing the profitability of an estate. It was almost axiomatic that a remodelled farm would attract a higher rental because prospective tenants could not value it against its returns in the past. Furthermore, some suggested that substantial holdings might entice men of capital and farming expertise who would in due course act as exemplars of more progressive agricultural practice to their conservative neighbours.[5]

The small farming class was under pressure for other reasons. In some areas, rising rentals and living costs in the later eighteenth century bore especially severely on this group. It was noted of the parish of Carluke in Lanarkshire: 'amidst these revolutions the poor farmer of a few acres at £10 or £20 rent who can with difficulty support his family on the produce of his small farm, suffers the most. He has little to sell, everything to purchase.'[6] Both in 1772–3 and 1782–3, tenant bankruptcies were often most numerous among the smaller men who had the least financial resilience.[7]

Given the range of intellectual and economic forces making for consolidation, it is not surprising that historians have seen this period of agrarian reorganisation as one of widespread tenant dispossession. The bigger holdings were built up and the smaller units systematically crushed as improvement gathered pace. Analogies have been drawn with the Highland Clearances.[8] Both lowland tenants and highland crofters shared a common fate or eviction and dispossession. As one scholar has put it: 'there was a general movement in every part of Lowland Scotland to lay down larger farms and nearly always larger farms meant fewer tenants; dispossession and eviction became a common experience … the overwhelming tenor of the evidence, in every county, is of holdings thrown together to make larger farms and tenants evicted.'[9] Another writer describes how 'the elimination of small tenancies forced their former occupants and their families to seek employment as wage labourers.'[10] These assertions convey clearly the perceived scale and extent of dispossession. The process is seen as a revolution which destroyed much of the old social fabric of the lowland countryside in the second half of the eighteenth century and caused immense dislocation and migration from the land. This view, to a greater or lesser extent, has become one of the central orthodoxies of Scottish history in this period.

Yet, to a considerable extent, the interpretation does not rest on especially strong historical foundations. There has been an over-reliance on information culled from the parish reports in the *Old Statistical Account*, where references to the consolidation and 'monopolising' of farms can indeed be found in abundance.[11] But the *OSA* must be used with great care on this subject. Despite its great value for other purposes, it is not a source which can be made to yield truly convincing data on tenant depletion. First, close study of some accounts reveals a confusing use of terminology by certain ministers. On several occasions, removal of small tenants was clearly being confused with the eviction of subtenants and cottars. As the next chapter will show, the dispossession of cottars in particular was indeed very widespread. But the cottar experience was not necessarily shared by the tenant class. Secondly, quantitative and chronological references in the *OSA* to tenant removal are usually rather vague. A typical comment would be: ' ... the throwing of a number of small farms together, which, at one period, was frequently practised in this country ... obliged a number of families to take up their residence in the towns and villages'.[12] Another report noted: 'when small farms enlarged small tenants crowded into towns or neighbouring villages ... and became burdens upon the public.'[13] Statements such as these reveal little about the scale, extent or timing of consolidation or about possibly distinctive patterns of dispossession in single and multiple tenancies.

The collection of harder and more revealing data requires the use of additional sources. A large number of rentals, 232 in all, have been examined for a dozen estates in the four counties of this study. The rental sample is divided across these areas as follows: Lanark, 41 per cent; Ayrshire, 14 per cent; Angus, 17 per cent; and Fife, 28 per cent. The concentration of the analysis was on the decades after 1750, the classic period of reorganisation. Yet, where the data allowed, the investigation was carried back to the later seventeenth century in order to construct indices of tenancy change over the years 1680–1815 and place the 'era of improvement' in a more general context. Research on rentals is exceedingly laborious and time-consuming and the data are not free from problems of interpretation. Farm names sometimes appear on a rental while others disappear. It is often difficult to determine whether a new name implies the renaming of an old holding, the name given to part of a former, now reorganised farm, or a purchase made by the proprietor. Conversely, the disappearance of a holding might signify either consolidation or disposal. Nevertheless, if used carefully and with a clear understanding of their limitations, rentals can be of enormous value in the analysis of tenant dispossession. They permit the construction of time series, the identification of single and multiple tenants, the quantification of tenant turnover and continuity, and the rate of depletion. Close inspection of rentals for the period suggest that they were maintained with considerable care and precision and there are unlikely to have been major omissions or discrepancies.

But even rentals do not tell the whole story. A simple count of tenant numbers can conceal significant changes within the social composition and holding size of the tenant class. In addition, therefore, an analysis of tacks and estate correspondence complemented the quantitative exercise. Equally important are sheriff court records. These have rarely been examined by historians of the 'Lowland Clearances' though, recently, they have been extensively used to document patterns of eviction in the nineteenth-century Highlands.[14] In Scots law, each tenant who was to lose his lease had to receive a notice of removal. The proprietor was required to follow this procedure, even on the expiry of a tack: it cold not be assumed that a tenant had to move merely because his tack had expired.[15] The proper procedure was clarified in the Act of Sederunt of 1756 passed by the Court of Session. This stated:

> It shall be Lawfull for an heritor or other setter of a tack on his option either to use the order of warning prescribed by the Act of Parliament of 1555 or to being his action of removing against the tennant before the Judge Ordinary at least forty days before the term of Whitsunday which shall be held as equal to a warning execute in terms of the said Act.

Prior to 1756 the precept of warning under the 1555 Act had to be 'red in the pareche-kirk quhair the lands byis, upon ane Sabbath-daye before Noone, the Time of Preaching and Prayers, and ane Copie left and affixed upon the moust patent Dure of the Kirke fortie dayes before the Terme'. The relevant procedures usually had to be followed very carefully because cases exist in sheriff court records of tenants successfully postponing the issue of a decreet of removal by demonstrating that the proper legal requirements had not been met.[16]

Partly because of this precision, processes of removal are a potentially important source for the analysis of tenant dispossession. The summons of removal was granted by a petition before a sheriff. The case material identifies the name and holding of the possessor, whether tenant or subtenant (since the latter was also covered by the Act), and often the reason for the petition, whether because of a breach of tack or rent arrears. Tenants could be removed after falling into more than one year's arrears. This information can all be tabulated and differences over space and time revealed. However, like rentals, the sheriff court processes also contain considerable pitfalls. The reasons for issue of summonses are not always given. In addition, the summons itself was not necessarily enforced. Evidence from a variety of estates show that the names of tenants continued to appear in the rental long after a summons of removal had been granted. Clearly, some proprietors followed the legal process to the letter in order to facilitate a change of tenant at the end of a tack, even if that eventually did not in fact take place. In this sense, a simple tabulation of summonses of removal will overstate the extent of tenant dispossession rather than underestimate it.

More importantly, there is the difficult problem of managing research on sheriff court records. It is hardly surprising that they have not attracted systematic scrutiny. Their sheer bulk is daunting. The sheriff court archive for Angus alone, one of the counties under close study in this volume, consists of 474 boxes for the period 1700–1810. In addition, within the records themselves, processes of removal and associated material do not occupy much space. An analysis of one sample bundle of cases for Cupar sheriff court in Fife indicated that over 50 per cent of processes concerned debts and less than 5 per cent were related to removals. The size and complexity of the records ensured that some form of sampling was inevitable. The processes of four courts in different geographical areas were sampled at decadal intervals between 1700 and 1800. The courts in question were Cupar, Peebles, Dunblane and Linlithgow. In addition, the processes for Lanark and Hamilton were examined for the period 1760–1800 on an annual basis to allow a more detailed survey of one county in the decades of most rapid change. In all, over seventy record-boxes of material were searched in the course of research.

II

The pattern of reduction in tenant numbers on eleven estates is set out in Table 7.1. In virtually all the properties surveyed, tenant numbers declined in the later eighteenth century. This finding is hardly surprising and is consistent with the orthodox view. More interesting, however, is the suggestion that the haemorrhage was, for the most part, relatively modest in extent and limited in scale. The data do not support the conventional interpretation of mass clearance of small tenants and significant depletion in tenant numbers as a whole. The mean reduction in all eleven properties, over varying periods, was around 16 per cent. The most serious losses were not more than about a quarter of the original number of tenants. But these figures in themselves, though suggestive, are not conclusive and other evidence must be used to extend the analysis. Data on tenant turnover and continuity are also revealing though there could well be several reasons for a higher than normal level of turnover which may be unrelated to policies of consolidation. Simultaneous expiry of leases of similar lengths set in the same year is one obvious explanation. Another is bankruptcy of tenants, a fate which befell many in the crises of 1772–3 and 1783–4. There is evidence too that mobility of tenants to other farms in the locality at the end of a lease was common before the second half of the eighteenth century.[17] In addition, the more competitive criteria attached

TABLE 7.1   Tenant numbers on 11 estates, 1735–1850.

Estate	Period	Change in tenant numbers	Percentage change
Bertram of Nisbet	1769–1850	42 → 31	-26
*Crawford	1771–2	38 → 32	-16
Douglas	1774–1815	99 → 72	-27
Hamilton	1758–98	142 → 123	-13
Glasgow (Shewalton)	1761–1806	25 → 19	-24
Cavens	1741–82	27 → 22	-18
Balbirnie	1770–1818	46 → 38	-17
Leven & Melville (Balgonie & Melville)	1750–80	114 → 131	+15
Morton (Aberdour)	1735–1811	50 → 38	-24
Panmure	1758–1826	177 → 176	-1
Airlie	1790–1821	122 → 103	-16
Eglinton (Coilsfield)	1757–1800	38 → 34	-11

NOTES   *The estate of Crawford figure only covers 2 years because it is derived from the original survey of farm reorganisation to be implemented in subsequent years.
   Bracketed reference is to a barony of the estate.
SOURCES   SRO, Bertram of Nisbet Papers, GD5/1/497–8; HPL, John Burrell's Journals, 631/1, Journal, 1771–2, 8 July 1771; NRA(S), Douglas-Home Papers, 859/62, 174, vols 74–8; NRA(S), Hamilton Muniments, 2177/778, EI.32, 33, 59, 73, 78, 65, 70, 89; NRA(S), Earl of Glasgow Papers, 0094/4,8–9; SRO, Oswald of Auchincruive Papers, GD213/22/54; SRO Balfour of Balbirnie Muniments, GD 288/4/122; SRO, Morton Papers, GD150/2061; SRO Leven and Melville Papers, GD26/5/251–95; SRO, Dalhousie Muniments, GD45/18/506–1091; SRO, Airlie Muniments, GD16/30A, vols 2–111. SRO, Eglinton Muniments, GD3/8360, 8361, 8359, 1846.

TABLE 7.2   Continuity and turnover of tenantry, Leven and Melville estates (Fife), 1675–1804.

Period	No. of tenants	No. in same possession	Percentage	
			Continuity	Turnover
Barony of Balgonie				
1675–1720	8	2	25	75 (17)
1720–30	19	14	74	26
1730–40	23	19	83	17
1740–50	25	17	68	32
1750–60	23	16	65	35
1760–70	23	18	78	22
1770–80	23	17	74	26
1780–90	22	19	86	14
1790–1804	18	6	33	67 (48)
Lordship of Melville				
1715–30	17	10	59	41 (27)
1730–40	12	7	58	42
1740–50	10	8	80	20
1750–60	7	5	71	29
1760–70	8	6	75	25
1770–80	8	8	100	0
1780–90	8	6	75	25
1790–1804	5	4	80	20 (14)

NOTES Figures in brackets are the period calculations converted to a mean decadal estimate. All percentages are rounded up or down to the nearest integer.

The number of tenants recorded is not the total number on the rent roll at the beginning of the period concerned, but the number of those in possessions that could be traced through to the end of the same period.

SOURCES Compiled from several rentals in SRO, Leven and Melville Muniments, GD26/5/251–95.

to the allocation of leases were also likely to accelerate tenant turnover independently of other estate strategies.

In Tables 7.2–7.5 the base number of tenants in anyone survey year was taken as that number which could be traced at least as far as the next such year and not only those which could be monitored throughout the whole period of

TABLE 7.3   Continuity and turnover of tenantry, Balfour of Balbirnie estate (Fife), (1770–1810).

Period	No. of Tenants	No. in same Possession	Percentage	
			Continuity	Turnover
1770–80	24	14	58.3	41.6
1780–90	24	18	75	25
1790–1800	25	19	76	24
1800–10	21	16	76.2	23.8

SOURCE SRO, Balfour of Balbirnie Muniments, GD288/4/1 and 2, Rentals, vols 1 and 2.

TABLE 7.4   Continuity and turnover of tenantry, Earl of Panmure estates (Angus), 1728–1824.

Period	No. of tenants	No. in same possession	Percentage continuity	Percentage turnover	Mean per decade
Panmure and Inverpeffer					
1728–36	89	54	60.7	39.3	49.1
1736–58	81	31	38.3	61.7	28.1
1758–75	44	26	59.1	40.9	24.1
1775–85	47	37	78.7	21.3	21.3
1785–96	44	34	77.3	22.7	20.6
1796–1824	34	16	47.1	52.9	18.9
Lethnot and Navar					
1728–36	37	28	75.7	24.3	30.4
1736–58	34	21	61.8	38.2	17.4
1758–75	33	15	45.5	54.5	32.1
1775–85	33	20	90.9	9.1	9.1
1785–24	25	19	59.4	40.6	10.4
Edzell					
1728–36	57	40	70.2	29.8	37.25
1736–58	50	20	40	60	27.3
1758–64	49	32	65.3	34.7	57.8
1764–75	43	33	76.7	23.3	21.2
1775–85	42	30	71.4	28.6	28.6
1785–1824	42	23	54.8	45.2	11.6

NOTE   The above tables were calculated by taking the number of tenants at the latter of 2 survey dates in possessions which could be traced back to the earlier date and using that figure as the denominator in the percentage calculations of continuity and turnover. This explains why there appears to be such a large variation in tenant numbers over the period examined. (See particularly the changes in Panmure and Inverpeffer.) Such considerations dictate that the conclusions drawn from these tables be treated more circumspectly than the others since it is not known to what extent this sample represents the whole picture of tenant turnover in this period.

In addition to this, an attempt was made to standardise these figures since the periods, being of varying lengths, did not allow direct comparison with each other. This was done by taking the percentage turnover figure, dividing it by the number of years in each individual survey period (to arrive at an annual figure), then multiplying this by 10 to produce a mean decadal rate of turnover.

SOURCE   SRO, Dalhousie Muniments, GD45/18/506–2091, *passim.*

rent examination. With this figure as the denominator, the enumerator becomes the total number of both those individuals who continued in possession and those who were of the same family. This latter category comprised those with a common surname to their predecessor and those who were known, from other sources, to be related.

Despite the variation in estate size and agrarian context, the data suggest a strikingly similar pattern throughout. Turnover was common but, in the light of the other powerful forces making for discontinuity described above, little evidence emerges of *radical* increase in consolidation. The results from an analysis of these estates are also consistent with the examination of tenant

TABLE 7.5   Continuity and turnover of tenantry, Douglas estate (Lanarkshire), 1737–1815.

Period	No. of tenants	No. in same possession	Percentage	
			Continuity	Turnover
Douglas parish				
1737–74	68	8	12	88[*]
1774–84	31	15	48	52
1784–95	29	19	66	34
1795–1805	31	20	65	35
1805–15	31	22	71	29
Carmichael parish				
1737–74	30	9	30	70[*]
1774–84	41	26	63	37
1784–95	34	26	87	13
1795–1805	39	34	87	13
1805–15	39	13	33	67
Roberton parish				
1737–74	22	1	5	95[*]
1774–84	27	15	56	44
1784–95	26	18	69	31
1795–1805	26	19	70	30
1805–15	28	20	71	29

NOTE   [*]These figures represent the percentage turnover of tenantry over the period of 37 years. When these are averaged out over this period then the decadal figures are as follows: Douglas = 23.8%; Carmichael = 18.9%; Roberton = 25.7%.
SOURCES   NRA(S) 859, Douglas-Home Papers, 62/1; 174/11; vols 74–8, 217–19, 254, 256, 258.

turnover on the Hamilton estate, considered in Chapter 6 (see Table 6.2). Equally, where the figures allow trends to be established for the whole of the century, the decades after 1760 do not stand out as ones of significantly greater upheaval than those which went before.

The extent of displacement can also be evaluated through an analysis of summonses of removal in sheriff court processes set out in Tables 7.6–7.10. The results of this exercise seem on the whole to be consistent with the trends derived from examination of rentals. There is little evidence of the sustained and widespread use of the legal process on a scale which would have been necessary if mass displacement of the smaller tenantry had taken place. Even at Hamilton, where the rate of issue of summonses of removal was higher than at other courts, the average number of decrees was thirty per annum. The average for all five courts for the sample years after 1760 was 16.8 per annum. We cannot assume that all, or even indeed the majority, were necessarily enforced. In addition, a substantial number represented the formal recognition of the end of a tack or an application for removal on the grounds of rent arrears or breaches of a tack. There is little support here for the notion of a

TABLE 7.6   Summonses of removal, Hamilton sheriff court, 1763–84 (available years).

Year	Cause of summons			
	End of tack	Arrears	Breach of tack regulations	Others
1763	8	4	2	2
1764	60	4	1	–
1765	4	3	1	–
1766	23	7	2	–
1767	58	–	1	–
1768	19	18	2	–
1779	–	14	1	–
1781	5	8	2	–
1782–4	9	13	2	–
Total (1763–84)	186(68%)	71(26%)	14(5%)	2 (0.7%)
Total (1768–84)	33(35%)	53(57%)	7(8%)	–

SOURCE   SRO, Sheriff Court Processes (Hamilton), SC37/8/7–20.

'clearance' of small tenants in the Lowlands with all its connotations of extensive removals and enormous social dislocation.

A comparison with the more notorious experience of the western Highlands and islands brings out the differences between the two regions in the scale of tenant displacement. In the north of Scotland, clearance reached its climax in the famines of the 1840s and 1850s when there was wholesale expulsion of crofters and cottars. The extent of coercion is clearly revealed in the sheriff court records of the time. On the island of Mull, for example, 1,277 summonses of removal were issued in the years 1846–52 at a rate of 213 per annum. During the same period, 1,429 summonses were served against tenants and cottars in Lewis at an annual rate of 285.[18] On these two Hebridean islands around 249 writs of removal were being served in these decades on an annual basis, a figure which was more than *fourteen* times the average annual sample indicated in the lowland courts of the later eighteenth century, considered above. This brief quantitative exercise suggests that there was a stark and dramatic difference in the level of coercion and the scale and speed of tenant displacement in the two regions.

Indeed, even when the lowland tenant lost land the process was much less traumatic than for his west Highland counterpart. Some tenants in the south, like the crofters of the north, held land on an annual basis or by a verbal tack. However, in the estates surveyed the vast majority possessed a written lease which normally endured for several years. Instant and collective tenant eviction on a large scale was unlikely in the Lowlands though common in the Highlands. Typically, consolidation from multiple tenancy to single control took some time. It was a gradual, piecemeal and attenuated process, as the following two examples illustrate. The farm of Carngillan on the Eglinton estate in Ayrshire had no less than eight tenants in 1757. This number fell to

TABLE 7.7 Cupar sheriff court: summonses and decrees of removal.

Year	End of tack		Arrears		Breach of tack	No written tack		Bankrupt	Other	Unknown		Totals
	Tnt.	Subtnt.	Tnt.	Subtnt.	tnt.	Tnt.	Subtnt.	tnt.	tnt.	Tnt.	Subtnt.	
1751	0	0	1	0	0	0	0	0	0	0	0	1
1760	2	0	2	0	0	0	0	0	0	5	0	9
1770	4	0	4	1	0	1	1	1	0	8	2	22
1780	0	0	2	0	0	0	0	0	0	1	0	3
1785	2	0	0	0	0	1	0	0	0	25	3	31
1790	11	0	2	0	0	7	0	0	0	7	2	29
1800	33	0	13	2	1	15	0	1	1	5	0	71
Totals	52		24	3	1	24	1	2	1	51	7	166
Percentages	31.3		14.5	1.8	0.6	14.5	0.6	1.2	0.6	30.7	4.2	100

SOURCE SRO, Sheriff Court Processes (Cupar), SC 20/5/1–62.

TABLE 7.8 Dunblane sheriff court: summonses and decrees of removal.

Year	End of tack		Arrears		Breach of tack	No written tack		Other	Unknown		Totals
	Tnt.	Subtnt.	Tnt.	Subtnt.	tnt.	Tnt.	Subtnt.	tnt.	Tnt.	Subtnt.	
1729–65	0	0	0	0	0	0	0	0	0	0	0
1766	0	0	1	0	0	2	0	0	3	1	7
1770	0	0	2	0	0	0	0	1	3	2	8
1780	3	1	2	0	1	5	0	0	2	1	15
1790	10	0	3	0	0	2	1	0	4	1	21
1800	13	0	2	1	0	3	0	0	3	0	22
Totals	26	1	10	1	1	12	1	1	15	5	73
Percentages	35.6	1.4	13.7	1.4	1.4	16.4	1.4	1.4	10.5	6.8	100

SOURCE SRO, Sheriff Court Processes (Dunblane), SC 44/22/1–62.

TABLE 7.9 Peebles sheriff court: summonses and decreets of removal.

Year	End of tack		Arrears		No written tack		Other	Unknown	Totals
	Tnt.	Subtnt.	Tnt.	Subtnt.	Tnt.	Subtnt.	Tnt.	Tnt.	
1662–1704	0	0	0	0	0	0	0	1	1
1750	0	0	0	0	0	0	0	2	2
1760	0	0	0	0	0	0	0	2	2
1770	0	0	1	1	1	0	1	2	6
1780	0	0	0	0	0	0	0	0	0
1790	0	0	0	0	0	0	0	0	0
1800	2	1	2	0	1	1	0	0	6
Totals	2	1	3	1	2	1	1	7	17
Percentages	11.8	5.9	11.8	5.9	11.8	5.9	5.9	41.2	100.2

SOURCE SRO, Sheriff Court Processes (Peebles), SC SF 42/5/1–53.

TABLE 7.10 Linlithgow sheriff court: summonses and decreets of removal.

Year	End of tack	Arrears	No written tack	Unknown		Totals
	tnt.	tnt.	tnt.	Tnt.	Subtnt.	
1737	0	0	0	0	1	1
1749	0	0	0	2	0	2
1770	1	0	2	2	0	5
1800	3	1	7	2	0	13
Totals	4	1	9	6	1	21
Percentages	19.0	4.8	42.9	28.6	4.8	100.1

SOURCE SRO, Sheriff Court Processes (Linlithgow), SC 41/6/1–22.

TABLE 7.11   Size of farms in Scotland, 1851–81.

Size of farm	1851	1871	1881
<10 acres	34	12	160
10–50	297	299	288
50–100	149	192	274
100–200	125	195	188
200–300	39	76	71
300–400	17	38	39
400–500	9	18	18
500–600	5	13	13
>600	14	49	49

NOTE   The totals in each period have been reduced to 1,000 to indicate the relative number of farms of different size in each decade.
SOURCE   John W. Paterson, 'Rural Depopulation in Scotland: Being an Analysis of its Causes and Consequences', *Trans. of the Highland and Agricultural Society of Scotland*, 5th ser., IX (1897), p. 261.

seven in 1767 and six in 1777. A further two tenants were lost in 1786 and again in 1797. By 1810 the holding was in the possession of two men, one of whom, John Morton, had gained a tack in 1767 and had advanced since then to joint control as the adjacent lands were consolidated.[19] Another variant of the process can be reconstructed from documents relating to the farm of Drumglay on the estate of the Earl of Strathmore in Angus.[20] It was possessed in runrig tenancy by five individuals in 1690. One tenant held one-third and the remaining four one-sixth shares each. This pattern had hardly altered up to 1762 except that a couple of smallholdings were created sometime between 1721 and 1737. These two were held by one individual in 1762. The first major reorganisation came in 1771 with an agreement between the Earl and three of his tenants on this holding, whose tacks were still current. The tacks of the other three tenants had all expired. Those with leases valid until 1777 were persuaded to surrender them by being promised preferential treatment in the allocation of farms after reorganisation had taken place. In effect, this ensured that these favoured three remained as main tenants in 1784 as the rental of that year demonstrates. Those who lost land belonged to that group whose tacks had expired before the agreement of 1771. The process of tenant removal was therefore absorbed within the broader and more familiar mechanism of the regular reletting of farms. In a sense, it was clearance by stealth. But the potential social dislocation and alienation associated with the Highland Clearances was largely avoided.

The argument that the scale of tenant consolidation from the 1760s was less extensive than is commonly suggested can also be supported from data on farm size contained in nineteenth-century censuses after 1851. The results of the analysis are set out in Tables 7.11 and 7.12. Two patterns are suggested. First, holdings below the 'improved' minimum threshold of 100 acres were still very common, especially in the western lowlands. In Lanarkshire, 52 per

TABLE 7.12 Number and percentages of farmers in farms of various sizes, 1871.

County	Farm sizes in acres								
	<10	10–49	50–99	100–200	200–300	300–400	400–500	500–600	>600
Forfarshire	111	358	269	318	214	124	53	37	114
(percentages)	6.9	22.4	16.8	19.9	13.4	7.8	3.3	2.3	7.1
Fife	51	155	134	234	170	90	41	23	98
(percentages)	5.1	15.6	13.5	23.5	17.1	9.0	4.1	2.3	9.8
Lanarkshire	136	415	496	604	168	61	36	17	81
(percentages)	6.8	20.6	24.6	30.0	8.3	3.0	1.8	0.8	4.0
Ayrshire	110	379	557	870	212	77	32	33	125
(percentages)	4.6	15.5	23.3	36.5	8.9	3.2	1.3	1.4	5.2
Scotland	4,664	11,583	7,441	7,576	2,942	1,428	723	490	1,923
(percentages)	12.0	29.9	19.2	19.5	7.6	3.7	1.9	1.3	5.0
Renfrew	19	145	236	268	60	9	3	2	16
(percentages)	2.5	19.1	31.1	35.4	7.9	1.2	0.4	0.3	2.1
Selkirk	10	6	4	8	4	3	6	5	72
(percentages)	8.5	5.1	3.4	6.8	3.4	2.5	5.1	4.2	61.0
Berwick	15	56	48	82	71	55	50	29	97
(percentages)	3.0	11.1	9.5	16.3	14.1	10.9	9.9	5.8	19.3
Peebles	7	23	13	20	27	12	7	13	57
(percentages)	3.9	12.8	7.3	11.2	15.1	6.7	3.9	7.3	31.8

TABLE 7.12 (Continued)

County	Farm sizes in acres								
	<10	10–49	50–99	100–200	200–300	300–400	400–500	500–600	>600
Edinburgh	1	43	46	101	66	40	23	19	77
(percentages)	0.2	10.3	11.1	24.3	15.9	9.6	5.5	4.6	18.5
Haddington	12	27	13	47	41	47	35	21	32
(percentages)	4.4	9.8	4.7	17.1	14.9	17.1	12.7	7.6	11.6
Stirling	29	165	276	253	67	27	10	4	31
(percentages)	3.4	19.1	32.9	29.4	7.8	3.1	1.2	0.5	3.6
Kinross	12	28	30	41	24	19	9	7	6
(percentages)	6.8	15.9	17.0	23.3	13.6	10.8	5.1	4.0	3.4
Kincardine	182	355	255	234	87	27	15	14	15
(percentages)	15.4	30.0	21.5	19.8	7.3	2.3	1.3	1.2	1.3

NOTES The percentages are of those farmers who returned the information in the census, NOT the total tenantry. In Lanarkshire the number of those not supplying this information was 76; in Ayrshire 93; in Scotland as a whole 1,421 in Renfrew 27; in Selkirk 5; in Berwick 5; in Peebles 5; in Edinburgh 12; in Haddington 0; in Stirling 5; in Kinross 5; and in Kincardine 6. The returns for Forfarshire and Fife were complete in this respect.
SOURCE Census, 1871 (Parliamentary Papers, 1873 LXXIII).

cent of farmers worked possessions of less than 100 acres; in Ayrshire, 43 per cent; and in Renfrewshire, almost 53 per cent. Elsewhere, and predictably in the south-east, larger farms were more dominant. But the Lothians pattern was far from typical. In Angus, 46 per cent of farmers possessed units below 100 acres and the figure in Fife was 34 per cent. The large, arable farm of the south-east type was one variant among several. Arguably more representative of the Lowland pattern as a whole was the smaller farm of less than 100 acres which, ironically, had been condemned as archaic by some improving propagandists of the later eighteenth century. The second feature to note is the evidence of substantial continuity between the old order and the new. The consideration of poll tax data in Chapter 1 and Appendices 2–6 suggested that the western region was dominated by small farms and the south-east by much bigger holdings.[21] The changes which had occurred over the decades between the later seventeenth and the early nineteenth centuries cannot be underestimated, especially the removal of multiple tenancy. But the basic distinction between the two zones remained. In 1850, as in 1700, the small sector remained important in the west, while larger farms were still significant in the south-east.

III

The discussion thus far has emphasised the continuities which prevailed in tenant structure in the later eighteenth century. Evidence has indicated that the rate of depletion and displacement was less than sometimes suggested. But three caveats need to be entered at this point. First, the survey of tenancies derived from selected estates in four lowland counties. Much more work will have to be completed on many other properties in other areas before it will be clear whether or not the patterns outlined here were typical of the lowland experience as a whole. Second, behind the modest erosion of single tenancies it is still possible to identify the continued and more extensive removal of tenants in multiple possessions. Only because much of the work of weeding out these possessions had already been carried far on many estates by the 1750s did their ongoing displacement not radically increase the figure of *total* tenant depletion.[22] However, on the Morton estates, the proportion of multiple tenants fell from 20 per cent in 1735 to 8 per cent in 1811.[23] On the Hamilton lands, the number of multiple tenants declined by 61 per cent between 1762 and 1809.[24] On estates where multiple tenancy was still prevalent in the 1760s, the number of removals was therefore likely to be much greater than suggested from the rental analysis conducted in this chapter.

Third, and most importantly, a significant local variation in tenant reduction should be noted. The patterns already described derive mainly from the rentals of estates where mixed husbandry was practised or where dairying was the norm. There would appear to have been much more tenant displacement in upland areas where arable farming was increasingly marginal and commercial pastoralism advancing rapidly. Only from such districts in the study region is there hard evidence of the kind of population loss which is reminiscent of the Highland Clearances. These areas were mainly confined to the southern parishes of Lanarkshire and Ayrshire, and the hill country of Angus.

Both contemporary observation and quantitative analysis suggest that dispossession was widespread in these zones. In the parish of Libberton in Lanarkshire, 'the ruins of demolished cottages are to be seen in every corner'. The minister had seen the population fall by more than half since the 1750s because, it was alleged, of 'the letting out the lands in large farms'.[25] In the nearby parish of Crawford, one report in 1771 suggested that 'the present plan of turning the whole farms into large store farms had so reduced the numbers of consumers and consequently the quantity of corn to maintain them ... '.[26] In Lamington, the number of communicants had fallen from 400 in the 1750s to about 200 in the 1790s. The decline was due to the 'union of farms' in the barony of Wandel where 4,000 out of 5,000 acres were now devoted to sheep pasture.[27] In south Ayrshire a similar trend was apparent. A typical description came from the parish of West Kilbride, where the conversion of arable farms to grazing land prevailed: '... in consequence whole baronies and large tracts of land, formerly planted thick with families, were thrown waste to make way for this new mode of management'.[28]

There seems little doubt that these comments were authentic responses to major social dislocation. Here, indeed, was evidence of the Lowland Clearances. On the Earl of Eglinton's vast Ayrshire estate, the reduction of small farms in upland districts was very extensive compared to the limited incidence of displacement elsewhere.[29] Again, on the Douglas lands, in the inhospitable hill country of southern Lanarkshire, tenant numbers fell by 54 per cent between 1737 and 1774, a much greater rate of depletion than that recorded for those estates considered earlier in this chapter.[30]

The pressures were similar to those in the Highlands. The penetration of market forces made for increased regional specialisation. These districts, as the case-study of the Douglas estate in Chapter 5 demonstrated, had probably been marginal grain producers for some time. Arable farming by the later eighteenth century was simply becoming uneconomic because of limitations of climate and terrain. There was a set of irresistible market pressures pushing these districts relentlessly towards large-scale pastoral farming and that, equally inevitably, meant the destruction of many traditional communities. The most compelling evidence that improvement did indeed produce immense and disruptive social changes in these areas comes from data on migration. Table 7.13 shows a varied pattern of mobility in the four counties in the later eighteenth century. Agrarian change did not cause depopulation; instead, it, and other factors, contributed to a complex pattern of inward and outward movement. Again, these results do not simply measure migration but probably also local differences in nuptiality and fertility. It is plain, nevertheless, that some parishes were losing people on a huge scale. Not all were located in pastoral districts and it would be much too simple to explain heavy losses

TABLE 7.13   Parishes gaining and losing population in the 4 study counties.

	Parishes losing		Parishes gaining		
	>30%	0–29%	0–29%	>30%	Totals
Angus:					
No. parishes	15	17	16	5	53
% of total	28.3	32.1	30.2	9.4	100.0
Fife:					
No. parishes	17	28	9	5	59
% of total	28.8	47.5	15.3	8.5	100.1
Lanarkshire:					
No. parishes	12	13	7	6	38
% of total	31.6	34.2	18.4	15.8	100.0
Ayrshire:					
No. parishes	12	10	11	12	45
% of total	26.7	22.2	24.4	26.7	100.0

NOTE   For methods of calculating net out-migration, see below, p. 146–7.
SOURCE   *OSA*

solely in terms of the impact of sheep and cattle ranching. However, Maps
7.1–7.5 do indicate a close correlation between areas of commercial pastoralism in three counties and high levels of out-migration.

It may be, therefore, that Highland-type tenant displacement was mainly
confined in the Lowlands to areas on the fringes of the Highlands and in
upland parishes in the south, adjacent to the Borders. Elsewhere, on the basis
at least of the evidence considered in this study, tenant depletion after *c.* 1760
in the arable Lowlands was more limited. The programme of large-scale
consolidation envisaged by some improving theorists was not always realised
in practice.

IV

In 1800, John Thomson, the agricultural reporter for Fife, noted the social
dangers of too much farm consolidation. While admitting that fragmentation
of land might create economic problems, he stressed the difficulties of removing too many smallholdings and concentrating the management of land in the
hands of a few big farmers. This, he suggested, would have grave effects on
social stability and threaten the entire political order. He drove home his
argument by referring to the unprecedented social turmoil in France as a
demonstration of how economic discontent could lead to revolution and
anarchy.[31] It is impossible to say how many Scottish landowners had these
thoughts in mind as they contemplated the social implications of improvement. Certainly little trace of any deep concern has been found in the archives
which have been examined. However, as evidence in Chapters 4–6 suggests,
proprietors and factors were conscious of the hostility that their policies

KEY TO MIGRATION MAPS

■ Parishes demonstrating net out-migration of more than 30%
⊞ Parishes demonstrating net out-migration of between 0 and 29%
☰ Parishes demonstrating net in-migration of between 0 and 29%
☐ Parishes demonstrating net in-migration of more than 30%

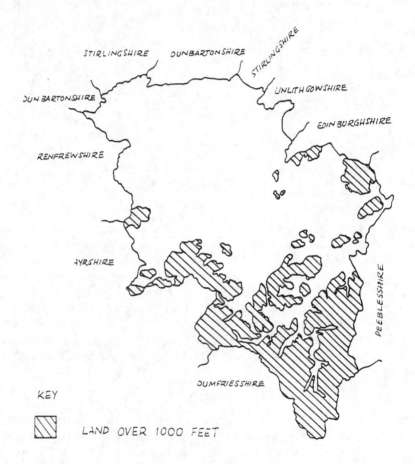

KEY

⬛ LAND OVER 1000 FEET

MAP 7.1   High land in Lanarkshire.

might provoke and were often at pains to avoid confrontation. A major
theme running through earlier discussion was that estates sought to use not
only the stick but also the carrot in changing tenant structure. This concern
also helps to explain why the displacement of small tenants was often
followed by the development of smallholdings and village settlements to
absorb some of the dispossessed population. It is very possible, therefore,
that an awareness of the potential threat to social stability was indeed a

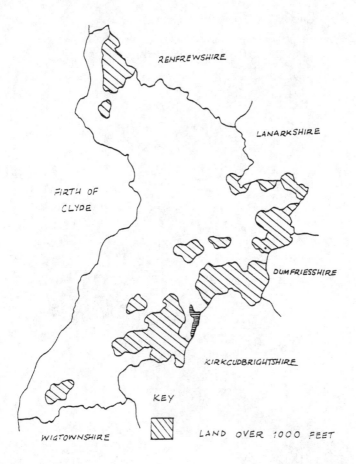

MAP 7.2   High land in Ayrshire.

significant constraint preventing the implementation of the more radical policies of the ideologues.

In addition, it is unlikely that the pre-improved rural economy had the financial resources to sustain widespread concentration of land in the hands of a few possessors. Earlier it was shown that the road to improvement was a difficult one, with progress constantly impeded by capital shortages, the crises of 1772–3 and 1783–4 and the difficulty of recruiting tenants from more advanced regions of the country.[32] The rapid increases in rent arrears, which took place during the years of difficulty but endured for several years after, hardly suggests a farming class with abundant surplus resources. Estates were therefore partly forced to consolidate holdings in a gradual and piecemeal fashion because the resources did not exist within the tenantry to permit faster progress. The essential point about Scottish agrarian transformation was that

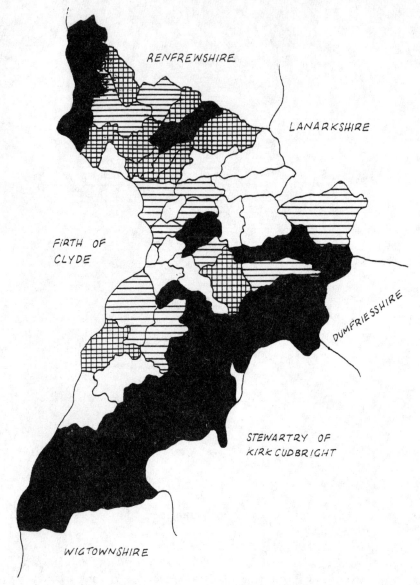

MAP 7.3   Migration in Ayrshire.

it happened in a relatively poor country. This basic fact prevented wholesale consolidation.

But the nature of the new agronomy also ensured that the small-farm sector was likely to survive. Historians have tended to focus on the consolidation process to the virtual neglect of other factors and have therefore failed to notice that some forces were operating in the opposite direction. In practice,

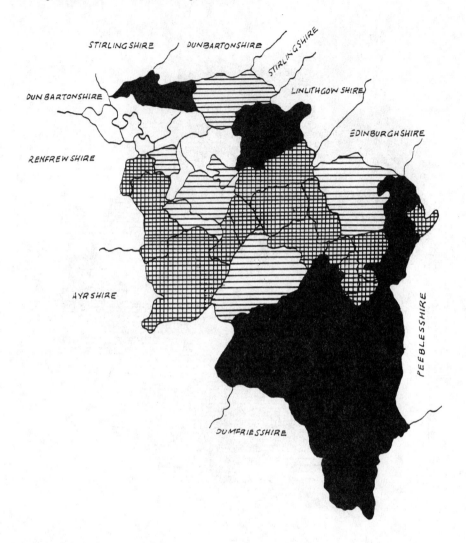

<small>MAP 7.4 Migration in Lanarkshire.</small>

the matter of holding size and shape was determined by a number of variables such as climate, terrain, market opportunity and agrarian specialisation. Thus the dairy farms and market gardens, which were prospering in Lanarkshire, Ayrshire and Renfrewshire on the burgeoning demand from the developing industrial towns, were most properly organised in smaller units.[33] Moreover, numerous examples have been discovered throughout this study of large farms being *divided* into several holdings because the existing unit was deemed too unmanageable. Surveyors seem to have judged each case on its merits and were not hidebound by a single orthodoxy.[34] Behind the bald figures of tenant

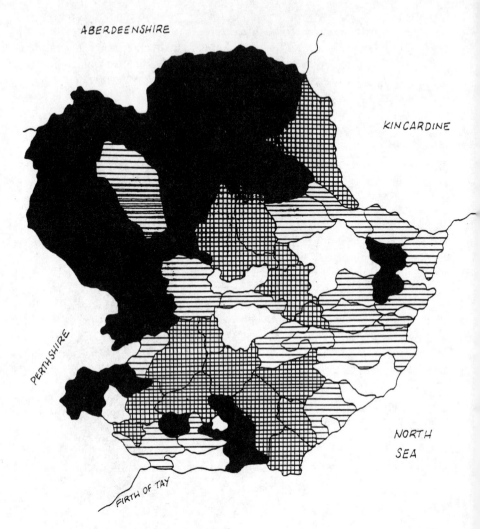

MAP 7.5   Migration in Angus.

numbers lay planning initiatives of great complexity with holdings adjusted, added to and also fragmented as particular circumstances demanded. A typical example of this process is outlined in Table 7.14.

In specific situations small tenancies were often regarded as inherently more profitable to the proprietor than larger holdings. This view was consistent with that important current in eighteenth-century thought which assumed that a growing population was necessary for economic progress. Many landowners sought to achieve the best of both worlds by pursuing farm consolidation on one part of their estates and division in another. Two circumstances favoured the latter approach. First, the cultivation of former waste, moor and commonty land was best achieved by establishing colonies of small tenants who would practise intensive agriculture. As is well known, this occurred on a large scale in the north-east lowlands but it was not simply confined to that region.[35] Secondly, the growing urban and industrial economy provided a new range of opportunities for the creation of small tenancies. While one force in the new system favoured consolidation, another, rural industrial expansion, suggested fragmentation. Small towns in the countryside grew apace. Villages and settlements were founded and extended. Linen and cotton industries were most important but the mining of coal and other minerals was also significant.[36]

In the region of study, industrial activity was a powerful force, especially in north Ayrshire and Lanarkshire, and Fife.[37] Many estates leased land to small tenants in and around areas of concentrated settlement. In 1791, the strategy of the Morton estate in Fife was partly influenced by the growth of the town of Aberdour: 'As the people both in Easter and Wester Aberdour are in great need for land and as this farm lyes so near the Town and a good Road, it should be reserved for acred land which will give a much higher rent and be better cultivated, than in a farm.'[38] There were similar hopes of high returns during the division of farms on the Crawford estate in Lanarkshire in 1772. Here the attraction was the provision of smallholdings for the leadminers of Wanlockhead. The surveyor specifically pointed out the attractions of small tenancies: 'This small parcel consisting of 21 acres of Crawford John with a small liberty of grassing milk cows is possest by William Watson, lead-driver, which about 13 years since only paid £15st. and now pays £25 at which to a demonstration shows how much may be made by small possessions in this farm … '[39]

In the counties studied in detail, the subdivision of land in this way was the norm in most of the estates considered because the majority were situated close to urban and industrial opportunities. The impact on tenant numbers could

TABLE 7.14 Proposed division of 2 farms, Leven and Melville estate (Fife), 1793.

Existing structure (acreage)		Proposed structure (acreage)
Bighty farm	71	120 (+69%)
Sheythrum farm	302	130 (-57%)
'lying betwixt	10	-100%
them possest by		
the tenant of		
Sheythrum mill'		
	383 acres	
Allowed for two roads		10
Allowed for ditches and plantations		20
Allowed for muir reserved for the fenars		20
For the inhabitants of the Coaltown		83
		383

SOURCE SRO, Leven and Melville Muniments, GD26/5/613, Memorandum for Lord Balgonie, 1793.

sometimes be spectacular. On the Earl of Strathmore's lands in Angus, tenant numbers rose from 219 in 1762 to 475 in 1784, owing mainly to the creation of smallholdings in and around Glamis and Newtown. At the same time the numbers of those in multiple-tenant possessions fell from 188 in 1762 to 58 in 1784.[40] It is likely that a form of resettlement and reallocation of land was undertaken which helped to maintain a farming population despite the consolidation of holdings underway elsewhere. The concentration of farms around a smaller tenant élite was a major feature of the rural social history of this period. But there were other forces at work which encouraged disaggregation and prevented the full implementation of the policies of consolidation which were often advocated. Historians have recognised the former development but have paid much less attention to the latter. The small tenantry survived in significant numbers, not as an archaic hangover from the past, but because they had a rationale and a niche in the new economic order.

The evolution of the composition of the tenant class before c. 1760 was also relevant. Earlier chapters have identified the progressive elimination of multiple tenancies in previous decades so that by the 1750s they were in the minority in most of the estates examined. Where they did exist they commonly consisted of only two to three tenants. One reason, therefore, why tenant displacement did not result in mass clearance in most lowland districts was that much of the work of consolidation had already taken place before the era of extensive improvement. A brief comparison with the western Highlands is again useful. There, multiple tenancies and large numbers of possessors per holding were much more common by the 1750s. Of the sixteen touns on the island of Tiree in 1735, all but four were held by multiple tenants. The mean number was 4.25 tenants per toun.[41] The contrast emerges strikingly in a comparison between tenancy structures on the Duke of Hamilton's Lanarkshire estates and his lands in the island of Arran. Of Arran's 112 farms in 1782, information exists for 59. The mean number of tenants per holding was 4.2. No farm was held by a single tenant and only 19 per cent were possessed by two individuals; 33 per cent of farms were held by five tenants or more. On the Lanarkshire estate in 1738 only 28 per cent of all farms were possessed by multiple tenants. In the same year, the mean number of tenants on these possessions was only two.[42] Tenant reduction in the later eighteenth-century Lowlands therefore threatened a much smaller proportion of the rural population than it did in the Highlands in the nineteenth century.

REFERENCES

1. Sir J. Sinclair, *Analysis of the Statistical Account of Scotland* (Edinburgh, 1825).
2. Sinclair, *Account of Husbandry*, II, p. 86.
3. NRA(S) 859, Douglas-Home Papers, vol. 256, Report of Robert Ainslie (1769), pp. 18–19.
4. Gray, 'Scottish Emigration', p. 135.
5. NRA(S) 859, Douglas-Home Papers, vol. 256, Report of Robert Ainslie (1769), *passim*.
6. OSA (Lanarkshire), p. 139.

7. Ibid.; HPL 631/3, John Burrell's Journals, 1771–4.
8. Devine, 'Social Responses to Agrarian "Improvement" ', pp. 148–68.
9. Gray, 'Scottish Emigration', p. 135.
10. T. Dickson, ed., *Scottish Capitalism: Class, State and Nation from Before the Union to the Present* (London, 1980), p. 149.
11. For the period 1760–1815 these arguments for most of the lowland regions rest virtually exclusively on the OSA and the *General Reports* of the 1790s and early 1800s.
12. OSA.
13. Ibid.
14. T. M. Devine, *The Great Highland Famine* (Edinburgh, 1988), pp. 178–89.
15. SRO, Sheriff Court Processes (Hamilton), SC37/8/20, Petition of W. Weir (1782); NLS, Session Papers, Hermand Collection, vol. 1, Petition of Janet Fulton (1770).
16. NLS, Session Papers, Douglas Collection, vol. 9. Answers for the Duke of Gordon (1770).
17. Whyte, 'Continuity and Change', pp. 163–4.
18. Devine, *Great Highland Famine*, pp. 327–32.
19. SRO, Eglinton Muniments, GD3/8346, 8359, 8360.
20. NRA(s) 885, Earl of Strathmore Papers, 160/9.
21. See above, pp. 5–6 and below pp. 171–93.
22. See above, pp. 25–9.
23. SRO, Morton Papers, GD150/206, Morton Rentals, 1694–1811.
24. See Appendix 10.
25. OSA (Lanarkshire), p. 498.
26. HPL 631/1, John Burrell's Journals, 8 July 1771.
27. OSA (Lanarkshire), p. 422.
28. Ibid. (Ayrshire), parish of W. Kilbride.
29. SRO, Eglinton Muniments, GD3/8459, 8277, Eglinton rentals, 1755–75.
30. NRA(s) 859, Douglas-Home Papers, 171/11; vol. 7/74, Douglas rentals, 1737–92.
31. Thomson, *General View of Fife*, p. 86.
32. See above, pp. 79–92.
33. T. M. Devine, ed., *Farm Servants and Labour in Lowland Scotland, 1770–1914* (Edinburgh, 1984), p. 61.
34. See, for example, SRO, Balfour of Balbirnie Muniments, GD288/241, Remarks upon Sundry of Mr Balfour's farms, 1769; OSA (Fife), 610; SRO, Morton Papers, GD150/2404/38X, Memorial for Lord Morton concerning his Fife estate, 2 Mar. 1791; SRO, Leven and Melville Muniments, GD26/5/613, Memorandum for Lord Balgonie, 1793.
35. Gray, 'North East Agriculture and the Labour Force'; NRA(s) 885, Earl of Strathmore Papers, 100/6, Lord Gray to J. Menzies, 14 June 1771; OSA (Angus), p. 532.
36. See below, pp. 152–4.
37. See Appendix 9.
38. SRO, Morton Papers, GD150/2404/36–8, Memorial for Lord Morton, 1791.
39. HPL 631/1, John Burrell's Journals, 12 June 1772.
40. NRA(s) 885, Earl of Strathmore Papers, 117/1; 169/1; 169/160. Strathmore rentals, 1737–1800.
41. E. Cregeen, ed., *Argyll Estate Instructions, 1771–1805* (Edinburgh, 1964).
42. HPL 631/1, John Burrell's Journals, Journal of 11 July–12 Nov. 1772.

8

Dispossession

Subtenants and Cottars

I

S YSTEMATIC analysis of subtenants and cottars is bedevilled by the blurring of distinction between the two groups on the part of both contemporary observers and later historians. Often the two are seen as a single class, the different terms meaning little of substance and merely reflecting changes of nomenclature. It is possible, however, as was suggested in Chapter 1, to argue for a degree of differentiation between them. While both possessed some land and were, in a legal and an economic sense below tenant rank, not all had the protection of a lease. Subtenants in the sense defined here possessed a written or verbal tack from the principal tenant, paid a rental and enjoyed definite rights of tenure under Scots law. Cottars were allowed patches of land in return for labour services, did not normally pay rental in the regions examined in this study and could apparently be evicted at the will of the tenant or subtenant. The paucity of references to cottar removals in sheriff court processes suggests that this was the position in practice. As one legal judgement stated in 1782, 'the possessors of houses and kail yards are everywhere removed without any formal process'.[1]

Subdivision of land among several small possessors was in conflict with the new orthodoxy of concentration of capital and territorial consolidation. But evidence of the removal of subtenants is difficult to obtain. Partly this is because estate records, a principle source for this study, rarely document them in any detail. Only occasionally do references to subtenants appear in the margin of rentals and rarely on the rental lists themselves. Their pattern of displacement, therefore, has to be pieced together from the few stray details which have survived. Certainly, controls on subtenancy do appear in contemporary leases. For example, a tack on the Earl of Strathmore's Angus estate specified the leasing of a farm in 1773: 'but excluding alwise assignees and subtenants (excepting only actual hired servants necessary for the labour of the farm to each of whom the said John Nicoll may subsett two acres of land or thereby) all and whole those parts of the town and lands of Drumglay ... '[2] A Lanarkshire tack of 1758 prohibited subleasing 'without signed consent' while a series of leases on the Earl of Glasgow's estate in Ayrshire stipulated similar conditions.[3] What is most striking, however, especially in the context of the conflict between farm subdivision and prevailing policies of consolidation, is the paucity of references to such controls in the majority of contemporary leases. Indeed, a scrutiny of several hundred tacks relating to several estates in the counties studied revealed only a small handful even mentioning subsetting. When they did, absolute prohibitions were rare. More often, tenants were enjoined to seek the permission of the proprietor before letting their lands through a subtack.[4] Estate surveys and factorial correspondence confirm the impression. Improvers were often hostile to small farms, for the reasons discussed in Chapter 7, but there is precious little evidence of a widespread attack on subtenure as such. Moreover, some estates were clearly permitting tenants to sublet throughout the last three decades of the eighteenth century. Active subleasing has been confirmed on the Hamilton, Douglas, Eglinton and Auchinharvie estates in Lanarkshire and Ayrshire in this period.[5] It also took place in some Angus parishes in the 1790s.[6] Even, therefore, if the process of reduction of subtenancies was accelerating, there was probably considerable variation in its speed and extent both between estates and across different parts of the country.

Sheriff court records provide further insights. Subtenants had the same legal protection as principal tenants. They could also subdivide their subtenancy and possessed written or verbal leases, some for as long as 9 or even 19 years. When it came to removal, however, even those with a verbal tack had to be given formal warning and the proper legal procedure followed. Under the Act of Sederunt of 1756 the principal tenant had to obtain an order from the sheriff and issue it to his subtenant at least forty days before Whitsunday. Importantly, this action could be taken without the permission of the proprietor. It follows that any substantial removal of subtenants *in addition to* the reduction of tenants already discussed in Chapter 7 would be likely to show up in sheriff court processes. An examination of the decadal survey of processes, however, does not suggest any comprehensive attack on subtenure. Summons of removal against subtenants formed 6.8 per cent, 10.96 per cent and 4.8 per cent respectively of all summonses in the Cupar, Dunblane and Linlithgow Courts' eighteenth-century sample. Only in Peebles was the figure somewhat higher at 17.6 per cent. However, a scrutiny of summonses of removal in the Lanark sheriff court records, for the years from 1765 to 1791, showed that only eight in all were awarded against subtenants. Two of these were because of rent arrears; the remainder because tacks had expired. Two periods, 1763–8 and 1779–83, were also examined in the Hamilton sheriff court processes. Over the nine years, 21 summonses of removal were issued against subtenants at a rate of around 2 per annum. In the case of 5 no reason was given; 1 was for breach of tack; no less than 8 summonses were served for rent arrears; in the case of 7 subtenants, their leases had expired.

It is very likely, therefore, that down to at least 1800, subtenancy was reduced on the estates examined as part of the process of general tenant reduction rather than as a systematic strategy of clearance designed to eradicate this particular tier in the rural hierarchy. A distinction can probably be made between the experience of the subtenants and that of the cottar class, to be considered later, in this regard. Equally, given the very marked regional variation in subtenure discussed in Chapter 1, it would be dangerous to assume that the patterns characteristic of Ayr, Lanark, Fife and Angus were necessarily replicated throughout the length and breadth of the Lowlands.[7]

Subtenants were potentially under threat from both landowners and principal tenants. But the rights of ownership of the proprietor were not removed by subletting. Subtenancy in the Lowlands was strictly regulated by written or verbal leases. It was not comparable to the endemic subdivision and squatting which afflicted Highland estates in the nineteenth century. The allocation of a lease meant that possession was finite as laid down in a binding contract between two parties. An examination of numerous cases in sheriff court processes suggests that the landlord's authority was not impaired by subletting. The proprietor could not remove a subtenant unless he also removed the principal tenant; however, subtacks only lasted as long as the principal tack was valid. When the landowner ensured that a tenant moved at the expiry of a lease, his subtenants had to leave their possessions as well.[8] It is interesting to note that the language of the summons itself always specified this, indicating that not only the tenant was to 'flit and remove' but so also were his 'Wife, Bairns, Family, Servants, Sub-tenants, Cottars, Corns, Cattle, Goods and Gear forth and from the said Lands, Houses and Pertiments thereof'. This essential legal control may have made it less necessary to mount a sustained assault on subtenure itself. Thus in Fife, Lord Balgonie's factor was unwilling to prohibit the practice so long as it was managed properly:

> I see no reason to depart from any article in the heads of the lease. They are all reasonable and particularly the Liberty to Subsett. I shall have no objections to Subsett a part but I would by no means allow the tenant to parcel out the farm that you could have done yourself and whatever is let to Subtenants the Tenant to be not only Lyable for the Rent and Conditions but if the principal tack falls so shall the subsetts ...[9]

The system could be phased out through the normal process of reletting tenancies. It is highly unlikely that subsetting appealed to principal tenants as much as it had done in earlier years. The sharp increase in produce prices in the later eighteenth century gave farmers a powerful incentive to exert direct control over all the productive capacity of their holdings. Subtenure may therefore have died a natural death.

Subtenancy meant that part of the income from the estate was creamed off by 'middleman' tenants who lived on the difference between what they obtained from their subtenants and what they were obliged to pay to the proprietor. It was in the landlord's long-term interest to expand the number of direct rentpayers. This may be another reason why subtenancy declined with little apparent fuss. Some landowners were converting subtenancies into small principal tenancies despite opposition from those who had previously sublet and had gained a valuable source of income at a time of rising rentals. Evidence of such upward mobility comes from most of the estates studied. Charles Brown, subtenant in Achnotrick on the Hamilton estate, offered £55 for three combined holdings in 1778. A year earlier, another Hamilton sub-tenant, William Walker, offered £26 for the nineteen-year lease of Annieshill. The proprietor was to furnish timber and lime for the repair of houses while the new tenant was to maintain the enclosures to be made.[10] In Fife, the Balfour of Balbirnie papers reveal a similar pattern. The farm of Finglassie on that estate was divided in 1789. The documents relating to the process indicate that George Ayton, the tenant, was subdividing the possession among three individuals. They were more than covering Ayton's rent and he was making about £48 per annum on the subsets. The factor had suggested that the farm be split into two but subsequent rentals reveal that the entire holding was taken over by one of the subtenants, David Ireland, in 1790 and that his son, Thomas, became the tenant after him in 1810.[11] Several examples of subten-ants taking over holdings, albeit of lesser size than this, also occurred on the Eglinton estate in Ayrshire in the 1790s.[12]

Information on subtenancy is too limited to be able to say how typical these cases were. They are much more likely to surface in estate records than the dispossession of subtenant families at the end of a lease and their decline into the ranks of the landless. Given the general momentum towards consolidated farms, downward mobility was probably much more common. Nevertheless, the movement of some individuals to full tenant status is not entirely surpris-ing. First, as shown in Chapter 7, proprietors often converted land into smaller units because in certain circumstances they produced more rental per acre than bigger holdings.[13] There was still a place for the tenant of modest means in many parts of the Lowlands. Second, some subtenants had the financial resources to bid for principal leases. On the Hamilton estate, evidence was gathered on twenty-two subtenants in the 1770s and early 1780s. The average subset of each was 26.13 acres, substantially above the 2–3 acres which were the typical size of the smallholdings being laid out in and around rural villages and towns in the same period. The average yield from oats in subtenancies in 1774 compares favourably with that of thirty-nine main tenants on the Ham-ilton estate. The subtenant average in that year was 5.3; for main tenants, 5.7.[14] Further, one tenant claimed that far from being an impediment, subtenants were often an asset when it came to improvement: 'though there be no particular course of labouring expressed in sub-tenants' tacks, yet they do labour regularly and for the profit of the farm … the subtenants have already improved the farm considerably and will do it more if continued, their Numbers, both as to their Families and Cattle, being of considerable assis-tance to that purpose.'[15]

II

Cottars had formed a numerically significant group in the old social order, in some areas accounting for between one-quarter and one-third of the rural population recorded in poll tax returns.[16] Cottar families were provided with smallholdings in return for supplying labour to main tenants at agreed times of the year. While the consolidation of direct tenancies and the erosion of multiple tenure took place over long periods of time, the removal of the cottars was concentrated in the last few decades of the eighteenth and the early years of the nineteenth century. In its scale, speed and effect it was more reminiscent of the patterns of clearance in the Highlands than any other aspect of lowland social change in this period.

There is abundant evidence that the cottar system was under widespread attack. In Lanarkshire, 28 per cent of parishes reporting in the OSA described the extensive removal of cottars. For Angus, the figure was 22 per cent and for Fife 33 per cent. But these data almost certainly underestimate the sheer scale of dispossession because most parishes in the OSA returns made no specific mention of cottars at all. For instance, of 60 Ayrshire parish reports, only 24 contain details on cottars. Of those which did, however, no less than 10 described clearance and removal. The testimony of contemporary observers adds weight to the quantitative conclusions. The agricultural reporter for Lanarkshire commented in 1798 that in that county, 'It is vain to say anything of the ancient cottages … the former nurseries of field labourers for they may be said to be now no more.' He went on to add that 'the few scattered ones which still remain can scarcely be called an exception'.[17] His colleague, who described agrarian change in Fife in the same decade, noted an identical trend in the northern part of the county.[18] These witnesses were at pains to emphasise the radical and comprehensive nature of the removals. This was partly shown in their colourful use of language. The minister of Kilmany in Fife referred to 'the annihilation of the little cottagers'.[19] The reporter for Marrikie in Angus described how 'many of the cottagers are exterminated'.[20] Other observers noted the existence of numerous buildings in their parishes, formerly inhabited by cottar families, which were gradually falling into ruins.[21] Elsewhere, cottar dwellings were being systematically demolished and the stone used to construct dykes and walls in the new farms.[22] All of this has a familiar ring. These were features usually associated with the Highland Clearances but the social dislocation in the rural Lowlands in the later eighteenth century has been overlooked until recently. The Highlands have stimulated a veritable scholarly industry but the Lowland Clearances still await their historian.

Ironically, however, while these great social changes have been virtually ignored by scholars, they did attract much contemporary concern. The removal of the cottars was occurring on such a scale that it was blamed for the rapid increase in the wage costs of farm labour in the later eighteenth century. Some critics pointed out that the attack on the cottar system had effectively destroyed the traditional 'nursery of servants'. The sons and daughters of the cottars had provided the main source of labour supply for local farms. Recruitment was now difficult because in many areas cottar families had been forced off the land.[23] This development, together with the attraction of more and better-paid opportunities in industry and the towns, had produced a crisis in the agricultural labour market. Other commentators, perhaps less convincingly, saw a relationship between the clearance of the cottars and the rising costs of the Poor Law in some of the larger towns.[24] The links between migration, urbanisation and the Poor Law were obviously more complex than this. Nevertheless, it is again indicative of the magnitude of cottar dispossession that it could be regarded by contemporaries as a vital influence on wider social developments in later eighteenth-century Scotland.

Perhaps, however, it is only by focusing on the locality that one can give a realistic impression of the actual scale of cottar removal at this time. Thus, on the lands of Inverdovat on the Tayfield estate in Fife in 1707, there were ten 'cotteries'. A few years later, this number had risen to thirteen. As late as 1733, several cottars remained in the township, though evidence for several decades after that is meagre. By 1813, however, when the social structure of the area can be documented once again, not one of the cottar holdings remained.[25] In the parish of Colmonell in Ayrshire the cottar class was still numerous in the 1760s: 'there was hardly a tenant who had not one or more cottagers on his farm'. By the 1790s, there were 'very few' in the entire parish.[26] Similarly in Kilwinning, in the same county, cottars were virtually omnipresent in the farms of the area in the early eighteenth century. But, by 1790, 'the cottages are now, in great measure, demolished'.[27] Virtually identical patterns were described in several areas of Angus at the other end of the Lowlands. A general decline in population was reported in the parish of St Vigeans. But the fall in the number of cottars was much greater. In one farm, for instance, there were eighteen cottars in 1754. By 1790 only one family had remained.[28] Inevitably, this comprehensive process of eradication did not take place at the same pace or on the same scale in all parts of the Lowlands. In the later eighteenth century, for instance, the cottar system was still relatively undisturbed in much of the north-east region.[30] Even in the four counties considered here, displacement varied in speed and extent. Of 78 parishes in the OSA which made reference to cottars in the four-county analysis, 27 (or 34 per cent) noted their existence without suggesting clearance. Nevertheless, the long-term trend was clear and the process of removal accelerated in later years. In the perspective of the study as a whole, the clearance of the cottars represented a remarkable change in the very structure of rural society. It was fundamental to the emergence of a predominantly landless labour force, the migration process within the countryside and the dissolution of the older settlement pattern. An entire tier of the traditional social order was removed in many areas over the space of a few decades.

One factor which facilitated (though did not in itself cause) the transformation was the nature of the legal process. Unlike tenants and subtenants, cottars, in the sense defined here, did not possess leases. In addition, they do not appear to have been protected by the legislation of 1555 and 1756 which laid down the formal procedures to be taken to enforce removal, in particular the need to issue a legal warning forty days before Whitsun and the possibility for that warning to be challenged at law. There is some evidence of writs of removal being issued against cottars. Thus, at Hamilton sheriff court in 1779, John Crawford of Aikerfin obtained a 'Lybell of Removing' against William Young and James Young, 'who possess a cothouse and two cows grass in Aikenfin'.[29] A similar decision was made in favour of Matthew Baillie of Carnbroe against five 'cottars in Carnbroe village with houses and yards'.[30] But such cases were unusual and probably refer to more substantial cottars. The lack of references to cottar removals in general in all the sheriff court processes examined implies that cottars were in fact evicted at will. This helps to explain why clearance could occur so rapidly and comprehensively.

As noted earlier, several observers took the view that the destruction of the cottar system had adverse effects. It made the recruitment of the next generation of farm servants more difficult. In addition, the cottar families had provided a vital and secure supply of labour at harvest time. Some argued that this was now more precarious and the health of the agrarian economy was endangered. Nevertheless, the widespread nature of cottar removal must have meant that many farmers were willing to accept these risks because they assumed that the risks were more than outweighed by considerable potential advantages. In fact, when the displacement of the cottars is examined in detail, it becomes apparent that it was entirely consistent with the requirements of the developing agrarian economy. The movement towards consolidation of single tenancies and the eradication of multiple tenancy enabled a rationalisation of labour requirements. When farms were amalgamated or the number of tenants on them reduced, it was likely that the number of cottars would also decline. This was especially the case where arable farms were replaced by large pastoral holdings with their more limited labour requirement.[31] The division of commonties and the intaking of waste land also weakened the cottars' position. Commonties, moors and mosses were crucial to cottar life. They provided many of the family's basic needs at no cost other than labour. Building materials, such as stone, wood, heather and bracken came from these sources. They also afforded peat and turf for fuel, and commonties were widely used by small tenants and cottars for grazing. In the second half of the eighteenth century, however, all of these traditional sources of subsistence were being removed or drastically reduced as the division of commonties intensified.[32] But this was part of a much broader trend where landowners sought to exploit all the territory of their estates 'at proper value'. Thus, on some properties, mosses were drained; in others, formerly marginal land was absorbed into regular cultivation. Moreover, just as proprietors laid claim to all the minerals on their properties, they also increasingly sought to control access to such formerly 'common' resources as peat and wood. Thus, there is much evidence of attempts to reduce or even eliminate traditional rights of access to mosses and peat bogs.[33] One example, from the Earl of Panmure's estate in Angus, illustrates the process:

> The Estate of Edzel and Newar is now mostly sett and the boundaries of the several possessions settled, and there is reserved the Moss of Mergie as is thought of about 800 or 1000 acres ... the muir of Slateford ought to be enclosed and planted and the thing should be set about immediately. It will be a most beautiful thing and in time will come to be of great value. For many years past this muir has been grossly abused by casting of turf in it. No less than thirty stacks or thereby yearly have the inhabitants taken out of it besides what the adjacent tenants and cottars take. The factor has prohibited these practices for the future under the severest penalty and has taken the tenants bound in the Minutes of Tack granted them not to cast turf themselves nor suffer others to do so, so far as they can hinder it.[34]

Cottars were also being squeezed by even more direct forces than erosion of customary rights to fuel and other necessities. If farmers had viewed them as a valuable resource these traditional needs could have been absorbed into the wage contract. However, it is clear that major influence encouraging removal was the perceived costs of the cottar system. Cottar families were normally provided with a few acres of land (usually 1–3) and additional grazing for both cattle and sheep. This was acceptable when several parts of a possession were underutilised within the infield–outfield structure. It was less tolerable when all the land was cultivated systematically and intensively on a regular sequence of rotations. Rental inflation in the later eighteenth century meant that farmers looked at the real costs of cottar holdings much more critically. In Colmonell parish in Ayrshire, the cottars had possessed a house, yard, small piece of land and enough grass for one or more cows. The value of the holding was 'thought to be trifling while rents were low'. But much higher rentals meant that to the farmer the value of grazing the cattle of cottars increased.[35] The balance of advantage had altered to encourage the use of cottar possessions for producing grain and stock for the market rather than for the maintenance of a reserve supply of labour.

Increasingly, also, other observers argued that cottars would place a burden on the Poor Law. This fear was not in itself new. Cothouses had long been seen as repositories of the poor, aged and infirm, and of migrants from other parishes. Thus the kirk session of Wiston in Lanarkshire proclaimed in 1752 that 'all persons who have coattages to set to beware that they bring no persons or families from other parishes who are not able to maintain themselves'. Those who did so would be obliged to support them without any assistance from the session.[36] But this concern may have become stronger in later decades when there was much greater mobility of population. At the same time, the tendency to support the poor through rating or assessment rather than primarily by means of voluntary giving was on the increase.[37] Also, as the number with rights to land declined, so the proportion of those seeking a settlement through obtaining a cothouse may have increased. Certainly, in some rural parishes, there was growing alarm about vagrancy in the last quarter of the eighteenth century. In Douglas in Lanarkshire, for example, reference was made in 1764 to 'the great number of vagrant persons and sturdy beggars' who were present in the area.[38] Again, in 1788, the lists of the poor were expanding in Douglas as a result of the influx of strangers who were attempting to gain possession of vacant cothouses. By demolishing the buildings, farmers ensured some protection from this threat.[39] As one commentator put it, those who retained cottars had 'to submit to the risk of being burdened with a heavier poor's rate'.[40] It is significant that in several of the *OSA* reports, it was indicated that uninhabited cottar dwellings were not simply allowed to moulder away. They were often completely levelled.[41]

Fundamentally, the cottar structure was in conflict with the new economic order. The old system was well suited to an agrarian regime where demand for labour tended to concentrate in brief periods in the year around tasks such as grain harvesting and fuel gathering. It was useful in these circumstances for farmers to have a reliable pool of labour which could be called upon in the busy seasons and then laid off without any cash cost until required again. However, the needs of improved agriculture were radically different. The more intensive cultivation of the land, thorough ploughing, the adoption of new crops – such as sown grasses, turnips and potatoes – and of innovative rotations ensured that the working year started to lengthen. There was, on the whole, an evening-out rather than an accentuation of seasonal labour requirements within mixed farming. Inevitably, this development favoured the hiring of full-time workers. These were sometimes married servants hired by the year, in some parts of Fife, but, more commonly, and especially in Lanarkshire and Ayrshire, single male and female servants employed for six months. Only these groups were suited to the regular toil increasingly carried out in improved lowland farms. Ironically, the married-servant class was similar to the cottars in several respects. They obtained a house, garden, fuel, the keep of a cow and other privileges as part of the wage reward. The crucial difference, however, was that they were full-time workers, entirely under the masters' control during their term of employment, and could be dismissed at the end of it.[42]

This position of subordination was crucial. While the independence of cottars can be exaggerated – they did possess land but only in mere fragments and they had to obtain work in larger holdings in order to make ends meet – they were obviously less subject to the discipline of the farming classes because they were not entirely dependent on the employment which the latter could offer. But the new agriculture demanded much higher levels of labour efficiency. Farmers were under pressure from two sources. Landowners were forcing up rentals in dramatic fashion and wages of agricultural workers were also rising rapidly from the 1770s and especially from the 1790s, as industrial and urban expansion lured many from the country districts to the towns.[43] Earlier in this work, one response to spiralling costs was noted. Farmers were increasingly able to extract more return from a given area through improved land management. Another and equally important reaction was the enforcement of policies designed to enhance the productivity of labour.

The clearance of the cottars can be seen in this context. In the most improved districts, where the old Scots plough was being replaced by James Small's plough, often using a team of one man and two horses, the clearest effect can be seen. Gradually the whole work routine centred around boosting the efficiency of the horses. Hours of labour and number of workers were closely related to the number of horse teams and their work rate. Ploughmen took responsibility for a particular pair and their entire routine from early morning to evening was devoted to the preparation, working and final grooming of the animals. The system required that the ploughmen be permanent servants, boarded within the farm steading or in a cottage adjacent or close to their animals. The part-time labours of the cottar were now redundant. It also became possible to tailor labour requirements to the numbers actually required for specific farm tasks. The cottar system assumed underemployment of labour for many months in the year. Removing cottars and relying increasingly on servants reduced underemployment. Since farmers who hired servants had fixed certain and clear obligations to their work force over periods of either one year or six months, they were forced to tailor their labour requirements exactly to the number required for the proper running of the farm. In addition, there was an urge to ensure that the work team was organised in such a way that it was fully employed when at work.[44] By now recognising the payments to servants as a distinct and measurable 'cost', masters were more likely to control them. The traditional reward to the cottar of land, house, grazing rights and occasional money fees was much less obvious on the balance sheet.

There were, therefore, clear economic incentives to clear the cottars. Yet there was one important constraint. Cottar families had been the main source of seasonal labour, especially at the crucial time of grain harvesting, gathering and processing. Harvest labour had not only to be available, it also had to be reliable. The harvest was the culmination of the farming year on which all else depended. To risk eliminating a traditional source of harvest workers without secure alternatives was to court disaster. This was especially so in those counties outside the south-east region and parts of Fife where farmers were increasingly dependent on unmarried servants. In western and central districts, single servants were in the majority. The family structures which could assist in the provision of seasonal labour were less common than elsewhere. Not surprisingly, it was principally from these areas that the complaints came that the attack on the cottar structure produced difficulties of labour supply. What facilitated cottar removal, then, was the development of alternative sources of seasonal workers. If they had not been available, it is probably that the cottars would have survived for longer. There were three main sources of seasonal labourers. First, in the 1780s and 1790s, seasonal migration from the southern and eastern Highlands was already occurring on a considerable scale.

Young men and women from the north were employed in cutting the harvest of the south.[45] Second, migrants from Ireland were active during the grain harvest season in the counties of the south-west.[46] Third, and crucially, the dissolution of the cottowns was paralleled by a remarkable growth in rural settlements, villages and small towns. This subject will be treated in detail later in this chapter. For the moment, however, it is sufficient to emphasise the scale of development.[47] It was primarily, though not solely, driven by the spread of textile industry in many lowland counties in the later eighteenth century and by the concentration of services ancillary to agriculture in small urban settings. Increasingly, the vacuum left by the cottars in the supply of seasonal labour was filled by the dependents of weavers, miners, iron-workers, day labourers and tradesmen recruited from adjacent rural villages and towns.[48] The clearance of the cottars could proceed with little economic impediment.

III

The dispersal and subsequent destinations of the evicted cottar families are not easily documented. Indeed, the absence of census data until after the great removals were completed in the early decades of the nineteenth century makes any precise analysis of the migration process virtually impossible. Other sources also have only limited value for this period. Testimonials or testificates extracted from kirk session records have been employed by some scholars to attempt the reconstruction of migration patterns in the seventeenth and eighteenth centuries.[49] These were certificates of good behaviour issued and received by parish authorities and given to individuals entering or leaving a parish. Material such as this, however, is less valuable for the last quarter of the eighteenth century than for earlier periods. There is evidence, revealed in a detailed scrutiny of Lanarkshire kirk session records, that the system was then breaking down rapidly, with parish clerks providing much less information than before and considerable gaps appearing in the lists.[50] This may reflect the changing social priorities of the church and the relaxation in some areas of the drive towards religious conformity. The rapid spread of dissenting congregations also ensured that the records of the established church no longer provided an entirely coherent guide to contemporary social developments. More seriously, testimonials rarely indicate the occupation or status of migrants. Even when they do, such as for the Lanarkshire parish of Wiston and Roberton, the ambiguity of the designations make it difficult to monitor the cottar class over time.

The level of migration into or out of any given area over a specific time period can only be accurately calculated if four vital statistics are known: the population levels at the start and end of the period, and the numbers of both births and deaths. The difference between the latter two reveals the natural rate of increase, while the difference between the two successive censuses gives the actual change in population level. By subtracting the natural increase from the actual population change a crude measure of the level of net in- or out-migration becomes apparent. However, variations in both nuptiality and fertility ratios can mean that gains and losses may imply other consequences than simply rates of human mobility.

Demographic data for the eighteenth century are sparse by comparison with later periods. On a national scale and prior to the first national census of 1801, only the Webster enumeration of 1755 and that of the *OSA* in the 1790s are of use to the historian in this context. Unfortunately, however, there are no data on fertility and mortality rates for later eighteenth-century Scotland comparable to those of enumeration. Thus, to even approximately measure the scale of migration, it becomes necessary to estimate the rate of natural increase. This has been done here by using the crude national average rate of population increase of 6 percent per decade or 0.6 percent per annum.

Table 8.1 and Appendix 12 provide population counts for the four counties at the two periods followed by the actual change in numbers. The estimated percentage multipliers on the county sheets are arrived at for each parish by multiplying the assumed national percentage yearly rise of population (i.e. 0.6 percent) by the appropriate number of years between the two population counts. For example, a parish which gave 1790 as the date of its *OSA* report would have an estimated multiplier of 35×0.6 percent or 21.0 percent. Thus, with this estimated natural increase, the estimated level of net in- or out-migration is deduced as described above and the figure can then be expressed as percentage of the original population level of 1755. The estimated mean percentage multiplier for each county, as indicated in Table 8.1, is simply the average figure calculated from the total of those multipliers of each parish as shown on the tables for each county in Appendix 12. It should be borne in mind, however, that local variation in both nuptiality and fertility could affect these figures.

To move beyond the generalised picture, a migration factor analysis was conducted. From the *OSA* reports, four independent factors were examined which might have influenced migration at the parish level. These were: reduction of cottar numbers, industrial presence, farm consolidation and the presence of villages or towns.[51] This exercise deals in the numbers and percentages of parishes in the four counties examined, *not* those of population as such. In other words, the importance of a specific factor and its impact on population movements, is not gauged here by the actual size of the estimated migration flows but by the number of cases of parishes demonstrating this coincidence of presumed cause and effect. For example, the absence of some kind of industrial presence was associated with out-migration in 33.3 per cent of the forty-five Ayrshire parishes analysed but this does not imply that the lack of some kind of industry accounted for one-third of out-migration from Ayrshire parishes.

Tables 8.2 and 8.3 lay out the numerical and percentage results of the single and (in some cases) combined factor analysis for the three counties. As can be seen, it is divided into two main sections: those parishes demonstrating net

TABLE 8.1   Estimated net out-migration from the 4 counties, 1755–90s.

County	Population 1755	Population 1790s	Actual change	Estimated mean percentage multiplier
Angus	68,593	91,601	+23,008	21.2
Fife	80,970	87,224	+6,254	21.3
Ayrshire	59,009	73,511	+14,502	21.8
Lanarkshire	80,300	151,234	+70,934	21.8

County	Estimated natural increase	Estimated Net out-migration	Net out-migration as percentage of 1755 population
Angus	14,542	+8,466	+12.3
Fife	17,247	-10,993	-13.6
Ayrshire	12,864	+1,638	+2.8
Lanarkshire	17,505	+53,429	+66.5

SOURCE   *OSA.*

out-migration and those demonstrating net in-migration. These two groups were isolated in turn from the database and then checked against the individual factors laid out in the left-hand column. For each of the two groups in each county the actual number of parishes with the particular factor present is given in the first column and this figure is then expressed as a percentage of the total number of parishes.

It should be noted that in all four counties, the denominator used to calculate percentages is slightly less than the actual total number of parishes because, in a few cases, there were no usable data given in the *OSA*. Note also that only where a particular factor, such as an industrial presence, was indicated in the parish account can the result be relied upon, since it is possible that in some cases, other factors – assumed here to be absent – were simply not mentioned in the *OSA* reports.

The results shown in Tables 8.2 and 8.3 give some indication of the explanatory power of the various factors *vis-à-vis* the in- or out-flows of population since they outline the percentage of parishes in which the specific and presumed causes and effects were associated with each other.

Tables 8.4 and 8.5 attempt to extend this analysis further by combining the results of both sides of a particular hypothesis. If it is assumed that in this period the absence of an 'industrial presence' from a parish would have acted as a 'push' factor and that, conversely, the existence of some kind of industry would have functioned as a 'pull', then in Ayrshire, for instance, this total hypothesis is supported by the results from 66.6 per cent of parishes, and so on. However, given the caveat entered above on the reliability of presumed 'negative' evidence, and the hypotheses built into the 'migration' figures, the results of this exercise must be treated with caution. Nevertheless, both the

TABLE 8.2   Estimated migration in the shires of Ayr, Angus and Fife, 1755–90s: factor analysis.

Factor(s)	Ayr (45 parishes)		Angus (52 parishes)		Fife (59 parishes)	
	no.	percentage	no.	percentage	no.	percentage
Parishes demonstrating net out-migration, 1755–90s						
No industrial presence	15	33.3	26	50.0	25	42.4
Farm consolidation	11	24.4	12	23.1	14	23.7
No villages, towns, etc.	3	6.7	24	46.2	26	44.1
Cottar nos reduced	3	6.7	8	15.4	8	13.6
Parishes demonstrating net in-migration, 1755–90s						
Industrial presence	15	33.3	11	21.2	10	16.9
No farm consolidation	19	42.2	16	30.8	13	22.0
Villages, towns, etc.	19	42.2	12	23.1	10	16.9
Cottars exist	2	4.4	6	11.5	5	8.5

SOURCE   *OSA.*

factor and combined factor analysis indicate a broadly similar result. The existence or reduction of the cottar class was not associated in more than about one-fifth of Ayr, Angus and Fife parishes with a static or increasing population on the one hand or a decreasing population on the other. Only the Lanarkshire figures marginally rise above this average. On the other hand, the industrial village/town and consolidation variables ranked very much higher as factors associated with mobility.

TABLE 8.3   Estimated migration in the shire of Lanark, 1755–90s: factor analysis.

Factor(s)	No. of cases	Percentage of total
Parishes demonstrating net out-migration, 1755–90s		
No industrial presence	8	21.1
Farm consolidation	10	26.3
No villages, towns, etc.	9	23.7
Cottar numbers reduced	8	21.1
Parishes demonstrating net in-migration, 1755–90s		
Industrial presence	8	21.1
No farm consolidation	11	28.9
Villages, towns, etc.	6	15.8
Cottars exist	3	7.9

SOURCE   *OSA.*

TABLE 8.4   Estimated migration in the shires of Ayr, Angus and Fife, 1755–90s: combined factor analysis.

Combined factors	Combined percentage figures for the 3 counties			
	Ayr	Angus	Fife	Mean
(O) No industrial presence + (I) Ind. pres.	66.6	71.2	59.1	65.6
(O) Farm consolidation + (I) No farm consolidation	66.4	53.9	45.7	55.3
(O) No villages etc. + (I) Villages etc.	48.9	69.3	61.0	59.7
(O) Cottars reduced + (I) Cottars exist	11.1	26.9	22.1	20.0

NOTES   (O) = Data set representing parishes that recorded net out-migration, 1755–90s.
    (I) = Data set representing parishes that recorded net in-migration, 1755–90s.
SOURCE   *OSA*.

This short statistical exercise suggests that the results of cottar displacement were far from simple. 'Cottar clearance' does not come through strongly as a key variable in the process of out-migration. Other influences seem to have been much more significant in causing mobility from one parish to another. Certainly there is no confirmation in this exercise of the contemporary claim that the removal of the cottars initiated a general flight from the land. That the disruption of rural life must have been one element in the migration to the growing towns and cities is undeniable. But there is a good deal of qualitative evidence to support the results of the statistical exercise that cottar clearance was not in itself a major force for depopulation and that opportunities for the dispossessed still existed in rural districts. John Naismith noted how in Lanarkshire in the 1790s the cottars had mainly gone and farmers now only

TABLE 8.5   Estimated migration in the shire of Lanark, 1755–90s: combined factor analysis.

Combined factors	Combined percentage figures for Lanarkshire
(O) No industrial presence + (I) Industrial presence	42.4
(O) Farm consolidation + (I) No farm consolidation	55.2
(O) No villages etc. + (I) Villages etc.	39.5
(O) Cottars reduced + (I) Cottars exist	29.0

NOTES   (O) = Data set representing parishes that recorded net out-migration, 1755–90s.
    (I) = Data set representing parishes that recorded net in-migration, 1755–90s.
SOURCE   *OSA*.

maintained unmarried servants who were boarded in their houses. But, while the cottars had disappeared from the farms, they had been replaced by a new class who lived in rural villages while still working on the land:

> 'The county ... is supplied with a new set of cottages. Several landholders partly perhaps to prevent the depopulation of the country, and partly for their own emolument, have let out, either in feu or long leases, spots of ground, for houses and little gardens, generally upon the sides of the public roads. Upon these, many little handsome cabins have been erected, which accompanied with neatly dressed gardens, supplied with pot-herbs, and frequently ornamented with a few flours, have a very pleasant effect. These are mostly clustered into villages, some of which are pretty populous.'[52]

This was not the dispersal of the cottars but their relocation. An almost identical development was described in Fife at the same time. There, in the parish of Ferry, a correlation was drawn between the decline of population in the rural districts and the dramatic increase in numbers in the village. Farmers were 'Not inclining to keep such large cottaries as formerly'. Several cottar families therefore moved into Ferry village, 'where they hire small houses and support themselves by their industry, either as tradesmen or day labourers'.[53] The parish minister of Sorn in Ayrshire noted a similar relationship between the removal of cottars in the district and village expansion. He commented in detail on the settlement of Dalgain. It lay beside the industrial village of Catrine and was founded in 1781 by a Dr Stevenson of Glasgow. He feued out small parcels of land on the north side of the Muirkirk road. By 1797 the population of the settlement had risen to more than fifty families. Significantly, the minister added that the majority of these 'formerly lived in cothouses, which are now in ruins. Most of these families are provided with gardens of various dimensions behind their houses ... '.[54]

These observations, describing contraction in the rural population and increases in village and small town numbers in the neighbourhood, were repeated in several other areas. For example, in Stonehouse in Lanarkshire, the 'country' population in 1696 was 600, the 'village' total 272. By 1792, a mere 467 resided in the rural area and 593 in the village.[55] Similarly, in Dalmellington in Ayrshire, total parish numbers declined from 739 in 1755 to 681 in 1792. However, this general trend concealed dramatic changes within the local demographic structure. It was observed that in the country area, population had 'considerably diminished' due to cottar removal but had risen 'in proportion' in the village of Dalmellington, which by 1792 contained over 500 inhabitants, or 73 per cent of the total in the parish at that date. In Dalry, the population of the parish had increased by around one-third from Webster's census in 1755 to 2,000 in 1792. But the country part had fallen while numbers in the village had almost doubled to 814 or 41 per cent for the total.[56] It would appear that the key to understanding much of the movement of the cottars lies in the village and small town expansion, in a rural context, of the later eighteenth century.

Historians have long been aware of the development of country villages in this period. Smout, for example, contributed a pioneering analysis of 'planned' villages between 1730 and 1830.[57] More recently, Lockhart has expanded on Smout's findings for the north-east region.[58] But perhaps insufficient attention has been paid to the crucial role of these settlements in reducing the social discontent which might have arisen from cottar removal and also in maintaining the labour supply so vital to the completion of the improvement process. Partly this may be because the share scale of small settlement development in this period may not have been appreciated. The 'planned' villages were obviously significant but they were but one part and, in some areas, only a fairly minor part of a much broader small-scale urban expansion. Increases in the population of rural small towns and existing villages should also be considered. The numbers gathering in unplanned settlements, several of them no bigger than population clusters of a few dozen houses, also need to be noted. For instance, the Smout list of 'planned villages' mentions only seven for the four counties considered in this study as being founded between c.1760 and c.1800. Table 8.6, by adopting a broader definition, sets out the total numbers of new and extended settlements. It suggests a remarkable growth in small-scale urban development in rural society in this period. When the analysis is extended to include all parish references to villages in these counties – whether existing, new or expanding – the total increases further. By this measure, 48 per cent of parishes in Fife, 83 per cent in Ayrshire, 35 per cent in Angus and 44 per cent in Lanarkshire had such settlements.

However, a simple enumeration of the incidence of villages and small towns does not do full justice to the dramatic growth of this sector. Increase in urban settlements associated with mining and factory development could be anticipated. But expansion was not confined to these.[59] The village of Larkhall in Lanarkshire rose in population by 44 per cent between 1755 and 1792. In the parish of Glassford in the same county, population was rapidly concentrating in 'three small but thriving villages'. One of them had 14 houses and 83 inhabitants in 1771. By 1791 the number of houses had risen to 44 and the population to 196. Clusters of small settlements were growing throughout the county. Six such concentrations existed in the parish of Cambuslang and were in flourishing condition in the 1790s. It was also common to find houses being built along main roads and at important junctions in several areas. Small-town growth was especially fast. Airdrie increased its population sixfold in the second half of the eighteenth century. In Fife, the town of Dysart and associated villages rose in numbers, to 2,688 in 1792, a 62 per cent increase from the 1750s. The pattern was repeated in the south-west lowlands. The town of Girvan in Ayrshire had no more than a couple of dozen houses and 100 people in the 1750s. By the 1790s, this figure had swollen to over 1,000 inhabitants. The parish minister was convinced that the town's expansion was in large part linked to 'the almost total exclusion of cottagers from the farms'.

TABLE 8.6   New and extended settlements, villages and towns in 4 Scottish Lowland counties.

County	Settlements		Villages		Towns		Percentage of parishes with additions
	New	Extended	New	Extended	New	Extended	
Ayrshire	1	0	8	7	0	11	47.8
Lanark	1	1	4	10	0	6	56.4
Fife	7	0	1	12	0	8	38.3
Angus	5	0	2	0	0	6	22.2
Totals	14	1	15	29	0	31	41.17 (average)

NOTES 'Settlements': this was the category used when the other two were not indicated. Such developments as a few houses built where the site was not specified and where land was feued for buildings were recorded here; perhaps generally where the scale, form or name did not suggest at least a small village.

'Village': recorded as such when the settlement was noted in the *OSA* as such.

'Town': again, recorded as such when so indicated in the accounts. Though in one or two cases a 'toun' could perhaps have been implied, there was by and large no doubt about this category.

SOURCE *OSA* parish reports for relevant counties.

The above is not intended to be an exhaustive account of settlement development. Nevertheless, it would seem apparent that the removal of the cottars was paralleled by a striking expansion and foundation of villages and other settlements. Migration data do not exist to confirm the point conclusively but it appears likely that the two developments were also inextricably linked in a causal sense. Several contemporary observers certainly thought so. What the available evidence suggests is that the cottar population was not so much expelled from rural society as relocated within it. The major determinant was the labour needs of the agrarian and industrial economies of the rural districts. But an additional factor was landlord action. On virtually all the estates examined in the course of this study, landowners showed an interest in village foundation or extension. Estate papers provide some clues to the varied forces which influenced this strategy. There was an awareness that laying down farmland in smallholdings close to a town or village could be highly profitable. It might attract artisans and 'manufacturers' who would pay high rentals and extend the local markets for agricultural produce.[60] In addition, as earlier sections of this book have shown, there was a general concern about depopulation and its adverse social and economic effects. Villages could absorb those who were displaced by improvement, maintain social stability and, by attracting industry, retain the dispossessed in the locality as an economically valuable population. At the same time, however, the village system was deemed vital to the progress of improvement itself. There was a recognition that the new agriculture demanded labourers as well as ploughmen, carters and other horsemen. Indeed, the growing specialisation of the function of permanent married and single servants described earlier in the chapter made the need for these other groups even more essential.

In the long run, the new agriculture enabled more food to be produced at lower cost. Labour productivity rose as a part of this process. Nevertheless, the creation of the new system demanded large numbers of workers in addition to those who cultivated the land. The creation of enclosures, the building of ditches, the intaking of waste, the construction of roads, bridges, farmhouses and mansions were all going on apace in late eighteenth-century Scotland. Tables 8.7 and 8.8 provide some representative examples of the kinds of work involved. The labour inputs were likely to be very great. On the Hamilton estate in May 1772 the 'putting out' of enclosure on the 131-acre farm of Over Abbyington involved no less than twenty-seven labourers or an average of 4.85 worker per acre.[61] Table 8.9 provides an insight into enclosing and planting labour requirements elsewhere on the same estate. On occasion, gangs of labourers were recruited from local villages as specialists in enclosure. Thus, on Lord Dumfries's estate in the Borders, one Robert Patrick 'dyker' was employed with sixty men and twenty-four horses, building dykes and planting hedges. His services and those of his men were available to other proprietors in the neighbourhood.[62]

It was unlikely that these demands could be solely or mainly met by the permanent servants who lived on the farm. As indicated earlier, agricultural activity was becoming more intensive and regular throughout the year and the horsemen were becoming more specialist workers. The routines of ploughing, sowing and reaping all remained very labour-intensive. In theory, the new ploughs associated with James Small and others ought to have saved labour by reducing the number of ploughmen to eventually one and horses to two. That certainly did happen in the long-term. However, before 1800 it is important to keep the impact of the new technology in perspective. A survey was conducted of those parishes in the *OSA* for the four counties which referred to ploughing. Full details are presented in Appendix 9. Only 27 per cent reported that the Small plough alone was used and most of these parishes were located in Fife; 20 per cent suggested that the traditional Scots plough was combined with modified versions and/or the Small plough; no less than 40 per cent of parishes indicated that the old plough was still in widespread use. This is not surprising, given the continued prevalence of ridges and the marginal land now being absorbed into regular cultivation for which the old plough was excellently suited. It is highly unlikely, therefore, that there was much in the way of surplus labour resources among the servant class. Labour-saving technology was still relatively limited and varied in its impact before 1800. At the same time, the new rotations imposed even more demand on labour. Complaints of the scarcity of servants were common and rapid increase in money wage rates testified to the tightness of the agricultural labour market as industrialisation attracted increasing numbers from farm employment.

It is against this background that the expansion of settlements, linked to

TABLE 8.7   Intended improvements on estate of the Earl of Eglinton, 1771.

 (i) to repair Mansion House and Castle and improve gardens etc.

 (ii) to compleate enclosure and subdivide Over, Mid and Laigh Moncurs, Chapple, Weirstoun, Ladyhall, Milnburn, Barnsleys and Auchinwinsey [Kilwinning] 'with ditches and Clapt Earth Quickset Hedges'.

(iii) Same to Meikle and Little Stones, Stonemoor and Stone Castle, Bowhouse and Lawthorn [Stone Barony].

(iv) New steading on Stonecastle and Little Stone 'which are quite fallen to ruin with lying waste several years'.

 (v) To enclose a subdividive in Ardrossan barony 'partly with snap stone dykes and partly with ditches and Clap quickset dykes'. Blackstone (stone dyke), Holmbyres, Towerleanhead, Yonderhouses, Gaithill (?), Burnhouse and Ittington (all with ditch and hedge). Meikle Busvie, Little Busbie (stone snap dykes), Ardrossan miln and Chappelhill (stone and ditches). Also to enclose and subdivide Sorbie, Darlieth, Coalhill Mains and Stanley Burn with ditches and quickset dykes.

(vi) Steading of houses on Knockvivoch, Coalhill and Chappelhill, north end of Little Busbie – 'all of which farm houses are gone to ruin' and little steading in Saltcoats lands.

(vii) In Roberton to enclose and subdivide properly with ditches and quickset dykes: Milntoun, Milnlands, Murehouse, Gatehead, East and West Murelands, Corsehouse, Annanhill and Knockentikes. To complete enclosures already begun and to subdivide Windyedge, Thornhill, Greenhills and Fordalhills (with ditches and quickset dykes).

(viii) In Dreghorn to enclose and subdivide with ditches and quickset dykes in the 2 Towend farms possessed by Jas. Orr and Hugh Galt and lands possessed about Kirktoun by Robt. Wilson, Jas. Cockburn, Jas. Mure, Hugh Bankhead, Andrew Fulton, David Dale and Hugh Dunlop and John Barnet. Also lands of Corsehill and Lowhill possessed by Gavin Ralston, Poundstone by Jas. Auld and Kirklands by Jas. Boyd.

(ix) to build steading of houses on lands of Jas. Auld, Hugh Dunlop And. Fulton (about 60 acres) 'whereon no house ever was'.

 (x) also steading of houses on Corselees, Sclates, Cleugh 'which were let down and gone to ruin the last nineteen years'.

(xi) In Eastwood to complete the enclosure and subdivision on Giffnook, Hillhead, Henry's Croft (all with hedges and ditches) and to complete manor house in Eaglesham.

(xii) A steading of houses on High Craigs, Temples, Stonebyres, Stepends, Walkers. And to enclose and subdivide these farms partly with stone dykes and partly with ditches and hedges.

(xiii) In Eaglesham to complete the enclosure and subdivision of Threepland, Nethercraigs, Polnoon, Mains, Kirklands, Hole, and 'the sundry inclosures marked out and begun about the Kirktoun of Eaglesham and also the farms of Brackenrigg, Borlands, Windhill, Rossmiln, Floors, Boggside, Tofts, Corselees, Picketlaw, Hills, Upper and Nether Braidflat, Over and Nether Kirkland Moore, Kirktoun Moors, Bonnytoun, Blackhouse, North Moorhouse, Langlee.

SOURCE SRO, Sheriff Court Records (Ayr), SC6/72/1, Register of Improvement on Entailed Estates.

TABLE 8.8   1803 references to improvement on Richard A. Oswald's possessions in Ayrshire.

Total expenditure: 14 May–31 Dec. 1803 – £2,624.12.8d.		
Places where some improvements took place	Work undertaken	Approximate number of mentions
Auchencruive	Draining (lawn)	2
Craighall	Repairing coachhouse	2
Gibsyeard	Repairing stables	2
Brocklehill Meadow	Altering dining-room	1
Mount Hamilton	Repairing cattle sheds	4
Little Ladykirk	Dyking	14
Ladykirk	Roofing	7
Barclaugh	Cutting & cleaning drains	5
Barquhay	Bridge work	3
Mainholm	Barn repair	2
Newdykes	Plastering	4
Raith	Sundry repairs	3
Orangefield	Building walls	6
Kerse	Carthouse work	5
Kersmine?	Hedging & ditching	8
Loanhouse	Roads – making & repairing	4
Mount Oliphant	Masonwork	12
	Poultry house building	1
	Pigsty building	1
	Wrightwork	5
	Repairing houses	5
	Paving	1

SOURCE   SRO, Sheriff Court Records, SC6/71/1, Register of Improvement on Entailed Estates (Ayrshire), 1771–1804.

the labour requirements of the new farms, should be seen. Small possessions of 2–3 acres, with a house, kailyard and garden, were established to accommodate 'day labourers' who could be hired and laid off when necessary. They were adjuncts to the improvement process, a reserve army of labour, but no longer with rights to a place on the land and with their living standards now dependent primarily on their capacity to obtain employment. In some ways, they resembled the cottars of old. Each group had subsistence plots and grazing rights. But the labourers and their families paid rental for their possessions and continued reoccupation depended ultimately on the fulfilment of that cash contract. Commercial connections had replaced customary relationships.

The movement of the cottars to new employment in the villages and small towns was not simply influenced by the changing system of working the land. In the older social order, many cottars were also tradesmen. The clearance of the cottars also removed this class from the new farms. But improved agriculture had an even greater need for the services of wrights, masons and ditchers than the traditional system. These craftsmen too increasingly congregated in

TABLE 8.9 Men employed in enclosing and planting Hamilton estates, Lanarkshire lands, March 1774.

Numbers employed	Farm	Purpose (if specified)
7	Merryton	–
6	One of Merryton field farms	Belt of planting
6	Field land of Over Dalserf	–
9	Cornhills	Belt of planting and hedge round farm
4	Field land of Carscallen	–
2	On coach road	Planting sweet briars
2	On Strathaven road	Belt of planting
2	Between Larkhall and Bottoms Gate	Belt of planting
2	Round South Garten	Hedge
*9	Carscallen	Enclosing farm
*4	Darngaber	Enclosing farm
*3	Green	Enclosing farm
*6	Newhouse	Enclosing farm
62		

NOTE * = employed by tenants; others employed by the estate.
SOURCE HPL, 631/1, John Burrell's Journals, vol. 2, 1773–8, 17 Mar. 1774.

villages and rural small towns. Their disappearance from the farms, however, ought not to be seen only as a result of coercion. It might also be argued that local demand for their services was increasing to the extent that they too could become detached from the land and pursue their trades on a full-time basis in a different milieu. It was not simply the farm servants who were becoming more specialised. Other groups such as day labourers and artisans, often part of the former cottar communities, were apparently now able to rely on wage labour for much longer periods in the year.[63]

IV

As is well known, the Highland Clearances produced considerable social protest at the time and a legacy of bitterness among subsequent generations. The removal of the cottars and subtenants in the Lowlands has attracted a different historiography. In the decades after 1760 there was little evidence of the angry peasant rebellions or the great surges of collective unrest which characterised much of French and Irish rural society. The relative stability of the lowland countryside was especially striking given the scale and speed of social dislocation and the systematic attack on customary rights and privileges documented earlier in this chapter. Basic changes were made to the rural social structure without provoking mass discontent. The economic transformation must have been painful for many but grievances apparently remained invisible and for the most part were concealed below the surface.[64]

Most scholars would accept that there was no hidden agrarian revolt in this period yet to be uncovered by more research. As one historian has remarked, 'it is highly unlikely that there exists a seam of undiscovered public rural violence in eighteenth-century Scotland'.[65] At the same time, however, some writers have criticised the orthodoxy of uniform stability. They make several points. First, it is argued that there were other ways of registering dissent apart from riot and other public demonstrations of discontent. These included sabotage, theft, arson and pilfering. Such techniques were, it is suggested, more appropriate and effective than open confrontation which would invite rapid retribution from the law. Second, the case for post-1780 tranquility is accepted but, since the earlier period is under-researched, the thesis of social stability before then 'has not been proven'. Third, rural unrest on a consider-able scale did exist in the Scottish Lowlands. But it was channelled in large part into religious dissent. Brown has asserted that patronage dispute, caused by opposition to the system whereby a hereditary patron had the right to 'present' (or select) the minister of a parish church, represented 'the most significant Scottish equivalent to rural protest in the rest of the British Isles'.[66]

The first and second of these contentions can be tested against the mass of sheriff court records and estate correspondence examined in the course of this study. One critic suggests that the forms of 'indirect' protest are 'harder for the historian to discern'.[67] In part this may be true. But as earlier chapters in this book have indicated, factors and ground officers maintained a very close surveillance of all aspects of activity on their estates. It is highly unlikely that serious or systematic destruction of property, physical assault or pilfering would have gone unrecorded in their correspondence, reports, memoranda and journals. The same can be said of the sheriff court records for Hamilton, Lanark, Cupar, Peebles, Dunblane and Linlithgow, considered in this study. Among the cases dealt with by these courts were actions relating to theft, grazing disputes and right of way, mobbing, assault and enclosing, disputes and breaking into private lands.

A careful scrutiny of both sets of material reveals little support for the notion that 'everyday forms of peasant resistance' were at all common. Only four cases were discovered, among the hundreds of removal actions examined, of refusal to vacate lands, resulting in 'letters of ejection' being issued to enforce dispossession. The sheriff court material revealed only one instance of dyke breaking in which the defenders, significantly, were described as 'White Boys or Levellers'.[68] But this was no agrarian protest. Those prosecuted were all colliers from Ceres in Fife who had broken down part of an enclosure which had formerly been an open field in order to gain easier access to the village kirk. A handful of cases of pilfering of wood were also discovered. But these 'thefts' often indicated economic need rather than hostile intent. Indeed, one process suggested that such pilfering was more the consequence of increas-ing landlord control over common lands than a subtle weapon of protest. What had previously been permitted as a customary right was now regarded as illegitimate. Thus, at the Dunblane court in 1790, seven women were charged with 'having broken down, leapt over, destroyed fences surrounding the enclosures of William Stirling of Keir, and carried away pailings of these fences'. Two of the women denied the charge but admitted carrying away 'two small burdens of rotten sticks'. Another went further, asserting that, 'If it was or is a Crime to carry off rotten Whins or Brooms from any Gentleman's possession the defender is ignorant of it, it being always the custom with the inhabitants of this place to go and carry off rotten Whins or Broom from any Gentleman's ground in the neighbourhood without every being challenged ...'[69]

Doubtless, other instances of petty criminality will come to light when even more court and estate records are examined. But the present study does not suggest that 'indirect' protest was at all common. Indeed, in such a grossly unequal society, undergoing rapid economic change, the small number of petty misdemeanours uncovered is remarkable. This is what the advocates of covert protest fail to acknowledge. The historically significant fact of this period is not the evidence, slight as it is, of scattered acts of hostility, but rather the extraordinary imbalance between the fundamental changes in rural social structure and the virtual absence of any overt popular opposition to them. Even if future research discovers more incidents of routine resentment, the meaningful question will still remain, not why there was some protest, but why there was so little in a country which experienced a rural social transformation unparalleled in its scale and speed in western Europe in the later eighteenth century.

The suggestion that the patronage riots and the emergence of dissent were a surrogate form of rural protest is also problematic. It is an argument which places two social trends, agrarian improvement and religious dissent, together and assumes rather than demonstrates a causal link between them. Religious protest also encompassed all types of community and occurred in virtually every area of Scotland. It cannot be associated solely or mainly with the rural parishes of the Lowlands where cottar and subtenant removal was concentrated. Equally, the implicit assumption that those who protested over patronage were driven by economic stress and class bitterness hardly convinces. The growth of religious dissent was a European phenomenon in this period occurring in numerous types of economic context. By 1826, around one-third of Lowland Scots belonged to presbyterian dissenting congregations. In 1851, 59 per cent of Scottish church-goers attended presbyterian dissenting places of worship. But at the same date, 47 per cent of English church-goers also belonged to nonconformist congregations. The fracturing of the national churches was based mainly on changing popular beliefs, the growing appeal of evangelical religion and the broad transformation of British society. It did not reflect peculiarly Scottish developments. The limited available evidence of the social composition of the dissenting congregations also indicates that a crude class-based analysis of religious dissent and opposition is difficult to accept. Thus in West Calder in West Lothian, one-third of the population were presbyterian dissenters. But this included 4 of the 44 landowners, 40 per cent of the tenant farmers but, significantly, only 21 per cent of cottars and day labourers. At Strathaven Burgher church, between 1767 and 1789, 58 per cent of the members' names on the baptismal role were those of tenants or portioners.[70] The sketchy evidence for other areas suggests similar patterns. Dissent drew heavily on the middle ranks of rural society. It hardly seems a movement which mobilised the masses of the poor and dispossessed or had a special appeal for them in particular.

The curious silence of the rural population does not necessarily mean the absence of pain, anxiety, insecurity or misery. But the relative tranquillity of the time does demand some explanation. After all, Scottish rural society was not naturally peaceful. Food rioting occurred in many parts of the country in 1709–10, 1720, 1740, 1756–7, 1763, 1767, 1771–4, 1778, 1783 and 1794–6. On occasion these eruptions could pose a strong challenge to local forces of law and order, as recent research has shown.[71] The scale and extent of patronage dispute and religious dissent, already discussed, are also revealing. They demonstrate that the Scottish people were not instinctively deferential or submissive to established authority. The fragmentation of lowland presbyterianism, which was accelerating in the later eighteenth century, suggests rather a society with a robust independence of mind and spirit derived in part from the Calvinist inheritance of the 'equality of souls' before God. It was a tradition which helps to explain the social and political radicalism of Scottish presbyterians in Ulster, most of whom were the descendants of small tenants, cottars and servants who had migrated across the Irish Sea from the western Lowlands in the seventeenth century.[72] The Scottish Militia Riots of 1797 which engulfed many lowland rural communities are also significant in this respect. Essentially, they represented an angry and rebellious response to legislation which brought in a form of conscription by ballot for the Scottish militia.[73] These very serious demonstrations of popular discontent showed that the mass of the lowland population were not naturally apathetic when customary rights were challenged. It seems likely, therefore, that social stability would indeed have been gravely threatened if the removal of the cottars had caused widespread hardship and destroyed traditional status. That it did not do so probably reflected the reality of the cottar function, the process of relocation in villages, small towns and settlements and the buoyant labour market of the rural Lowlands in the later eighteenth century.

By the later eighteenth century the cottars can be described more as proletarians than as peasants whose links with the land were becoming very tenuous. They did possess small patches of land but had to provide labour on neighbouring larger holdings to gain a full subsistence. This was not simply at the busy seasons. Cottar families also worked for farmers by the day or by the month for cash at other times of the year. In addition, both Justice of the Peace and sheriff court records suggest that, in law, servants and cottars were regarded as dependent labourers and not as independent possessors of land.

The gulf between the two groups, as was shown in Chapter 1, was often more apparent than real. Since most farm servants outside the south-eastern counties and parts of Fife were unmarried, masters had to depend on the cottar and small-tenant class for the new generation of hands. Equally, at marriage, some former servants must have become cottars. Both groups were intimately connected through the life cycle of the rural family structure and shared work experiences.

Some information extracted from the records of Cupar sheriff court in Fife confirms the point. Normally, the cottars are a shadowy and elusive group in the historical documentation but depositions given in a legal case of 1758 cast a vivid light on some aspects of their way of life. This evidence is presented in Table 8.10. These short biographies illustrate how cottars had servant and labouring experience, that their families included both cottar and labouring children and that there was considerable lateral and vertical mobility among them. On the face of it, the distinction between them and the servant class seems very blurred.

Potential discontent was therefore defused because dissolution of the cottar system coincided with a rapid increase in employment opportunities as a result of agrarian improvement and the first phase of industrialisation. Inevitably there were years of crisis in each of the last three decades of the eighteenth century, and in pastoral districts the reduction of population on the land was not necessarily followed by the development of new agricultural and industrial opportunities in the immediate neighbourhood. But elsewhere and in most years, the rural labour market was extremely tight for both farm and industrial workers in the last three decades of the eighteenth century. Parish ministers commented on the fact that there was usually enough employment in the locality for all those who wanted it. The supply of labour was only growing modestly. The Scottish national rate of population increase at 0.6 per cent per annum between 1755 and the 1790s was relatively slow by western European standards. Higher wages and more varied opportunities in the cities and large towns attracted many away from the rural districts. The onset of war with France also drew young males to the army and navy.[74]

At the same time, the rural economy was becoming very active and its demands for more workers increasingly voracious. Crucial to the fortunes of the cottars was the dynamic development of the linen and cotton manufactures. Many cottar families had textile skills and they were likely to gain significantly from the new opportunities. An examination of the social structure of six rapidly expanding small towns in the countryside, Cambuslang, Carstairs, Larkhall, Balmerino, Galston and Kirriemuir, in the OSA reports confirms the overwhelming importance of textile spinning and weaving, not only for adult males but also for women and girls. Textile industrialisation was in many ways a rural phenomenon in this period and it is hardly surprising that the resettlement of cottar tradesmen and their families in local villages was necessary to service it. Equally, standards of living rose on country

TABLE 8.10   Life histories of 6 cottars, Monthrive, Fife, 1758.

Henry Reickie: 'in Pratis'; married; 52 years = born 1706

History: herded for 1 summer in Monthrive 38 years ago (c.1720) and was a cottar and had beasts pasturing there 3 years sometime after his herding and had lived in Pratis (which adjoins Monthrive) ever since.

William Morgan: 'In Pratis Cottoun'; married; 55 years = born 1703

History: Born and raised in Monthrive, his father being a cottar there. Herded therein 1715 than went to Nether Pratis and other places, returning in 1721 to herd for one year at Monthrive. Then 2 years in Baliarmo. Then a fewar in different places till 10 years ago when he returned to Nether Pratis, has been a workman at Balbirny's Quarry at Clutty Den, for last 7 years.

David Dowie: 'in Lethem Cottoun'; married; 44 years = born 1714

History: Born and raised in Monthrive; 1722–5 herded his father's beasts; lived at Monthrive till 1727 when he went to Over Pratis for 2½ years; then returned to live with his father for 5 years who was a cottar at Monthrive; has been at Lethem ever since.

William Lindsay: 'in Skelpie Cottoun'; married; 36 years old, thus born in 1722.
History: 1739–51 – herd and servant in 'The Room of Monthrive'.

Thomas Honeyman: 'Cottar in Carskerdo'; married; 56 years – born, 1702.
History: 1715–16 – herd in West Quarter of Monthrive; 1726–32 – servant in ditto.

Thomas Braid: 'Cottar in Muirhead'; married; 56 years = born 1792
History: c.1713–14 – Herd in Muirhead; c.1714–15 – 'in the Keam in the neighbourhood … '; c.1715–20 – servant in Monthrive; then ½ year in Cairny as servant; following all as servant: 2½ years Clatto; 2½ years Greenside; ½ year Waltoun; 6 years Cassindilly; 5 years Muirhead; 6 years Tarritmiln; 11 years Scotstarvit; since then in Muirhead.

SOURCE   SRO, Sheriff Court Records (Cupar), SC20/5/12.

districts as the economic transformation gathered pace. One estimate, covering the mid-west, south-west and east central regions, suggests that the adult agricultural workforce experienced an improvement in their standard of living of between 40 and 50 per cent between 1760–70 and 1790.[75] Even that figure may understate the extent of the improvement because it fails to take into account the fact that many day labourers and rural artisans were able to supply much of their own food from the village potato patches and vegetable gardens which had replaced the cottar holdings of former days. What is likely, however, is that material improvement for the majority must have done much to ease the transition to a new economic and social order.

REFERENCES

1. NLS, Session Papers, Hermand Collection, vol. 8, Petition of John McLauchlane, 3 July 1782.
2. NRA(s) 885, Earl of Strathmore Papers, 160/9, Contract between J. Menzies and J. Nicol (1772).

3. NRA(S) 9904, Earl of Glasgow Papers, 2/8, Miscellaneous Tacks; SRO, Bertram of Nisbet Papers, GD5/1/520, Tack of Kersewell Crofts (1759).
4. See, for example, SRO, Leven and Melville Muniments, GD26/5/613/2, R. Beatson to Lord Balgonie, 1 Apr. 1794; GD26/5/728, Letter of estate factor to Messrs. Oliphant and Gibson, W. S., 9 Oct. 1803.
5. HPL 631/1, John Burrell's Journals, 16 Mar. 1774; NRA(S) 859, Douglas-Home Papers, 139/2, Memorial of Robert Ainslie (1792); SRO, Eglinton Muniments, GD3/8346, Remarks on rental margin, 1798; SRO, Cunninghame of Auchinharvie Papers, RH2/8/75, Petition of R. R. Cunninghame (1816).
6. *OSA* (Angus), pp. 122 and 494.
7. See above, pp. 11–13 and Appendices 2–6.
8. HPL 631/1, John Burrell's Journals, 16 Mar. 1771; SRO, Sheriff Court Processes (Lanark), SC38/22/14, Lybell of Removing by J. Menross, 1765; SC38/7/10, Register of Decreets (1750); SRO, Sheriff Court Processes (Hamilton), SC37/8/20, Petition for W. Weir, 1782; NLS, Session Papers, Hermand Collection, Petition J. Malauchlaine, 3 July 1782.
9. SRO, Leven and Melville Muniments, GD26/5/613/2, R. Beatson to Lord Balgonie, 1 Apr. 1794.
10. HPL 631/1, John Burrell's Journals, 3 July 1784 and 29 Sept. 1777.
11. SRO, Balsour of Balbirnie Muniments, GD288/99/1, Estimate and Report for setting the Farm of Finglassie, 15 Apr. 1789; GD288/4/1 and 2, Balbirnie Rentals.
12. SRO, Eglinton Muniments, GD3/8346, Rentals for 1798.
13. See above, pp. 131–4.
14. HPL 631/1, John Burrell's Journals, 2 Apr.–3 Nov. 1774.
15. NLS, Session Papers, Kilkerran Collection, vol. 10, Petition of James Ogston, writer in Edinburgh, 26 Feb. 1745.
16. See above, pp. 12–13 and Appendices 2–6.
17. Naismith, *General View of Clydesdale*, pp. 52–4.
18. Thomson, *General View of Fife*, pp. 380–1.
19. *OSA* (Fife), p. 471.
20. Ibid. (Angus), p. 532.
21. Ibid. (Lanarkshire), pp. 185 and 193.
22. Ibid. (Angus), p. 9.
23. Ibid. (Fife), p. 331; ibid. (Angus), p. 674.
24. Naismith, *General View of Clydesdale*, pp. 52–4.
25. NRA(S) 874, Berry Papers, 12/6; vol. 14 and vol. 16.
26. *OSA* (Ayrshire), parish of Colmonell.
27. Ibid., parish of Kilwinning.
28. Ibid. (Angus), p. 624.
29. *OSA* (Aberdeenshire), *passim*.
30. SRO, Sheriff Court Processes (Hamilton), SC37/8/18, Lybell of Removing by J. Crawford (1779); SC37/8/20, Lybell of Removing by M. Baillie (1783).
31. See above, pp. 126–7.
32. See above, p. 51.
33. NRA(S) 859, Douglas-Home Papers, 256, Robert Ainslie's Report (1769), p. 39; SRO, Leven and Melville Muniments, GD26/5/288, Regulation of Peats in Letham Mure, Aug. 1765.
34. SRO, Dalhousie Muniments, GD45/18/2268, Memorandum on Edzell Estate (1767).
35. *OSA* (Ayrshire), parish of Colmonell.
36. SRO, CH2/376/3, Kirk Session of Wiston, 7 June 1752.
37. R. Mitchison, 'The Making of the Old Scottish Poor Law', *Past and Present*, 63 (1974), pp. 58–93.
38. SRO, HR581/4, Heritors' Meetings, Douglas parish, Nov. 1764.
39. Ibid., May 1788.
40. *OSA* (Lanarkshire), p. 143.
41. For example, ibid., pp. 254 and 575.
42. T. M. Devine, 'Scottish Farm Service in the Agricultural Revolution' in Devine, ed., *Farm Servants and Labour*, pp. 1–9.

43. V. Morgan, 'Agricultural Wage Rates in Late Eighteenth Century Scotland', *Econ. Hist. Rev.*, 2nd ser., XXIV (1971), pp. 181–201.

44. Devine, 'Scottish Farm Service', pp. 1–9.

45. T. M. Devine, 'Temporary Migration and the Scottish Highlands in the Nineteenth Century', *Econ. Hist. Rev.*, 2nd ser., XXXII (1979), pp. 344–59.

46. J. Handley, *The Irish in Scotland, 1798–1845* (Cork, 1943).

47. See below, pp. 152–3.

48. See various references in several *OSA* reports.

49. R. A. Houston, 'Geographical Mobility in Scotland 1652–1811', *Journal of Historical Geography*, 11 (1985), pp. 379–94.

50. SRO, CH2/376/3 (Wiston); CH2/397/2 (Crawfordjohn); CH2/15/1 (Dunsyre).

51. See Appendix 9.

52. Naismith, *General View of Lanarkshire*, pp. 52–4.

53. *OSA* (Fife), p. 372.

54. Ibid. (Ayrshire), parish of Sorn.

55. Ibid. (Lanarkshire), pp. 583–6.

56. Ibid. (Ayrshire), parishes of Dalmellington and Dalry.

57. Smout, 'Landowner and the Planned Village' in Phillipson and Mitchison, eds, *Scotland in the Age of Improvement*, pp. 73–106.

58. D. G. Lockhart, 'The Planned Villages' in Parry and Slater, eds, *Scottish Countryside*, pp. 249–70.

59. The data which follow are derived from *OSA* parish reports.

60. SRO, Morton Papers, GD150/2404/36–8X, Memorial for Lord Fife concerning his Fife estate (1791); HPL 631/1, John Burrell's Journals, June–Aug. 1772; SRO, Dalhousie Muniments, GD45/18/2269, Observation ... to the Earl of Panmure anent Edzell estate, 10 Oct. 1767.

61. HPL 631/1, John Burrell's Journals, 28 May 1772.

62. SRO, Oswald of Auchincruive, GD213/54, John Maxwell to Sir R. Oswald, 7 Dec. 1772.

63. For a local demonstration of this point see A. Gibson, 'Proletarianisation? The Transition to Full-Time Labour on a Scottish Estate, 1723–1787', *Continuity and Change*, 5 (1990), pp. 357–89.

64. Devine, 'Social Responses to Agrarian "Improvement" ' in Houston and Whyte, eds, *Scottish Society*, pp. 148–68.

65. Whatley, 'How Tame were the Scottish Lowlanders?' in Devine, ed., *Conflict and Stability*, p. 21.

66. Ibid., pp. 21–2; Brown, 'Protest in the Pews', pp. 83–105; and C. G. Brown, *The Social History of Religion in Scotland since 1700* (London, 1987), p. 104.

67. Whatley, 'How Tame were the Scottish Lowlanders?', p. 21.

68. SRO, Sheriff Court Records (Cupar), SC20/5/29.

69. Ibid. (Dunblane), SC44/22/33.

70. Brown, 'Protest in the Pews', p. 99.

71. Whatley, 'How Tame were the Scottish Lowlanders?', pp. 14–15; K. J. Logue, *Popular Disturbances in Scotland, 1780–1815* (Edinburgh, 1980).

72. T. M. Devine, 'The Failure of Radical Reform in Scotland in the Late Eighteenth Century: The Social and Economic Context' in Devine, ed., *Conflict and Stability*, p. 53.

73. Logue, *Popular Disturbances in Scotland*.

74. These points are explored in more detail in Devine, 'Failure of Radical Reform', pp. 51–64.

75. Treble, 'Standard of Living', pp. 194–200.

Conclusion

A Model of Scottish Agrarian Change

A RECENT general history of Scotland faithfully reports the current ortho-doxy about the pace, nature and impact of agrarian change in eighteenth-century Scotland:

> Agriculture was undoubtedly the most important bottleneck which had to be passed through before general economic growth could establish itself. But far from provid-ing the best case of a 'revolution', where there was a sudden and dramatic transfor-mation of habits of work and investment, agricultural development is the most persuasive example of long-term patterns of change.[1]

Some historical geographers share this view. As one writer has concluded, the rural economy, was 'in a constant state of flux due to a continually varying set of pressures and aims'.[2] Innovation did take place in the later eighteenth century but one of its principal features, enclosure, 'was often a failure, a fashion in a period when being "progressive" was desirable'.[3]

The detailed examination of four representative lowland counties, which has been carried out in this book, is in conflict with these assertions. It has been argued that there was a radical departure from the patterns of the past in the last quarter of the eighteenth century, not simply measured in terms of physical enclosure, but also in the more effective use of land involving liming, sown grasses and the organisation of labour. It was a structural change, not simply a perpetuation and intensification of existing trends, since it produced a dramatic increase in crop yields, allowing Scottish cultivators to catch up on English levels of output in the space of a few decades, and resulted in a visible alteration of the rural social system in an equally short time. To a considerable extent this was a revolution from above, with landlord power a principal influence and the landlord's craving for more revenue a central force. Never-theless, it could not have come about at such speed but for the emergence of a new and much more dynamic force in the later eighteenth century. An additional element, and one which became even more crucial over time, was the existence of a pool of tenants within the existing social order with the capital resources and the commercial expertise to respond rapidly and ener-getically to the new opportunities. The transformation was certainly far from complete by 1815; the revolution had still to run much of its course. But on the evidence presented in this book, the changes of the later decades of the eighteenth century set several regions in the Lowlands on a new path. In its whole-hearted orientation towards the market, evolution of compact farm tenancies, erosion of the cottar system and enhanced productivity, rural society in 1815 was different from that of 1760.

The argument for discontinuity in the last quarter of the eighteenth century depends in part on an understanding of agrarian structure before 1750. It was not wholly static and there were key connections with the later period of accelerated development. However, in the later seventeenth century, despite ongoing changes within the structure of tenancy, there was little clear sign of agrarian advance outside the south-east region. Enclosing, improved rotations and communication developments were thin on the ground. Access to land on the part of a majority of rural dwellers was widespread through the proliferation of very small farms, multiple tenancies and cottar holdings. The prevalence of rental in kind suggested that the forces of commercialisation, though intensifying, were still relatively weak outside some favoured areas. This was in stark contrast with the agrarian economy of England. There, the seventeenth century has been identified as the decisive period of commercialisation and innovative land management.[4]

In lowland Scotland, the first few decades of the eighteenth century saw market influences becoming more significant. Conversion of rentals in kind to money was common and multiple tenancy was in rapid retreat. These two trends ensured that by the 1750s the number of tenants with enlarged holdings who were committed to servicing the market must have been much greater than in earlier decades. This indeed was a fundamental link with the era of Improvement. Agrarian innovation would have had little practical impact but for the embryonic capitalist farming class emerging from the ranks of the tenantry before 1750. But there was an imbalance in this earlier period between changing social organisation on the one hand and continuity in agricultural technique on the other. There was apparently little evidence of improved land management in the areas examined in detail. It was only in later decades that the transformation was really set in motion, because only then did major improvements in agricultural productivity, rapid commercialisation and profound alterations in social structure come together to move the rural economy in a quite new direction.

REFERENCES

1. M. Lynch, *Scotland: A New History* (London, 1991), p. 379.
2. G. Whittington, 'Agriculture and Society in Lowland Scotland, 1750–1870' in G. Whittington and I. D. Whyte, eds, *An Historical Geography of Scotland* (London, 1983), p. 143.
3. Ibid., p. 144.
4. B. A. Holderness, *Pre-industrial England: Economy and Society, 1500–1700* (London, 1976), p. 70; J. R. Wordie, 'The Chronology of English Enclosure, 1500–1914', *Econ. Hist. Rev.*, 2nd ser., XXXVI (1983), pp. 483–505; A. Kussmaul, *A General View of the Rural Economy of England, 1538–1840* (Cambridge, 1990), pp. 170 ff.

Appendix 1

Poll Tax Data Collection
and Problems

1. RECORDS USED

THERE were at least three poll taxes in the 1690s. Most of the surviving records seem to relate to the first one of 1693 (generally collected in 1694). The third one of 1698 was limited to a smaller, richer section of society. The roll of pollable persons for the parish of Aberdour of 1698, for example [SRO E70/5/1], listed only 20 individuals, the least wealthy of which possessed no less than 1,000–5,000 merks' worth of 'frie stock'. Clearly then, the records of this last poll tax are of little use for an examination of social structures.

All usable and known extant poll tax records relating to rural parishes of Lowland Scotland have been studied with the exception of a handful of parishes for the Lothians. The reasons for the rejection of these particular parishes were various: their fragmentary state, their lack of social status designations or possession names. Time and effort were spent upon those parishes that would give the best results.

In addition, the voluminous returns for the shire of Aberdeen necessitated a selective approach and the method of sampling is explained in Section 3 below.

The two main series that were not examined were those for Edinburgh, Leith, Canongate and those for Orkney.

2. METHODS

The enumeration sheet shows the socio-economic designations used for analysis. These are naturally strongly influenced by the classes used in the poll tax itself, an outline of which is shown in M. W. Flinn's *Scottish Population History*, p. 55. The final designations were arrived at after initial attempts at data collection and preliminary analysis. A copy of the enumeration sheet can be found at the end of Appendix 1.

The major groups of servants and cottars were themselves broken down into several sub-groups and these were adapted, where necessary, so that the particular nomenclatures of the different regions could be recorded: for example, 'hind' in the Lothians, 'in harvest servants' in Renfrewshire.

The three sub-groups of cottars were also recorded for all parishes where the information was given.

Individuals classed as 'others' were those whose socio-economic status was in doubt. In some cases there is a strong suspicion that at least a sizeable proportion of these belonged to one of the other specified groups. In these cases the percentages have been recalculated and are indicated in the tables. These figures should perhaps be treated with some circumspection.

3. SELECTION OF SAMPLE FOR ABERDEENSHIRE PARISHES

The whole county of Aberdeen was divided into 4 broad geographical regions for the purposes of this analysis. These were decided on after a study of maps from the following sources:

> Carter, I, *Farm Life in North-East Scotland* (Edinburgh 1979); the two maps on pp. xii and xiv.

> Allan, J. R., *The North-East Lowlands of Scotland* (London, 1952); the folding map at the rear of the book.

> Keith, G. S., *General View of the Agriculture of the County* of Aberdeenshire (1814); map at the front of the volume.

> Whyte, I. D., *Agriculture and Society in Seventeenth Century Scotland* (Edinburgh, 1979), figure 9, p. 142.

The first 3 noted above illustrated a very broad division of the county into 3 or 4 distinct geographical areas: first, a very definite highland area of the Grampians; second, moving north-east, an area of highland and alluvial valleys interspersed with lower-lying land; third, a definite lowland area centred on the Buchan but also including some of the Fortmartin district; finally, a narrow coastal strip, particularly evident in the *G.V.A.* map (1814) and identifiable by its predominantly clay soil.

Whether or not the pedology of this coastal strip would have had any impact on socio-agrarian structures was obviously unknown at the outset. However, other work (see Whyte, *Agriculture and Society*, pp. 142–3) has already shown that the more obvious topographic features did affect the incidence of single as opposed to multiple tenancies and therefore the attempt to identify a fourth area on a physical basis seemed worthwhile.

4. PROBLEMS OF INTERPRETATION

The identification of domestic servants proved to be difficult. In some cases certain domestic servants were obvious, being listed in the household of the aristocracy, having the designation 'Mr' and having a wage far in excess of other servants. But where the first two pointers were not apparent, the third, on its own, proved to be insufficient evidence, since the gradations of pay obscured any clear-cut differences in this respect between domestic and out-door servants. In the Renfrewshire parish of Mearns, for instance, male servant fees of £7, £8, £10, £16+, £18 and £20 and female servant fees of £4,

£12–13+, £14–16+ were all noted. In consideration of this problem then, the results of any attempt to separate out the domestic servants (those recorded as 'S' in the tables) from the rest should be treated with caution.

Sometimes it was difficult to be sure of the residence of individuals. For example, in the Renfrewshire parish of Neilstoune, 'The Lands of Commore' listed several people under its head, before it listed 'James Andersoune, of Kilburne'. Does 'of' in this case mean that he was a tenant or resident in Kilburne and had a possession in Commore and do the subsequent named individuals reside in the former or the latter place? It has usually been assumed that 'of' meant 'in' and thus Andersoune above is recorded as being resident in a place called 'Kilburne'. This will not affect the analysis of parochial social structures, but may have a slight impact on the calculations of multiple/single tenures and any individual farm counts or analyses undertaken.

Because of these problems of interpretation, the percentage figures should perhaps be regarded as a guide (albeit a reasonably good one) rather than as a precise quantification of social formations of these parishes in the later 17th century.

5. RENTAL DATA

Some parish poll tax returns supplied usable rental data. Rather than record each individual rental, the total range of these was divided into different rental classes prior to data collection and those paying a proportion of the valued rentals were assigned to their appropriate rental classes.

In some instances, the tenant numbers in these calculations do not tally with those of the socio-economic breakdowns, for various reasons. Perhaps the main ones are:

(a) Tenant farmers sometimes classed themselves as 'gentlemen' and paid the appropriate higher personal tax. Accordingly, these were classed as 'above tenantry' in the socio-economic count, but as tenants in the rental analysis since they were paying a proportion of the valued rent.

(b) Tradesmen who were small tenants paying a part of the valued rental were classed as tradesmen in the socio-economic count. In the subsequent rental analysis these would have been recorded as tenants.

6. INTRODUCTION TO TABLES

SOCIAL STRUCTURES: This table simply gives the percentages of each major social class, i.e. it does not break down servants, cottars and others into their constituent sub-groups.

Note that all the socio-economic percentages use a different denominator to those used by I. D. Whyte and K. A. Whyte ('Some Aspects of the Structure of Rural Society in Seventeenth-Century Lowland Scotland' in T. M. Devine and D. Dickson, eds, *Ireland and Scotland, 1600–1850* (Edinburgh, 1983), pp. 32–4). They used the number of male heads of family and single males to calculate percentages whereas those given here use female heads of families (widows) and single females in addition. The counts include individuals with specified socio-economic status, heads of households (both sexes) and single males with no specified status. It excludes spouses and children.

Except for the first columns in these tables, all the figures are percentages, rounded up to the nearest decimal place.

Anyone listed as 'merchant', irrespective of amount of stock, was listed under column 3 in the enumeration.

Where individuals appear in 'others' column and are the only ones for the possession, there was no indication of their status or valued rental and thus they were not recorded as tenants.

SINGLE/MULTIPLE TENANCY: Sometimes possessions do not appear to have a named tenant. This means that when possessions are classed as either single or multiple, some are left out of this dual classification and thus percentages do not add up to 100.

COTTARS, SUBTENANTS AND GRASSMEN/WOMEN: All three of these categories of individuals have been counted as being in the same class for the purposes of this particular analysis. The count simply gives the percentage of possessions in a given parish which had at least one cottar, subtenant or grassman/woman.

7. SOURCES

J. Stuart, ed., *List of Pollable Persons within the Shire of Aberdeen, 1696* (Aberdeen, 1844), 2 vols; D. Semple, ed., *Renfrewshire Poll Tax Returns* (Glasgow, 1864). See also SRO, T335; SRO, E70/8; SRO, GD 86/770A; SRO, GD 178/2; J. B. Greenshields, *Annals of the Parish of Lesmahagow* (Edinburgh, 1864).

Appendix 2

Poll Tax Tabulations, Aberdeenshire, 1696

TABLE A   Percentage of tenantry in each rental class (and cumulative percentages), Aberdeenshire – 1696.

Parish	Rental classes (£ Scots)										
	0–10	11–20	21–30	31–40	41–50	51–60	61–70	71–80	81–90	91–100	101+
Highland:											
Crathie	21.7	6.5	28.3	4.3	10.9	8.7	19.6	0	0	0	0
(cumulative)	21.7	28.2	56.5	60.8	71.7	80.4	100.0	>	>	>	>
Highland/Lowland:											
Monymusk	18.3	7.0	11.3	32.4	12.7	8.5	0	1.4	4.2	2.8	1.4
(cumulative)	18.3	25.3	36.6	69.0	81.7	90.2	>	91.6	95.8	98.6	100.0
Tillinessell	4.2	8.3	4.2	20.8	62.5	0	0	0	0	0	0
(cumulative)	4.2	12.5	16.7	37.5	100.0	>	>	>	>	>	>
Fyvie	10.1	13.7	13.7	10.1	13.7	32.9	5.0	1.4	2.2	0	>
(cumulative)	10.1	23.8	37.5	47.6	61.3	88.6	91.5	96.5	97.9	100.1	>
Lowland:											
Auchterless	41.7	12.5	8.3	12.5	8.3	8.3	8.3	0	0	0	0
(cumulative)	41.7	54.2	62.5	75.0	83.3	91.6	99.9	>	>	>	>
Kingedward	6.7	6.7	20.0	9.3	12.0	5.3	10.7	16.0	8.0	5.3	0
(cumulative)	6.7	13.4	33.4	42.7	54.7	60.0	70.7	86.7	94.7	100.0	>
Peterculter	0	0	13.6	18.2	63.6	0	0	0	0	0	4.5
(cumulative)	0	0	13.6	31.8	95.4	>	>	>	>	>	99.9
Deer	10.4	13.9	11.3	4.3	31.3	14.8	3.5	4.3	0.9	3.5	1.7
(cumulative)	10.4	24.3	35.6	39.9	71.2	86.0	89.5	93.8	94.7	98.2	99.9

TABLE A   (Continued)

Parish	Rental classes (£ Scots)										
	0–10	11–20	21–30	31–40	41–50	51–60	61–70	71–80	81–90	91–100	101+
Coastal strip:											
Crimond	6.8	18.2	22.7	9.1	22.7	0	2.3	4.5	9.1	0	4.5
(cumulative)	6.8	25.0	47.7	56.8	79.5	>	81.8	86.3	95.4	>	99.9
Fraserburgh	28.4	10.4	11.9	7.5	10.4	11.9	3.0	6.0	3	0	7.5
(cumulative)	28.4	38.8	50.7	58.2	68.6	80.5	83.5	89.5	92.5	>	100.0
Cruden	29.9	14.5	9.4	6.8	12.8	8.5	5.1	6.8	2.6	0	3.4
(cumulative)	29.9	44.4	53.8	60.1	72.9	81.4	86.5	93.3	95.9	>	99.3
Foverane	9.7	22.3	16.5	9.7	14.6	12.6	2.9	1.9	4.9	2.9	1.9
(cumulative)	9.7	32.0	48.5	58.2	72.8	85.4	88.3	90.2	95.1	98.0	99.9

TABLE B Social structure of parishes in Aberdeenshire as derived from the poll tax returns of 1696.

Parish	Total counted	Above tenant class	Tenants	Sub tenants	Merchants & richer tradesmen	Servants Male	Servants Female	Tradesmen	Cottars & Grass men/women	Others
Highland:										
Crathie	254	4.7	17.3	41.7	0	9.4	6.3	3.1	8.7	8.7
Tullich*	204	6.4	31.9	0	0	15.2	9.3	4.4	2.5	30.4
Glengarden	148	2.7	57.4	0	0	16.2	6.8	2.7	4.7	9.5
Glenmuick	187	4.8	51.9	0	0	20.3	12.8	3.7	4.8	1.6
Glenbucket	96	3.1	64.6	0	0	10.4	7.3	6.3	4.2	4.2
Highland/Lowland:										
Gartly	221	2.3	14.9	2.3	0.5	19.0	12.2	1.4	44.4	3.2
Glass	247	2.0	28.8	1.2	0.4	25.1	17.4	4.9	19.4	0.8
Monymusk	481	1.0	15.0	0	0.9	22.9	13.3	12.3	15.2	20.4
Fyvie	812	2.3	17.0	1.4	0	25.9	11.0	10.7	22.7	8.1
Tillinessell #	153	2.6	12.4	0.7	2.0	24.2	17.0	16.3	2.0	22.9
Forbes	82	1.2	19.5	0	0	35.4	14.6	4.9	17.1	7.3
Lowland:										
Auchterless	471	1.1	15.1	0.2	0.4	23.1	10.4	15.7	29.7	4.2
Kingedward	467	1.5	15.0	2.8	0	19.3	13.9	18.6	16.1	12.8
Peterculter $	177	1.7	18.6	19.2	0	14.7	14.1	11.9	0	19.8
Deer	783	2.4	15.8	1.2	0.4	21.7	13.5	17.2	26.5	1.2
Udnie	507	1.6	12.6	0.2	0.8	27.6	13.6	14.2	16.8	12.6
Coastal strip:										
Crimond	260	2.7	17.7	9.2	0	20.0	13.8	17.3	7.7	11.5
Fraserburgh	420	3.1	12.4	9.0	6.4	16.7	16.7	19.0	4.8	11.9
Cruden	731	2.5	12.0	7.5	0	24.9	13.4	8.8	28.2	2.7
Foverane	519	5.8	15.6	0.4	0.2	21.4	14.1	13.5	18.4	10.8

NOTES * = If the individuals classed here as 'others' are included in the tenant class (see parish notes for the reason) then the tenant total rises to 62.3%.
= If the individuals classed here as 'others' are included in the cottar class (see parish notes no. 3 for reason) then the cottar etc. category total rises to 25.6%.
$ = If the individuals classed here as 'others' are included in the cottar class (see parish notes no. 3 for reason) then the cottar etc. category total rises to 19.8%.

TABLE C Proportions of multiple- and single-tenant possessions in Aberdeenshire parishes as derived from the poll tax returns of 1696.

Parish	Total no. of possessions	No. of multiple-tenant possessions	% of multiple-tenant possessions	No. of single-tenant possessions	% of single-tenant possessions
Highland:					
Crathie	11	7	63.6	4	36.4
Tullich	34	8 (21)	23.5 (61.8)	6 (7)	17.6 (20.6)
Glengarden	24	17	70.8	4	16.7
Glenmuick	32	18	56.25	10	31.25
Glenbucket	16	11	68.75	3	18.75
Highland/Lowland:					
Gartly	20	10	50.0	10	50.0
Glass	37	19	51.4	13	35.1
Monymusk	39	16	41.0	19	51.4
Fyvie	75	28	37.3	33	25.3
Tillinessell	24	1	4.2	16	66.7
Forbes	10	3	30.0	7	70.0
Lowland:					
Auchterless	53	11	20.8	36	67.9
Kingedward	75	5	6.7	57	76.0
Peterculter	28	6	21.4	20	71.4
Deer	106	16	15.1	76	71.7
Udnie	66	6	9.1	43	65.2

TABLE C　(Continued)

Parish	Total no. of possessions	No. of multiple-tenant possessions	% of multiple-tenant possessions	No. of single-tenant possessions	% of single-tenant possessions
Coastal strip:					
Crimond	23	8	34.8	10	43.5
Fraserburgh	25	8	32.0	13	52.0
Cruden	52	20	38.5	18	34.6
Foverane	49	13	26.5	26	60.5

NOTES　The polls for Crathie, Glenmuick, Glass, Fyvie and Forbes all recorded the ministers' families, but these were excluded from the calculations.

Tullich: Figures in brackets are the recalculated ones counting those in the 'others' class in the tenant class. See the explanation in the notes of the tables of social structure.

Tillinessell: Excludes Laird of Whythaughs.

Auchterless: Excludes Laird of Haltoun.

Kingedward: Excludes Sir John Guthrie and 'subtennents' marked as possessions in the enumeration.

Peterculter: Excludes Laird of Culter and 'younger'.

Fraserburgh: Excludes Laird of Techmuirie and Lord Saltoune. The 2 Fraserburgh entries are counted as 1.

Cruden: Excludes Earl of Errol and Laird of Auchleuries.

Foverane: Excludes Lord of Foverane and Mr Forbes of Foverane. Those tenants classed as 'Gentlemen' were counted as tenants for the purposes of this table.

TABLE D   Proportions of possessions with cottars, subtenants and grassmen/women in Aberdeenshire parishes in 1696.

Parish	No. of possessions	No. with cottars, subtenants & grassmen/women	% with cottars, subtenants & grassmen/women
Highland:			
Crathie	11	10	90.9
Tullich	34	3	8.8
Glengarden	24	6	25.0
Glenmuick	32	5	15.6
Glenbucket	16	3	23.1
Highland/Lowland:			
Gartly	20	17	85.0
Glass	37	20	54.1
Monymusk	39	19	48.8
Fyvie	75	55	73.3
Tillinessell	24	4	16.7
Forbes	10	8	80.0
Lowland:			
Auchterless	53	39	73.6
Kingedward	75	41	54.7
Peterculter	28	21	75.0
Deer	106	79	74.5
Udnie	66	43	65.2
Coastal strip:			
Crimond	23	13	56.5
Fraserburgh	25	16	64.0
Cruden	52	39	75.0
Foverane	49	35	71.4

Appendix 3

Poll Tax Tabulations, Renfrewshire, 1695

TABLE A   Social structure of parishes in Renfrewshire as derived from the poll tax returns of 1695.

Parish	Total counted	Above tenant class	Tenants	Merchants & richer tradesmen	Servants		Tradesmen	Cottars	Others
					Male	Female			
Egleisholme	362	1.4	35.6	0.6	23.5	16.9	11.6	6.4	4.1
Mearns	245	14.7	42.0	0.0	10.2	16.7	8.2	8.2	0.0
Neilstoune	511	3.9	32.5	0.2	19.2	23.5	3.9	14.3	2.5
Cathcart	167	8.4	15.0	0.0	19.2	30.5	10.2	16.2	0.0
Eastwood	268	1.1	22.4	0.0	19.0	25.8	17.2	11.6	3.0
Paisley	790	2.4	26.3	0.9	15.4	27.6	13.5	9.1	4.7
Renfrew	151	0.7	27.8	0.0	19.9	42.4	4.7	4.0	0.7
Inchinnan	246	1.2	20.3	1.2	23.2	32.5	9.8	7.7	4.1
Erskine	345	2.3	20.6	0.0	22.3	31.6	9.3	4.9	9.0
Houstoune	155	0.7	36.8	0.0	18.7	20.0	7.1	12.9	3.9
Killellane	186	2.2	28.0	0.0	22.6	26.3	10.8	7.5	2.7
Kilbarchane	531	2.6	29.8	1.9	13.8	23.2	17.1	4.7	7.0
Lochwinnoch	547	16.1	23.8	0.2	15.0	18.5	15.7	5.3	5.3
Killmacomb	551	2.5	22.5	3.5	7.1	18.2	14.7	7.4	24.1
Greenock	318	0.3	30.8	3.8	6.9	8.2	24.5	6.9	18.6
Innerkip	510	1.4	59.6	1.6	4.1	9.4	13.5	4.1	6.3

NOTES   The 79 heritors in Lochwinnoch have all been classed as 'above Tenantry'.
Killmacomb parish enumeration includes Neuport, Glasgow and the Bay.
Greenock enumeration includes Carsdyck feuars but excludes those in the town of Greenock.

TABLE B Percentage of tenantry in each rental class (and cumulative percentages), Renfrewshire – 1695.

Parish	Rental classes (£ Scots)										
	0–10	11–20	21–30	31–40	41–50	51–60	61–70	71–80	81–90	91–100	101+
Egleisholme	10.3	43.7	19.8	14.3	6.3	4.0	1.6	0	0	0	0
(cumulative)	10.3	54.0	73.8	88.1	94.4	98.4	100.0	>	>	>	>
Mearns	7.4	18.5	32.6	10.4	17.8	4.4	0.7	1.5	1.5	0	5.2
(cumulative)	7.4	25.9	58.5	68.9	86.7	91.1	91.8	93.3	94.8	94.8	100.0
Neilstoune	4.3	24.7	31.7	19.4	10.8	3.8	1.6	0	1.1	1.1	1.6
(cumulative)	4.3	28.0	59.7	79.1	89.9	93.7	95.3	>	96.4	97.5	99.1
Cathcart	2.6	7.9	5.3	5.3	23.7	7.9	13.2	13.2	2.6	2.6	15.8
(cumulative)	2.6	10.5	15.8	21.1	44.8	52.7	65.9	79.1	81.7	84.3	100.1
Eastwood	5.0	11.7	20.0	21.7	8.3	11.7	6.7	1.7	6.7	5.0	1.7
(cumulative)	5.0	16.7	36.7	58.4	66.7	78.4	85.1	86.8	93.5	98.5	100.2
Paisley	8.7	19.7	25.3	14.4	9.6	6.6	3.9	4.4	0	3.5	3.9
(cumulative)	8.7	28.4	53.7	68.1	77.7	84.3	88.2	92.6	>	96.1	100.0
Renfrew	0	7.1	11.9	28.6	11.9	11.9	7.1	4.8	0	0	16.7
(cumulative)	0	7.1	19.0	47.6	59.5	71.4	78.5	83.3	>	>	100.0
Inchinnane	5.8	17.3	13.5	23.1	13.5	9.6	3.8	0	5.8	1.9	5.8
(cumulative)	5.8	23.1	36.6	59.7	73.2	82.8	86.6	>	92.4	94.3	100.1
Arskine	4.9	21.0	12.3	14.8	8.6	11.1	14.8	0	0	6.2	6.2
(cumulative)	4.9	25.9	38.2	53.0	61.6	72.7	87.5	>	>	93.7	99.9
Houstoune	16.3	12.2	22.4	22.4	8.2	6.1	6.1	2.0	0	0	4.1
(cumulative)	16.3	28.5	50.9	73.3	81.5	87.6	93.7	95.7	>	>	99.8
Killellane	21.1	21.1	17.5	10.5	8.8	3.5	0	7.0	1.8	3.5	5.3
(cumulative)	21.1	42.2	59.7	70.2	79.0	82.5	>	89.5	91.3	94.8	100.1

TABLE B (Continued)

Parish	Rental classes (£ Scots)										
	0-10	11-20	21-30	31-40	41-50	51-60	61-70	71-80	81-90	91-100	101+
Kilbarchane	8.8	32.2	25.1	10.5	9.4	3.5	1.8	0	2.3	1.8	4.7
(cumulative)	8.8	41.0	66.1	76.6	86.0	89.5	91.3	>	93.6	95.4	100.1
Lochwinnoch	7.2	31.1	20.6	19.1	12.0	4.3	1.9	0	0	1.9	1.9
(cumulative)	7.2	38.3	58.9	78.0	90.0	94.3	96.2	>	>	98.1	100.0
Killmacomb	13.1	22.3	27.0	13.1	10.8	5.4	2.3	1.5	0	0	4.6
(cumulative)	13.1	35.4	62.4	75.5	86.3	91.7	94.0	95.5	>	>	100.1
Greenock (not town)	15.9	40.0	20.6	6.3	4.8	4.8	3.2	0	1.6	0	3.2
(cumulative)	15.9	55.9	76.5	82.8	87.6	92.4	95.6	>	97.2	>	100.4

TABLE C   Proportions of multiple- and single-tenant possessions in Renfrewshire parishes as derived from the poll tax returns of 1695.

Parish	Total no. of possessions	No. of multiple-tenant possessions	% of multiple-tenant possessions	No. of single-tenant possessions	% of single-tenant possessions
Egleisholme	77	29	37.7	40	51.9
Mearns	73	25	34.2	29	39.7
Neilstoune	80	30	37.5	47	58.8
Cathcart	13	5	38.5	2	15.4
Eastwood	12	7	58.3	2	16.7
Paisley	160	42	26.3	85	53.1
Renfrew	15	10	66.7	5	33.3
Inchinnan	36	12	33.3	18	50.0
Erskine	53	17	32.1	18	34.0
Houstoune	31	11	35.5	20	64.5
Killellane	18	9	50.0	7	38.9
Kilbarchane	133	33	24.8	67	50.4
Lochwinnoch	129	27	20.9	57	44.2
Killmacomb	105	28	26.7	45	42.9
Grenock	61	19	31.1	29	47.5
Innerkip	127	56	44.1	65	51.2

NOTES Mearns: 'Kirk of Mearns' excluded.
Eastwood: 'Minister' excluded.
Houstoune: 'Sir Patrick Houstoune of that ilk' excluded.
Killmacomb: 'List of the Bay' and Neuport excluded.
Greenock: 'Landward of Greenock Parochine', 'Carsdyck feuars' and 'Laird of Blackhall' excluded.
Innerkip: 'Laird of Kellie' excluded.

TABLE D Proportions of possessions with cottars, subtenants and grassmen/women in Renfrewshire parishes in 1695.

Parish	No. of possessions	No. with cottars, subtenants & grassmen/women	% with cottars, subtenants & grassmen/women
Egleisholme	77	14	18.2
Mearns	73	15	20.5
Neilstoune	80	35	43.8
Cathcart	13	6	46.2
Eastwood	12	5	41.7
Paisley	160	43	26.9
Renfrew	15	4	26.7
Inchinnan	36	9	25.0
Erskine	53	15	28.3
Houstoune	31	11	35.5
Killellane	18	6	33.3
Kilbarchane	133	14	10.5
Lochwinnoch	129	18	14.0
Killmacomb	105	12	11.4
Greenock	61	12	19.7
Innerkip	127	13	10.2

Appendix 4

Poll Tax Tabulations, Midlothian and West Lothian, 1694

TABLE A　Social structure of parishes in Midlothian and West Lothian as derived from the poll tax returns of 1694.

Parish	Total counted	Above tenant Class	Tenants & Richer Tradesmen	Merchants	Servants		Tradesmen	Cottars	Others
					Male	Female			
Midlothian:									
Carrington	189	1.1	12.2	0	40.7	19.1	10.6	13.8	2.7
Cockpen	236	3.0	14.4	0	24.2	16.1	17.8	21.6	3.0
Cranston	210	1.0	8.6	0	28.6	15.2	14.3	26.2	6.2
Fala	140	4.3	6.4	0	39.3	9.3	18.6	7.9	14.3
Kirknewton	143	0.7	18.2	0	25.9	12.6	7.7	28.0	7.0
Pennicook	298	1.3	16.8	0	35.6	17.5	1.3	24.2	3.4
Ratho	413	2.2	16.0	0	29.1	17.9	7.8	23.5	3.6
Stow	319	3.8	13.2	0	20.4	24.5	1.3	32.9	4.1
Temple	395	1.5	12.9	0	31.7	15.4	12.4	17.2	8.9
Dalkeith	755	3.2	2.4	13.1	11.3	16.6	24.8	21.1	7.7
West Lothian:									
Bathgate	461	2.4	19.3	1.7	19.7	17.4	10.9	26.5	2.2
Kirkliston	447	2.5	10.7	0.2	31.8	18.1	13.4	21.3	2.0
Dalmeny	458	1.8	12.2	0.2	31.7	21.4	6.3	21.8	4.6
Livingstone	583	3.8	27.6	0.5	18.7	14.1	4.3	26.8	4.3
Torphichen	396	4.0	30.6	0.3	11.6	12.9	4.6	30.1	6.1

TABLE B   Proportions of multiple- and single-tenant possessions in Midlothian and West Lothian parishes as derived from the poll tax returns of the 1690s.

Parish	Total no. of possessions	No. of multiple-tenant possessions	% of multiple-tenant possessions	No. of single-tenant possessions	% of single-tenant possessions
Midlothian:					
Cockpen	5	3	60.0	1	20.0
Fala	4	2	50.0	2	50.0
Kirknewton	19	5	26.3	14	73.7
Pennicook	32	10	31.25	18	56.25
Ratho	30	13	43.3	13	43.3
Stow	45	6	13.3	28	62.2
Lasswade (sample)	22	7	31.8	10	45.5
(No possessions named in parishes of Carrington, Cranston, Temple, Dalkeith and Duddingston)					
West Lothian:					
Bathgate	65	12	18.5	46	70.8
Kirkliston	19	14	73.7	5	26.5
Dalmeny	28	11	39.3	17	60.7
Livingstone	33	20	60.7	11	33.3
Torphichen	75	28	37.3	37	49.3

NOTES   Fala: Laird of Prestonhall's family excluded.
Pennicook: 'Families within Pennicook' excluded and 'Sir John Clerk and Family' excluded.
Ratho: 'Sir John Gibsone' and 'Lord Hatton's Family' excluded.
Lasswade: 'coalyers and coalbearers' and 'Rosline Muire Coalyers' excluded.
Kirkliston: 'Baronie' included. Some other' possessions' look very big = villages?

TABLE C   Proportions of possessions with cottars, subtenants and grassmen/women in Midlothian and West Lothian parishes in 1694.

Parish	No. of possessions	No. with cottars, subtenants & grassmen/women	% with cottars, subtenants grassmen/women
Midlothian:			
Cockpen	5	4	80.0
Fala	4	3	75.0
Kirknewton	19	12	63.2
Pennicook	32	21	65.6
Ratho	30	21	70.0
Stow	45	28	62.2
Lasswade (sample)	22	16	72.7

(No possession names were given for the parishes of Carrington, Cranston, Temple and Dalkeith; no socio- economic status given for Duddingston)

Parish	No. of possessions	No. with cottars, subtenants & grassmen/women	% with cottars, subtenants grassmen/women
West Lothian:			
Bathgate	65	45	69.2
Kirkliston	19	13	68.4
Dalmeny	28	16	57.1
Livingstone	33	24	72.7
Torphichen	75	38	50.7

TABLE D Percentage of tenantry in each rental class (and cumulative percentages), Midlothian & West Lothian –1694.

Parish	Rental classes (£ Scots)										
	0–10	11–20	21–30	31–40	41–50	51–60	61–70	71–80	81–90	91–100	101+
Midlothian:											
Carrington	0	23.5	0	0	0	0	0	0	11.8	17.6	47.1
(cumulative)	0	23.5	>	>	>	>	>	>	35.3	52.9	100.0
Cockpen	72.7	0	0	9.1	0	0	0	0	0	0	100.0
(cumulative)	72.7	>	>	81.8	>	>	>	>	>	>	100.0
Kirknewton	3.8	19.2	30.8	7.7	15.4	0	3.8	3.8	3.8	3.8	7.7
(cumulative)	3.8	23.0	53.8	61.5	76.9	>	80.7	84.5	88.3	92.1	99.8
Ratho	0	2.8	30.6	5.6	8.3	0	8.3	5.6	2.8	8.3	27.8
(cumulative)	0	2.8	33.4	39.0	47.3	>	55.6	61.2	64.0	72.3	100.1
Stow	0	0	4.8	0	2.4	0	4.8	0	9.5	0	78.6
(cumulative)	0	0	4.8	4.8	7.2	>	12.0	>	21.5	>	100.1
West Lothian:											
Bathgate	0	16.7	12.5	8.3	0	4.2	16.7	0	0	0	41.7
(cumulative)	0	16.7	29.2	37.5	>	41.7	58.4	>	>	>	100.1

NOTE Torphichen data unreliable: perhaps Bathgate data too.

Appendix 5

Poll Tax Tabulations, Berwick and Selkirk, 1694

TABLE A   Social structure of parishes in Berwickshire and Selkirkshire as derived from the poll tax returns of 1694.

Parish	Total counted	Above tenant class	Tenants	Merchants & richer tradesmen	Servants		Tradesmen	Cottars	Others
					Male	Female			
Berwickshire:									
Aytoun	249	3.2	18.5	0	33.7	12.9	16.5	13.7	1.6
Edrom	444	3.2	9.7	0	37.8	18.0	12.4	15.3	3.6
Swintone	104	1.0	11.5	0	47.1	13.5	8.7	14.4	3.9
Eyemouth	251	2.4	17.1	2.4	17.5	15.5	20.3	8.8	15.9
Greenlaw	363	3.0	16.5	0	31.7	11.3	12.7	17.6	7.2
Polwarth	139	3.6	5.8	0	35.3	15.8	18.7	19.4	1.4
Selkirkshire:									
Selkirk	388	2.3	20.6	0	32.0	18.3	8.8	16.5	1.5
Ettricke	334	1.5	18.6	0.3	35.4	30.0	1.8	7.8	4.8

NOTES   Town of Selkirk excluded from the enumeration.
Two possessions listed but said to be in Robertoun parish are listed in the enumeration but excluded from the calculations.

TABLE B   Proportions of multiple- and single-tenant possessions in Selkirkshire and Berwickshire parishes as derived from the poll tax returns of the 1690s.

Parish	Total no. of tenant possessions	No. of multiple-tenant possessions	% of multiple-tenant possessions	No. of single-tenant possessions	% of single-tenant possessions
Selkirkshire:					
Selkirk	28	16	57.1	10	35.7
Ettricke	34	16	47.1	11	32.4
Berwickshire:					
Aytoun	21	7	33.3	11	52.4
Edrom	30	6	20.0	20	66.7
Swintone	3	2	66.7	0	0.0
Eyemouth	7	4	57.1	2	28.6
Greenlaw	38	7	18.4	27	71.1
Polwarth	7	2	28.6	3	42.9

NOTES   Ettricke: 'Minister' and 'servants in Andres House' excluded.
Aytoun: 'Minister' excluded.
Eyemouth: 3 Eyemouth entires counted as 1.
Polwarth: 'Minister' excluded.

TABLE C　Proportions of possessions with cottars, subtenants and grassmen/women in Selkirkshire and Berwickshire parishes in 1694.

Parish	No. of possessions	No. with cottars, subtenants & grassmen/women	% with cottars, subtenants & grassmen/women
Selkirkshire:			
Selkirk	28	15	53.6
Ettricke	34	15	44.1
Berwickshire:			
Aytoun	21	10	47.6
Edrom	30	17	56.7
Swintone	3	2	66.7
Eyemouth	7	2	28.6
Greenlaw	38	25	65.8
Polwarth	7	6	85.7

Appendix 6

Lesmahagow Poll Tax Return, 1695

WHILE much of the information recorded in the return is reasonably clear, there are certain individuals whose social status appeared less so. Thus, the results given below are based on an approach which contains certain assumptions.

1. Tenants were generally taken as those who were definitely specified as such, together with those whose 'valuation' identified them similarly. In addition, a few others were counted in this group where, despite the lack of either of the above indications, it seemed reasonable to assume that they were in fact functioning as tenants.

2. In the few cases where individuals were recorded as both tradesman and cottar, they have been listed in the latter class only.

3. 'Herds' were simply classed as servants.

4. The heads of families were used to classify the whole of the individuals in that family and thus the denominator used to calculate percentages was not that of the total parish population but only the denomination of those heads of families and other individuals actually counted.

5. The Blackwood quarter of the district was omitted from the parish return.

Social structure of Lesmahagow, 1695.

Socio-economic class		Number	Percentage of total
Tenants	definite	277	
	probable	21	
	Total	298	54.8
Servants	definite	132	
	probable	3	
	Total	135	24.8
Cottars	definite	62	
	probable	2	
	Total	64	11.8
Tradesmen	definite	46	
	probable	1	
	Total	47	8.6
Total of Totals		544	100.0

Appendix 7

Enumeration Sheet, Poll Tax Data

POSSESSION	ABOVE TENANTRY	TENANTS	MERCHANTS & RICHER TRADESMEN	SERVANTS							COTTARS			
				MALE			FEMALE			TRADES MEN	COTTARS	NO TRADE	TRADES MEN	OTHERS
				SERV.	HERD	IN HARV.	SERV.	HERD	IN HARV.					

Appendix 8

'Improving lease', Lockhart of Lee Estate, Lanarkshire, 1799

ARTICLES AND REGULATIONS,

SETTLED BY THE

TUTORS & CURATORS OF CHA. LOCKHART-WISHEART, Esq; of Lee;

TO BE OBSERVED BY

The TENANTS of the Lands belonging to him, whose Tacks shall be made to bear relation to the same.

Dated 21ft
And recorded in the books of Session,24th January, 1791

I.

All assignees, whether legal or voluntary, and all sub-tenants, are excluded.– Heirs portioners are also excluded, the eldest being to succeed without division; but power is given to a tenant having children, to appoint any of his children he pleases to succeed him in his lease.

II.

The tenants must reside with their families upon their farms, and always have a sufficient stock thereupon.

III.

The lands shall be managed and cropped by the tenants during their tracks in the following manner, viz.–The old croft land, together with such a proportion of the field lands as the tenants shall be taken bound to labour and cultivate, must within the first five years of the tack, be put into ten divisions, as nearly equal as the nature of the fields will admit; five of these divisions at least must be in grass, the other five may be in tillage, and cropped in the following order.

1. Oats,		1. Oats.
2. Peafe,		2. Barley.
3. Barley,	or	3. Oats.
4. Oats,		4. Peafe.
5. Fallow,		5. Fallow.

When land is new plowed out of old lee, the rotation of crops may be:–

1. Oats,		1. Oats.
2. Oats,		2. Oats.
3. Barley,	or	3. Peafe.
4. Oats,		4. Oats.
5. Fallow,		5. Fallow.

The division or field that falls yearly to be in fallow, must be equal to a tenth part of the lands to be cultivated; but it must get at least four plowings in the season, and be manured at the rate of sixty cart loads of good dung, or ten cart loads of lime shells to the acre. Turnips may be sown on the fallow field after it has been laboured and manured as aforesaid, and along with the following crop, it must be sown with grass feeds, at the rate of two bushels of rye grass, and twelve pounds of clover feed to the acre. Thereafter it must remain in grass five years, in one of which years it may be cut for hay. The farms being all thus fallowed and manured, the same round of fallowing and manuring as above specified is to be begun again. The tenants are bound strictly to observe, that the part of the fallow field to be first limed in the second round of fallow, is to be that which got no lime in the first round. Tenants who may have less than the half of the manured land in tillage after the whole has been once fallowed and manured, shall only be obliged to fallow and manure yearly one-fifth part of what they reap in tillage. Liberty is given to tenants to put their respective farms into eight divisions in place of ten; but, in this cafe, one eight part of the lands to be cultivated shall be yearly fallowed and manured as above mentioned, till the whole is gone over, and thereafter one-fourth part of what is in tillage is to be in fallow. Thofe who follow this method may leave the pease crop out of the rotation. The field lands that may be by agreement left out of the above-mentioned divisions and method of management, shall at no time be plowed, unless it be to have them fallowed and manured with dung or lime, thereafter to be sown with grass feeds, along with the third crop, and not be plowed again unless when it is to undergo the same course of management. At any rate, it must remain in pasture grass fix years after being sown off.

The small possessions in the crofts of Carnwath, and other places, must be put into four equal divisions; one of which divisions shall be yearly fallow, or turnips; one barley; one red clover; one oats. The half of the fallow division may be potatoes in place of turnips; but when it is, it must be dunged after the crop is taken out of the ground. No lint is to be sown, except upon the oat division, when the land is to be in fallow the following season. Declaring, That if the tenants shall at any time contravene any of the articles of management above mentioned, he shall be obliged to pay the sum of Three Pounds Sterling of additional rent, for every acre managed contrary to the regulations above specified, and that along with the first rent falling due after the contravention has taken place; and shall also pay Six Shilling Sterling for each cart load of lime-shells, and One Shilling Sterling for each cart load of lime-shells, and One Shilling Sterling for each cart load of dung that is not laid on the fallow field, or division, as before specified.

IV.

The tenants shall be bound to allow the proprietor, or in-coming tenant, to sow grass along with the last crop, and to hain and preserve the grass that shall be fo sown by them the last year of their possession, and not to pasture, or allow any of their bestial to trespass thereupon, after the separation of the crop from the ground, under the penalty of paying One Pound Sterling for every horse, cow, or other cattle, that may be found pasturing on the same.

V.

The tenants shall be bound to consume with their cattle, upon their respective farms, the whole straw and fodder (hay excepted) that shall grow thereupon, and to lay on the whole dung that shall be made upon the same; and upon no account to fell or five away any of their fodder or dung; and they shall be obliged to leave the whole dung made upon their farm the last year of their possession, carefully gathered together, for the ufe and behoof of the proprietor to whom the same shall belong. Declaring, That if they, notwithstanding hereof, take upon them to fell or give away any of the faid fodder or dung, they shall be bound to pay the proprietor the sum of Four Shillings for every threave of straw or fodder, and Two Shillings for every cart-load of dung fo fold or given away.

VI.

The proprietor, at any time within the first five years of the lease, is to have it in his option and power to inclose and subdivide the old croft land, and twenty acres of the field-land of each respective farm, with ditch and hedge, stone or seal dykes, or drains, whichever of these is best adapted to soil and situation; the rentee being obliged to pay 5 per cent. per ann. for the coft or money laid out on such inclosing. The which coft or outlay is to be ascertained by the workmen's receipts, or an accompt certified under the hand of the perfon employed to direct the work. Where the proprietor does not incline to make any inclosures, in terms of this article, the tenant himself may inclose as above; and, at the end of the tack, he shall be entitled to receive from the proprietor the original coft of making such inclosures; provided that the fences be then in good order and repair; and that the lines of division of the inclosures be first approved of by the factor or doer on the eftate, at the time such inclosures are made.

VII.

The tenants shall be bound and obliged to maintain and uphold, in good and sufficient condition and repair, yearly, the whole houses, offices, dykes, ditches and hedges, and drains or gates, that are upon their respective farms at their entry, or which may be built thereupon during the currency of their tacks; and to leave them, at their removal, in the like good and sufficient repair, all upon their own charges and expences.

VIII.

In cafes where a tenant may find it necessary to alter the situation of any of the houses, or to repair or rebuild any of them upon a better plan, he is to have liberty to bring a proof of the value of the faid houses (they always being considered as in good and sufficient repair and condition at the time if such proof is brought); and the value being ascertained, it is to be recorded in the court-books of the barony of Carnwath; and, at the expiry of the lease, the houses shall be again valued, and the proprietor shall allow to the tenants the increase of value of the houses, provided that the alteration and improvement of the same have been executed on a plan approved of by the proprietor, his factor, or doer, at the time such alterations shall take place.

IX.

In cafe the proprietor (his factor or doer for the time) shall, at any time, find the houses, dykes, drains, hedges, ditches, and gates neglected, and in disrepair, power and liberty are expressly reserved to him to order the same to be put in proper and sufficient repair and condition; and the expence thereof being ascertained by the workmen's receipts, or by an accompt certified by the factor, the tenants shall be obliged to pay the same, with interest from the date of the receipts or faid certified accompts.

X.

In cafe it shall be judged proper to make any alteration in the farms, either by straighting marches, or by excambing lands with neighbouring heritors or tenants, the tenants shall be obliged to concur and acquiesce therein; and the variations thereby occasioned in their rent, whether increase or decreafe, shall be determined by two neutral perfons to be named by the proprietor and tenant.

XI.

The proprietor reserves all mines, metals, and coal, quarries of stone and lime, marl, and other fossils whatsoever of the like kind, within the bounds of the lands let, with liberty to work, win, and carry away the same; for that purpose, to fink pits, build houses, make roads, and erect any necessary works thereupon, the tenants being allowed such surface damages, and such abatement of rent as shall be determined by two neutral perfons, to be mutually appointed by the parties.

XII.

The tenants are to be thirled to the mills to which their respective lands have been in ufe to be astricted, and shall pay mill-dues, and perform services to mill and kiln, confirm to ufe and wont.

XIII.

The tenants are to have the liberty and privilege of casting, winning, and leading home peats for feuel, for the ufe of their families residing in their respective lands, from such moss or mosses, or parts of the same as shall be allotted and set off to them yearly by the officer of the barony, or others having the proprietor's authority for that purpose.

XIV.

The tenants shall attend the courts of the barony within which their respective farms lie, when summoned thereto, and obey the acts, decrees, and regulations thereof according to law.

XV.

Whatever the term of entry may be, the term of removal from that part of the farm that is in tillage the last year of the tenant's possession, shall be at the separation of the crop from the ground of each respective field, fo that whenever one field is cleared, the incoming tenant may enter to it, for the purpose of plowing only, although the crop may not be separated from the other fields. And we, as tutors foresaid, consent to the registration hereof in the books of Council and Session, or of any other proper Court, therein to remain for preservation; and constitute

our Procurators. In witness whereof, these presents, consisting of this and the four preceding pages, are written upon stamped paper, by Robert Stewart, writer in Edinburgh, and subfcribed by a majority and quorum of the faid tutors at Edinburgh, the twenty-first day of January, One thousand seven hundred and ninety one years, before these witnesses, James Haldane, writer in Edinburgh, and Jofeph Thorburn, servant to the faid John Wauchope.

{William Miller.
Signed {James Haldane, witness.   {John Pringle.
          {Joseph Thorburn, witness.   Signed   {Geo. Cumin.
                                                    {John Wauchope.

SOURCE   NLS, Acc. 4322, Lockhart of Lee Papers, Box 17

Appendix 9

OSA ABSTRACTS, ANGUS, AYRSHIRE AND FIFE

INTRODUCTION

Only those categories of factors analysed in the tables which require some explanation are discussed below.

Industrial Presence: This factor was noted when it appeared to present a real alternative to agricultural work.

Consolidation/Junction of Farms: This factor was noted in several different ways. The most commonly used phrase was probably 'the junction of Farms', but 'monopolising', 'the throwing of farms into one' were also used. Note also that the reduction of tenant numbers implies the same thing and that a note indicating that this was the case is usually, if not always, appended.

'Monopolising' could have meant, of course, that one individual was tenant of more than one farm and this, at least in some cases, is obviously what was implied by the author of the report. These cases were classed under this heading.

Market Penetration: The main assumption here was that if the parish was exporting agricultural or other produce then there was obviously a market connection. If this was not indicated then other evidence was sought, such as the existence of a market or trading place within the parish, the presence of dealers (in e.g. cattle, grain, etc.) or an industrial presence which implied production for a market.

The supplementary notes give indications of the produce or goods exported from the parishes and, when given, the location of the market place.

Plough Technology: If more than one type of plough is noted in the *OSA*, then the most prevalent is indicated in the table. If there appears to be a near-even split between two types then this is indicated by the use of asterisks. Note that two-horse ploughs were always assumed to be of the newer type unless stated differently in the account. However, there are one or two anomalies. The old Scots plough is usually said to have been drawn by larger plough teams (originally oxen teams) because of its greater weight relative to the newer iron ploughs of the later 18th century. However, the assumption that larger teams implied the use of the old plough and vice versa, though true in the majority of cases, was not so in every one. This was perhaps because of the different construction in different localities and because of the modifications that were introduced. Note that in Symington parish in Ayrshire, the ploughs were said to be of the Scotch kind, drawn by three horses, whereas in Barrie parish in Angus, Small's plough, drawn by four horses was in general use.

Where doubt remained, a note was made and these are attached to the individual tables.

TABLE A   Angus.

Parish	Enclosure Part	Enclosure Most	Enclosure All	Enclosure Unspecified	Industrial presence	% weavers of population	Cottars Exist	Cottars Reduction	Consolidation / junction of farms	Approx. Villages existing or newly created	Market penetration	Comments	Date of onset of changes
Aberlemno	✓ (²⁄₃)					7.2					✓	Grain exported	since 1766
Airly				✓		5.7			✓		✓	Grain exported	c. 1770
Arbirlot					✓					Town	✓	Trade centre	
Arbroath	✓				✓		✓				✓	Grain exported: Dundee	since 1776
Auchterhouse						6.7		✓		Town			
Barrie		✓			✓	12.5	✓	✓		✓	✓	Grain exported: Dundee & N.W. England. Cattle exported	
Brechin					✓						✓	Trade centre	c. 1770
Careston		✓				0.4			✓	Town	✓	Grain, cattle, sheep exported	'of late'
Carmylie													c. 1770
Cortachy & Clova	✓					0.7							
Craig	✓				✓	2.7				✓ (Fishing)	✓	Montrose	c. 1730
Dun	✓				✓✓			✓					c. 1766
Dundee					✓✓	14.8[1]	✓			Town (mechanics)[2] (weavers)	✓[3]	Trade centre	c. 1760
Dunnichen													
Edzell	✓					1.3	✓	✓		✓	✓	Grain, livestock, dairy produce exported	c. 1760
Essie & Nevay	✓				'No manufactures'	4.6	✓	✓	✓				c. 1760
Fern	✓					0.8		✓	✓			Grain exported?	c. 1760–5
Fernell				✓	'No manufactures'			✓	✓		✓		
Forfar	✓				✓	9.5[4]	✓			✓ (Beside town)	✓	Trade centre	c. 1750
Glamis					✓	3.4				✓	✓	Grain exported; livestock exported: England	c. 1730?
Glenisla	✓					0.8					✓[5]		

TABLE A (Continued)

Parish	Enclosure Part	Most	All	Unspecified	Industrial presence	% weavers of population	Cottars Exist	Cottars Reduction	Consolidation junction of farms	Approx. Villages existing or newly created	Market penetration	Comments	Date of onset of changes
Guthrie	✓					3.0							
Inverarity				✓									
Inverkeilor						2.6	✓	✓	✓[6]	✓(small fishing)	✓	Cattle exported: England Grain too?	c.1780
Kettins	✓					5.6				✓	✓	Cattle exported: England	
Kingoldrum				✓					✓		✓	Grain exported: Dundee, Kirriemuir	c.1760
Kinnell				✓	✓				✓		✓[7]		c.1770
Kinnettles	✓					9.3	✓				✓	Cattle exported Grain exported	c.1750–60
Kirkden	½					3.6[8]	✓				✓	Grain exported. Also cattle, horses & dairy	
Kirriemuir	✓				✓	5.2		✓	✓	Town	✓	Livestock, dairy, wool exported. Trade centre	
Lethnot	✓					1.4	✓[9]		✓		✓	Livestock exported. Grain exported: Brechin & Montrose	c.1740
Liff & Bervie	✓				✓	9.6	✓			✓[10]	✓[7]	Cattle exported	
Lintrathen	✓[11]					2.2		✓			✓[12]	Livestock exported	c.1793?
Lochlee					✓[14]	0.5		✓			✓?[13]	Sheep, cattle exported?	
Logie & Pert	✓					1.0	✓	✓	✓	✓	✓	Half annual produce exported	c.1750–60
Lunan	✓					4.5	✓	✓			✓		
Lundie & Foulis	✓[15]								✓[16]		✓	Grain exported	
Mains of Fintry				✓		3.7			✓		✓		c.1760
Maryton					✓						✓	Surplus exported: Montrose	

TABLE A . (Continued)

Parish	Enclosure Part	Most	All	Unspecified	Industrial presence	% weavers of population	Cottars Exist	Reduction	Consolidation junction of farms	Approx. Villages existing or newly created	Market penetration	Comments	Date of onset of changes
Menmuir	✓					1.3	✓				✓	Grain & Livestock exported. Dairy produce: Brechin & Kirrieumuir	
Monifeith		✓					✓			✓[17]		Grain exported	c.1750
Monikie						3.1				✓[18]			c.1750–60
Montrose					✓			✓	✓	Town	✓	Trade centre	
Murroes of Muirhouse					✓			✓	✓		✓	Cattle exported	c.1760
Newtyle						25.2		✓		✓	✓	Grain exported	
Oathlaw	No usable data for this parish												
Panbride				✓			✓				✓	Articles of provision exported	
Rescobie	No usable data for this parish												
Ruthven	✓				✓[19]		✓		✓			Grain exported: Leith & Glasgow. Cattle exported: Arbroath	c.1755 c.1754
St Vigeans					✓	6.7		✓		✓ (Fishing)	✓		
Strathmartin	✓[20]										✓	Cattle exported	c.1780?
Strickathrow											✓	Grain & cattle exported: Brechin & Montrose	
Tannadice	✓						✓		✓			Surplus produce exported	
Tealing	✓				✓	11.2		✓				Grain, livestock, dairy produce, linen, whisky exported: Dundee	c.1760?
Totals (54 parishes)	11	14	3	7	15	32 had at least some weavers	16	13	16	14	40		
		36											
Percentages	10.4	25.9	5.6	14.8	27.8	59.25	29.6	22.2	31.5	25.9	72.2		
Overall percentage	56.7				27.8	59.25	51.8 either exist or reduced		31.5				

NOTES   The 'Percentage of weavers' figure is the recorded number of weavers expressed as a proportion of the total population.

1 This figure has been calculated by assuming that the number of looms, i.e. 1,850 = the number of weavers, and adding 1,340 spinners, plus 370 servants making yarn thread. Thus, 3,560 divided by a population of 24,000 = 14.8%. Treat this figure with caution; the ratio of looms to weavers in the parish of Liff and Bervie was 1.6 to 1.

2 Lethan, 1788. This planned village, given the name of Restenneth, is listed in the appendix to T. C. Smout's article in N. Phillipson and R. Mitchison, eds, *Scotland in the Age of Improvement* (Edinburgh, 1970), p. 105.

3 All the 'in kind' rentals were said to have been converted to cash. Thus, market penetration was assumed.

4 400–500 looms. Assume 450 = 450 weavers, divided by a population of 4,756 = 9.5%.

5 Almost 1,700 black cattle and an unspecified number of sheep in the parish in 1791. Must (?) be for market = market penetration.

6 Junction of farms in only 'a few instances'.

7 Much more produce was said to have been grown/raised than was necessary to support the parish.

8 'Most' women in the parish were employed in spinning yarn for the Osnaburgh weavers.

9 Subtenants are described in some detail.

10 There seem to have been 4 or 5 'hamlets' where weaving was the principal occupation.

11 In 1793, the author of the *OSA* account wrote that there were, 'No enclosures'. In 1799, the new minister wrote that 'the greater farmers' had enclosed 'very considerable parcels of land within these few years'.

12 In 1793, 'little trade'. In 1799, £1,000 worth of livestock was sold from the parish per year.

13 9,200 sheep and 600 black cattle were bred. Only wool prices are given in this account.

14 Limeworks and Bleachfields employ 'a considerable number of hands'.

15 Lundie has a very little land enclosed; Foulis 'most enclosed'.

16 'Enlarging of Farms'.

17 3 villages here with populations of 132, 175 and 230, but they do not appear to be 'industrial'.

18 2 villages with 25 and 30 families in them and 2 or 3 less populous ones. Again, they do not appear to be 'industrial'.

19 Only a 'few manufacturers'.

20 'Not much inclosed'.

TABLE B Ayrshire.

Parish	Enclosure Part	Most	All	Unspecified	Industrial presence	% weavers of population	Cottars Exist	Cottars Reduction	Consolidation junction of farms	Approx. Villages existing or newly created	Market penetration	Comments	Date of onset of changes
Ardrossan				✓	?[1]		✓			Town			
Auchinleck	✓				✓	1.9				?[2]	✓	Coal exported: Ireland	c.1750s
Ayr						4.5				Town	✓	Sheep: shires of Lanark & Renfrew	
Ballantrae							✓			✓			
Barr						1.6			✓[3]	✓	✓	Breed cattle & sheep	
Beith	✓				✓	5.1	✓			Town	✓	Dairy and silk gauze exported	
Colmonell	✓?					2.2	✓	✓	✓	✓?[4]	✓	Crops exported: Girvan, Ballantrae	
Coylton	No usable data												
Craigie	✓							✓	✓		✓	Butter, cheese exported: Ayr, Kilmarnock, Paisley & Glasgow	
New Cumnock							✓			✓[2] (new)	✓	Bear, dairy products exported	
Old Cumnock				✓		1.7				✓	✓	Butter, cheese exported: Catrine, Muirkirk	
Dailly	✓				✓[5]	1.6				✓	✓	Cattle exported: England	c.1760
Dalmellington					✓				✓	✓	✓	Coal exported: Galloway	
Dalry	✓				✓	7.2		✓	✓	✓	✓	Dairy products exported: Greenock, Paisley & Glasgow	c.1750–60
Dalrymple						1.6							

TABLE B (Continued)

Parish	Enclosure Part	Most	All	Unspecified	Industrial presence	% weavers of population	Cottars Exist	Reduction	Consolidation junction of farms	Approx. Villages existing or newly created	Market penetration	Comments	Date of onset of changes
Dreghorn	✓										✓	Coal exported: Ireland	
Dundonald		✓			✓					✓[6](new)	✓	Grain, cheese, cattle exported	
Dunlop		✓			✓	1.5				✓	✓?[7]	Grain exported: Paisley, Glasgow. Cattle exported: Glasgow, Irvine	
Fenwick										✓	✓	Grain exported.	
Galston	✓				✓?[8]	4.2				✓	✓	Cheese exported: Kilmarnock, Paisley, Glasgow, & Edinburgh, Calves exported: Edinburgh	
Girvan				✓	✓?	5.8?[9]		✓	✓	Town	✓	Cattle exported: England	
Irvine					✓	2.6+		✓	✓		✓	Coal exported: Ireland. Carpets, muslins, gauze, silk exported: Ireland, Paisley	
Kilbirny West Kilbride					✓[11]	5.6			✓[10] ✓[12]	✓Town		Linen exported: Glasgow & Paisley	
Kilmarnock				✓	✓[13]	3.0				Town	✓	Coal exported: Ireland, Highlands	
Kilmaurs	✓					2.4	✓		✓[14]	Town	✓	Oats, meal exported: Glasgow, Paisley	

TABLE B (Continued)

| Parish | Enclosure | | | | Industrial presence | % weavers of population | Cottars | | Consolidation junction of farms | Approx. Villages existing or newly created | Market penetration | Comments | Date of onset of changes |
	Part	Most	All	Unspecified			Exist	Reduction					
Kilwinning				✓	✓	9.9		✓	✓	Town	✓	Cheese exported: Glasgow, Paisley, Edinburgh. Yarn exported, Glasgow and Paisley.	
Kirkmichael	✓					2.1	✓		✓		✓	Cattle exported: England	c.1760s
Kirkoswald				✓		1.2	✓		✓?[16]	✓[15]	✓	Oatmeal, bear, potatoes exported: manufacturing towns. Dairy produce exported: Ayr, Paisley	c.1770s
Largs					✓?	7.4			✓	Town	✓	Cattle exported: Greenock & other towns. Wool exported: Kilmarnock	
Loudon	✓				✓	14.5				✓[17]	✓	Meal, dairy, veal exported: Edinburgh, Glasgow, Paisley	c.1740s-5
Mauchline				✓	✓	1.1				Town			
Maybole						c.10							
Monkton & Prestwick	✓					2.4				✓+ Burgh	✓?	Black cattle for 'market'	
Muirkirk					✓[18]					✓	✓?	14,000 sheep = market?	
Newton Upon Ayr										Town			
Ochiltree					✓	6.0				✓	✓	Coal exported	

TABLE B (Continued)

Parish	Enclosure Part	Most	All	Unspecified	Industrial presence	% weavers of population	Cottars Exist	Reduction	Consolidation junction of farms	Approx. Villages existing or newly created	Market penetration	Comments	Date of onset of changes
Riccarton	✓	✓								✓	✓[19]		
St Quivox	✓	✓			✓	0.2				✓	✓	Dairy products: Glasgow. Cotton exported	c.1730s?
Sorn						4.0[21]		✓[20]		✓			
Stair	✓				✓[22]								
Stevenson	✓					2.9	✓			Town	✓	Coal exported: Ireland. Sea Trade Centre	
Stewarton	✓					c.5.0[23]	✓			Town	✓[24]		
Straiton				✓		1.3+	✓		✓	✓	✓[25]		
Symington				✓		1.6				✓	?[26]		
Tarbolton				✓						✓	✓	Cheese, butter exported	c.1740
Totals	2	13	8	7	19		8	7	16	38 (including towns)	36		
Percentages	4.3	28.3	17.4	15.2	41.3		17.4	15.2	32.6	82.6	78.3		
Overall percentage	65.2				41.3		32.6 either exist or reduced		32.6	81.6	78.3		

NOTES 1 Coal on Auchinleck estate – no scale indication.
2 Village of Auchinleck 'on the decline'.
3 1 farmer holds more than 1 farm in several cases, *but* no specific mention of the junction of farms. (*NB*: some farmers held up to 5 farms.)
4 34 thatched houses in this village.
5 Coal production = 9,000 tons per annum.
6 New village built because of coal works there.
7 Over 10,000 stones of cheese produced = market.
8 Weaving of gauze and lawn = main manufacture. Silk exported to Glasgow and Paisley = 'industrial presence'.
9 100 looms for weaving cotton = 100 weavers? = 5.8%
10 Setting of large farms to one person = policy of letting. 11 Flourishing silk manufactures, and coal and lime in 'great abundance'.
12 Large arable farms converted to grazing = depopulation.
13 2,000–3,000 employed in trades = 30–45% of total population.
14 'Amalgamation' of some farms.
15 Only 17 families, no real industrial presence there.
16 Earl of Cassilis took lead in 'enlarging and improving' farms.
17 3 of these 4 mentioned villages appear to have been created and expanded by the Loudoun family.
18 Iron and coal-tar manufactures.
19 Wallacetown in this parish houses dealers in grain, meal, malt, etc. = market?
20 Most of the families in village of Dalgain formerly lived in cothouses = reduction of cottar class and relocation.
21 445 people employed at cotton twist mill (= 16% of population) plus 226 women 'pick cotton' in their homes = 671 people = 24% of population.
22 8.2% of total populace employed in coal mining. Also salt, shipbuilding, rope-manufacturing, brewing here in Saltcoats.
23 Exact population of parish unknown; thus weavers/population percentage is an approximation.
24 Said to be 'great demand' for the cheese made here = market penetration?
25 20,000 sheep and 2,100 black cattle must be for market production.
26 Prices of provisions are regulated by markets of Ayr and Kilmarnock.

TABLE C   Fife.

Parish	Enclosure Part	Most	All	Unspecified	Industrial presence	% weavers of population	Cottars Exist	Reduction	Consolidation junction of farms	Approx. Villages existing or newly created	Market penetration	Comments	Date of onset of changes
Abbot's Hall	✓				✓		✓		✓	Town	✓	Livestock sold	
Abdie				✓	?	2.8		✓		✓	✓	Wheat and barley exported	
Aberdour				✓									
Anstruther Easter													
Anstruther Wester					✓ (shipping)	4.1	✓				✓	Grain exported	
Auchterderran	✓						✓			✓	✓	Cattle exported: Dunfermline, Dysart, Kinghorn	
Auchtermuchty	✓				✓	14.2				Town	✓	Cattle exported: England	
Auchtertool	✓				✓	5.1			✓		✓	Cattle exported	
Ballingry									?		?	Cattle = 'one of principal productions': Dealers	
Balmerino					✓	7.1						Grain and cattle exported	
Beath	✓							✓					
Burntisland					✓		✓				✓	Trade centre	c.1760
Cameron		✓	✓			1.7							
Carnbee		✓	✓		✓	1.4	✓				✓	Cattle exported	
Carnock					✓	7.2			✓		✓	Grain, flax, potatoes exported	c.1760s[1]
Ceres				✓	✓	5.9[2]	✓			✓[3]	✓	Livestock, corn, flax linen, coal, lime exported	c.1750–60
Collessie				✓				✓	✓✓				
Crail	✓					2.0		✓		Burgh of Crail	✓	Potatoes, grain, beans exported: Glasgow[4]	
Creich	✓								✓		✓	Barley exported & wool	

TABLE C (Continued)

Parish	Enclosure Part	Most	All	Unspecified	Industrial presence	% weavers of population	Cottars Exist	Reduction	Consolidation junction of farms	Approx. Villages existing or newly created	Market penetration	Comments	Date of onset of changes
Cults													
Cupar of Fife	✓⁶			✓	✓	6.0⁵				Town	✓	Market centre	c.1770s
Dairsie				✓	✓⁸						✓⁷	Cattle exported	c.1770
Dalgety				✓					✓		✓⁹	Coal exported	c.1770
Denino				✓		1.0							c.1770s
Dunbog							✓						
Dunfermline				✓	✓	9.0		✓		✓¹⁰	✓	Limestone exported and coal. Also cloth?	c.1760
Dysart				✓	✓	12				✓¹¹	✓	Trade centre. Cloth to England	c.1770s
Elie		✓			✓¹³			✓					
Falkland				✓	✓	10.5	✓			✓ Town +	✓	Market centre 4 villages	
Ferry-Port-on-Craig					✓	8.7		✓		✓	✓	Barley and wool exported	
Flisk	No usable data for this parish												
Forgan													
Inverkeithing				✓	✓	1.6	✓			✓ Town+ 1 village	✓	Trade centre	
Kemback													
Kennoway		✓			✓¹⁴					✓	✓	Linen exported: Edinburgh & Stirling	
Kettle	✓			✓	✓	4.4+	✓			✓	✓	Linen exported: Cupar & Auchtermuchty. Corn and cattle exported	c.1788
Kilconquhar					✓¹⁵	4.4	✓			✓ 4 villages	✓	Corn, pease, beans exported	
Kilmany	✓			✓				✓	✓				
Kilrenney													

TABLE C (Continued)

Parish	Enclosure Part	Most	All	Unspecified	Industrial presence	% weavers of population	Cottars Exist	Cottars Reduction	Consolidation/junction of farms	Approx. Villages existing or newly created	Market penetration	Comments	Date of onset of changes
Kinghorn	✓				✓				✓	Town[16]	✓	Corn, livestock exported	
Kinglassie	✓							✓	✓	✓?	✓	Linen, livestock exported	
Kingsbarns						3.7	✓			✓?[17]	✓	Linen, livestock exported	
Kirkcaldy	✓				✓					Town	✓	Market centre?	
Largo			✓			2.1[18]				Town	✓	Cattle exported: Edinburgh and England	
Leslie				✓	✓?					Town	✓		
Leuchars				✓		5.5[19]			✓	✓	✓	Grain, pease, beans exported	
Logie	✓				✓	1.4				✓	✓	Cattle exported?	
Markinch						5.7	✓				✓	Wheat, barley exported	
Monimail				✓		3.2					✓		
Moonzie											✓	Black cattle bred for sale: Cupar	
Newburgh					✓	16.2				Town	✓	Linens etc.: London & Leeds Malted barley: Edinburgh	
Newburn	✓									Town	✓		
Pittenweem	✓					20	✓				✓	Lobsters: London	
St Andrews & St Leonards	✓					1.0	✓				✓		
St Monance	✓				✓[22]	1.2			✓[21]	Burgh	✓	Grain exported	
Saline	✓					1.2					✓	Grain, beans exported	
Scoonie					✓[24]	8.4[23]		✓		✓	✓	Shipping trade centre	
Strathmiglo	✓					5.1[25]		✓	✓	✓	✓	Exports: not specified	
Torryburn				✓	✓[26]						✓		
Wemyss	✓				✓[27]	4.0				[28]	✓	Fish, coal, salt	

TABLE C   (Continued)

| Parish | Enclosure | | | | Industrial presence | % weavers of population | Cottars | | Consolidation junction of farms | Approx. Villages existing or newly created | Market penetration | Comments | Date of onset of changes |
	Part	Most	All	Unspecified			Exist	Reduction					
Totals (60 parishes) 7	15	2	17		29	32 had at least some weavers	14	9	15	29	44		
Percentages	11.7	25	3.3	28.3	48.3	53.3	23.3	15	25	48.3	73.3		
Overall percentage				68.3	48.3	53.3	38.3 either exist or reduced		25	48.3	73.3		

NOTES   1   Manners, customs, dress, etc. of populace has altered within these last '50, or even within these last 20 years'.

2   138 looms = 138 weavers(?) = 5.9%.

3   740 people residing in the 'village', i.e. Ceres.

4   Sent to Glasgow via Forth-Clyde Canal.

5   223 looms = 223 weavers(?) + 37.2 = 6.0%.

6   Dairsie was said to be generally unenclosed which implies some small part was enclosed.

7   Cattle said to bring 6–10 guineas in market at 3–4 years old.

8   Colliery of Sir John Henderson of Fordel.

9   Prices given for 'great numbers of excellent Black Cattle'.

10   3 considerable villages (Pittencrief, Limekilns and Charlestown, built in 1777–8) besides the burgh of Dunfermline – 8 villages in total.

11   At least 4 villages in parish.

12   700–750 looms = c. 725 weavers? = 14.9% *but* 2,000–3,000 people employed in manufactures = 2,500 = 51.4%.

13   No numbers given but there is shipbuilding here, 8 vessels involved in trade to foreign parts, and manufacture of cloth.

14   Weavers and other tradespeople in the village (c. half population in village) as a 'considerable quantity of coarse brown linen is sold … '.

15   'Considerable' number of coalfields in parish.

16   Village of Kinglassie = c. 250 population. No suggestion of 'industry' here.

17   Village of Kingsbarns contains c. half population of parish; 30–40 weavers there.

18   This figure seems to be misleading since the information on pp. 105–6 of the relevant *OSA* volume clearly shows for there to have been a substantial industrial presence in Kirkcaldy.

19   This figure is calculated by assuming that 90 looms = 90 weavers + 1,620 = 5.5%.

20   The account notes that there were 89 handicraftmen = 89 weavers? + 15 apprentices = 104 + 1157 = 8.9% *but* it also states 'No manufactures' here.

21   Number of tenants was said to be decreasing = junction of farms.

22 Coal, salt and fishing.
23 140 looms = 140 weavers? = 8.4%.
24 'Industry' includes fishing, coal, weaving and roperie.
25 '50 Manufacturers' = 50 weavers? = 5.1%.
26 Coal; great body of population are day-labourers, mechanics or sailors.
27 'Industry' includes coal, salt, fish, weaving, spinning, etc.
28 Village in the making – not planned.

TABLE D   Angus.

Parish	Plough technology			Sown Grasses	Turnips	
	Old Scots	Modified	New or Small's		Exist	Extent of cultivation
Airly						
Arbirlot	*					
Arbroath						
Auchterhouse			*		✓	180–200 cattle fattened on turnips p.a.
Barrie				✓[1]	✓	'considerable quantity'
Brechin			✓[2]	✓?[3]	✓	'excellent crops'
Careston				✓[4]	✓	Enough grown to feed 'a great number of cattle'
Cortachy & Clova	✓			✓	✓	for fattening cattle in winter
Craig					✓	'Seldom grown' except in vicinity of Cortachy
Dunn				✓	✓	Used as cattle feed by same
Dundee		✓		✓	✓	Cultivated by at least 1 of the 15 or so farmers
Dunnichen				✓	✓	May(?) have been introduced 30 years ago
Edzell	✓[5]			✓	✓	Raised by everyone to greater or lesser degree
Essie & Nevay	See[6]			✓		
Fern	✓[7]			✓		
Fernell						
Forfar	*					
Glenisla			*		✓	Used in lower part of parish first, now upper also
Guthrie			9		✓	c.2.7% of arable acreage
Inverarity				✓[8]	✓	

TABLE D   (Continued)

Parish	Plough technology			Sown Grasses	Turnips	
	Old Scots	Modified	New or Small's		Exist	Extent of cultivation
Inverkeilor			✓[10] [9]	✓	✓	Common in every part of parish now 'general'
Kingoldrum				✓	✓	
Kinnell	✓[11]			✓[12]	✓	c. 4.1% of *total* acreage
Kinnettles					✓	
Kirkden					✓	
Kirriemuir				✓[13]	✓	
Lethnot					✓	2.5% of arable acreage; turnips introduced in last 20 years
Liff & Bervie				✓	✓	[14]
Lintrathen		✓		✓	✓	
Lochlee	*	*		✓	✓	'lately … introduced'
Logie & Pert	*	*	*	✓		c. 4.1% of *total* acreage used for fallow, turnips, potatoes
Lunan	See[16]			✓[15]	✓	c. 4.6% of *total* acreage in either turnip or cabbage
Lundie & Foulis			✓	✓	✓	
Mains of Fintry			✓[18] ✓	✓[17]	✓	3/5 ground under grass, turnips, kail & potatoes
Maryton	✓			✓	✓	
Menmuir				✓	✓	
Monifeith	See[19]			✓	✓	Introduced in 1753
Monikie		✓		✓	✓	'several acres' raised by farmers each year to fatten cattle
Montrose	See[21]		✓	✓[20]	✓	c. 2.3% of *total* acreage
Muirhouse				✓	✓	'a few', 'Not general'
Newtyle				✓	✓	
Rescobie				✓	✓	
Ruthven	See[22]			✓	✓	c. 2.9% of *total* acreage raised on almost every farm

TABLE D (Continued)

Parish	Plough technology			Sown Grasses	Turnips	
	Old Scots	Modified	New or Small's		Exist	Extent of cultivation
St Vigeans						
Strathmartin		✓[23]		✓	✓	
Strickathrow	See[24]			✓	✓	Rotations include 'a field of turnips'
Tannadice	See[25]		✓			
Tealing				✓	✓	20 acres of flax, turnip and potatoes on every farm

Total number of parishes = 54
Number with Old Scots plough = 5 (9.3%)
Number with Modified plough = 4 (7.4%)
Number with New or Small's plough = 7 (13.0%)
Number with sown grasses = 38 (70.4%)
Number using turnips = 44 (81.5%)

NOTES   * = Both types appear to be used; no indication of which kind predominates.
1 Rye-grass only is mentioned.
2 Small's plough, but drawn by 4 horses.
3 Clover = sown grass?
4 Of the parish's 1,500 acres, 700–800 acres are laid down in grass p.a.
5 Old Scots plough used till lately but now Small's plough is 'introduced'.
6 2–4 horses used per plough = new and old or modified?
7 60 ploughs in total; 40 drawn by 4 horses, 20 by 2 horses = majority of Old Scots?
8 Grass said to occupy c. 32.7% of total arable acreage. This was in addition to pasture lands (quantified in OSA) area. Thus the former was, almost certainly, 'sown' grasses.
9 Plough type not specified, but higher wages induced farmers to do more work with fewer hands.
10 Most are 2-horse ploughs.
11 The 31 ploughs of the parish are all 3- or 4-horse ones.
12 'Cutting grass' acreage is given separately to pasture acreage, thus = sown grass?
13 Red and white clover and rye-grass = 12% of arable acreage.

14 In 1793 'some plots of turnip ... sown grass appear ... '. In 1799, the parish had at least 600 acres in 'proper culture', i.e. using turnip and sown grass in new rotations.

15 33.3% of total acreage in sown grasses.

16 The 16 ploughs are drawn by 4 horses or oxen which usually suggests the old 'Scots' plough, *BUT* in seedtime they are drawn by only 2 horses which suggests a new or at least modified plough.

17 'Grass' is part of a 5-year rotation (which includes turnips) on *c.* one-third of arable land. This implies 'sown' grass.

18 Most ploughs are drawn by 2 horses.

19 Farms have ploughs drawn by 2–4 horses, whereas before they used 10 oxen for draught. Thus, new ones = modified ?Scots.

20 *c.* 32.5% of total acreage in sown or artificial grasses.

21 37 horse ploughs and only 3 cattle ploughs suggests move to a modified or new type but this is not specified.

22 In 1742 in Ruthven, there were 31 ploughmen and 86 'work-cattle'. In 1792 there were 37 ploughmen but no work-cattle. The number of work-horses had only increased by 2 to 52 by the latter year.

23 Scots ploughs drawn by 2 horses; worked by 1 man.

24 The 'ordinary' sort of plough used.

25 Ploughs made 'after the best form'.

TABLE E Ayrshire.

Parish	Plough technology			Sown Grasses	Turnips	
	Old Scots	Modified	New or Small's		Exist	Extent of cultivation
Auchinleck					No	
Ayr				√		
Beith				√		
Colmonell		√?[1]				
Craigie				√	No	
Old Cumnock				'Few'		
Daily				√	√	'introduced last year'
Dalry	√		2	√	√	'2 Farmers have used'
Dreghorn				√		
Dunlop	√?[3]			√		
Galston				√	?	soil well adapted for turnips, but little yet raised
Girvan				√	√	On 1 farm
Kilmaurs				√	No	'Never sown'
Kilwinning		√?[4]		√		

TABLE E (Continued)

Parish	Plough technology			Sown Grasses	Turnips	
	Old Scots	Modified	New or Small's		Exist	Extent of cultivation
Kirkoswald						
Largs	✓				✓	'little practised' except for Lord Cassilis
Loudoun						
Monkton &		✓				
Prestwick			✓⁵	✓	✓	'just beginning'
St Quivox	✓			✓		
Storm				✓⁶		
Stair				✓	✓	
Stevenson				✓	✓	'Never attempted'
Symington	✓⁷			✓	✓	'sown in small quantities'
Tarbolton				✓	✓	Not fully established but increasing

Total number of parishes = 46

Number with Old Scots plough = 5 (10.9%)
Number with Modified plough = 3 (6.5%)
Number with New or Small's plough = 2 (4.3%)
Number using sown grasses = 18 (39.1%)
Number using turnips = 9 (19.6%)

NOTES   1 'Chiefly of light Scottish sort'.
2 'Some gentlemen who practise fallowing and turnip farming have English and East country ploughs of light construction'.
3 System of ploughing uses 4 horses + 3 men = Old Scots.
4 Scotch plough 'of the lightest and best kind' generally used. This uses 3–4 horses and 1 man, 1 boy.
5 Plough 'after the English form' using 3 or 2 horses.
6 Introduced in 1737.
7 Drawn by 3 horses.

TABLE G   Fife.

Parish	Plough technology			Sown Grasses	Turnips	
	Old Scots	Modified	New or Small's		Exist	Extent of cultivation
Abbot's Hall		✓ ½	✓ ½	✓[1]	✓	2.7% of *total* acreage in turnip and cabbage
Abdie	✓[3]		✓[2]		[4]	
Aberdour	✓[5]				✓	'some turnips and cabbages are introduced'
Anstruther Wester				✓	✓	c. 2.3% of *total* acreage in turnips and cabbage
Auchterderran				✓	✓	c.3.2% of *total* acreage in turnips and cabbage
Auchtermuchty				✓[6]	✓	
Auchtertool	*		*	✓[7]	✓	
Ballingry			✓	✓	✓	usually a 'heavy crop'
Balmerino			✓	✓?[8]	✓	
Beath			✓		✓	on every farm
Carnbee			✓	✓[9]	✓	1/7 of arable = turnips and fallow
Carnock	✓			✓	✓	
Ceres			✓	✓	✓	
Crail			✓[10]	✓	✓	
Cults			✓[11]	✓	✓	
Cupar			✓[12]	✓	✓	only recently introduced
Dairsie				✓[13]	✓	increased much of late as cattle fodder
Dalgety				✓[14]	✓	
Denino	*		*	✓[15]	✓	c.2.5% of arable acreage
Dunfermline				✓	✓	c.0.9% of *total* acreage
Dysart			✓	✓	✓	'No great quantities'
Falkland			✓		✓	raised in small quantities
Ferry-Port-on-Craig				✓	✓	
Forgan				✓	✓	soil much adapted turnips
Inverkeithing			✓[16]			
Kemback			✓	✓	✓	on every farm
Kennoway				✓[17]	✓	'every farm raises'
Kettle						

TABLE G (Continued)

Parish	Plough technology			Sown Grasses	Turnips	
	Old Scots	Modified	New or Small's		Exist	Extent of cultivation
Kilconquhar			✓	✓	✓	'very general'
Kilmany			✓[18]	✓[19]	✓	c.3.6% of arable acreage
Kinghorn			✓		✓	c.3.3% of *total* acreage in turnips and potatoes
Kinglassie	See[20]				✓	
Kingsbarns					✓	
Kirkcaldy		✓		✓[21]	✓	c.4.2% of arable acreage successfully raised
Largo				✓	✓	
Leslie				✓	✓	raised for young stock
Leuchars			✓	✓	✓	in considerable quantities
Logie	✓[22]			✓	✓	turnip husbandry is spreading
Markinch		✓[23]			✓	
Monimail	See[24]			✓	?	Turnips little used as yet
Newburgh					✓	Introduced many years ago
Newburn				✓		
Pittenweem				✓		
St Andrews & St Leonards			✓[25]	✓	✓	
St Monance			✓	✓	✓	to rear young cattle
Scoonie			✓	✓	✓	
Torryburn					✓	
Wemyss					✓	

Total number of parishes = 60

Number with Old Scots Plough = 4 (6.7%)
Number with Modified plough = 2 (3.3%)
Number with New or Small's plough = 23 (38.3%)
Number using sown grasses = 37 (61.7%)
Number using turnips = 39 (65%)

NOTES 1 Sown grass accounts for 5.2% of *total* acreage of parish.
2 2-horse ploughs are most usual = new kind?
3 Old Scots plough in general use, though Small's plough is introduced.
4 Root crops used – not specified.
5 Small's plough is introduced but 34 of the total of 51 ploughs are still drawn by oxen.
6 Sown grasses account for *c.*6.7% of *total* acreage.
7 Sown grasses account for *c.*6.3% of *total* acreage.
8 Farmers said to lay a lot of ground down in grass = sown grasses?
9 ¹/₇ in sown grasses (i.e. of arable land).
10 Mostly 2-horse ploughs are used.
11 Instruments of husbandry are of the 'Newest and best construction'.
12 Every 2 ploughs is said to employ 3 men: 2 for the ploughs, 1 for barn work = new or Small's ploughs?
13 *c.*15.3% of arable acreage in sown grass and hay.
14 *c.*10% of *total* acreage in sown grasses.
15 'hay' like turnips, is sown in 'No great quantities'.
16 'Of best construction' = new ploughs?
17 'Grass for hay' and 'Arable pasture for hay' suggests sown grasses?
18 All ploughs are drawn by two horses.
19 Hay acreage = 10.8% of arable total; this is separate from pasture (27.4%) = sown grasses?
20 Whereas cattle were used for draught for plough 'some years ago', now horses are used. Number of these and type of plough are not specified.
21 Sown grass = 54.8% of arable acreage (62.6% with clover).
22 2-horse ploughs.
23 Also, English plough is fast coming into use.
24 The ploughs are made to different designs.
25 Ridges are straightened.

Appendix 10

Tenant Structure, Hamilton Estate, Lanarkshire, 1680–1810

Column 2: Tacks. Extracted from NRA(S) 2177, Hamilton Papers, 1134–6. May not include all tenants.

Column 3: Renewals. Date of renewal listed if included in sources for Column 1. Black line continues to Column 4 if name appears in 1738 rental – it does not mean that tack has been constantly renewed through those years, only that name appearing in early tacks does so again in 1738 rental.

Column 4: 1738 Rental. Note: in barony of Dalserf the date on this column changes to 1740 rental.

Column 5: 1745. This is a list of tenants provided for Murray's requisition of horses for Prince Charles Edward Stuart in October 1745. NRA(S) 2177/397.

Column 6: 1747–9 List of those tenants delivering meal to Duke's girnels 1747–9. NRA(S) 2177/386. Dotted lines = n/d for that barony.

Column 7: 1758 Rental. Thick black lines = tenant issued with summons of removing in 1760s. NRA(S) 2177, E1.59 and SRO, SC37.8.7.

Column 8: From lists of arrears 1762 and 1769. These lists obviously may not include all the tenants. NRA(S) 2177/778; E1.75

Column 9: 1774 is drawn from any reference to the tenant or the farm in the Burrell Journals before 1778. Useful for indication of change but not as reliable as rental.

Column 10: Rental 1778.

Column 11: Rental 1795.

Column 12: From list of rents uplifted 1809–may not be complete. NRA(S) 2177/E.3.89

Column 13: As above, 1817 may not be complete but probably is.

Complete line indicates tenant's name appearing in each list – even if change of first name indicates son or other near-relative. Change of name, of course, could indicate a son-in-law – might be the case in Darngaber, for example, in Hamilton barony in 1795 where Torrance is replaced by Hamilton but reappears in 1809. Dotted lines indicate tenant's name does not appear in that particular list but may reappear later *or* that there is no list of that date for that particular farm or barony. Vertical line indicates termination of tenancy.

Hamilton barony

1 Farm	2 Tacks		3 Renewals	4 1738	5 1745	6 1747-9	7 1758	8 1762-9	9 1774	10 1778	11 1795	12 1809	13 1817
Allanton	Forrest	1710						Corbet					
	Naismith	1710		Burns / Law		Muir							
Merryton	Hinshaw	1713											
	Frame	1714										Greenshiels	Alston
	Boyd												
	Brownlie	1714											
	Watt	1707											
	Cuthbert	1709			Lawson		Corbet						
	Hamilton				Wilson								
	Burns	1710											
	Burns												
Quarter	Haddow	1714					Robertson		Frame		Henderson		
	Galder	1714											
	Wilson (W)	1714											
	Wilson (J)	1707	1726										
Thinacres	J. Clark	1713				Haddow	Wardrop			Russel / Hamilton		Bell	
	J. Paterson	1713				Nielson				Russel			
	G. Burn	1714					Alston	Boyd					
	Alston		1732										
	Barrie	1715		Davidson									
	J. Brown	1715		Loudon				Semple					
	A. Burn	1715											
	Semple	1712		R. Arbuckle	Naismith	Meikle							
Crooked stone	Wilson				Campbell			(5 tenants 1769–)					
	Carscallen	1713		W. Fleming									

Hamilton barony (Continued)

1 Farm	2 Tacks	3 Renewals	4 1738	5 1745	6 1747–9	7 1758	8 1762–9	9 1774	10 1778	11 1795	12 1809	13 1817
	J. Wilson 1713								Hamilton 1780	Lindsay		Barr
	J. Mackie 1713											
	J. Torrance 1713											
	Jas. Machie 1711	1731										
	A. Torrance 1715											
Crooked stone Muir												
Brounted	A. Lang 1714		Wilson		Yuill					Lindsay	Herries	Herries Hamilton
Carscallen	A. Yuill 1712 Myreton		Wilson				J. Mackie		Steel	Lindsay Bannatyne	Herries Bannatyne	
	Hamilton J. 1713		Curr			Corbet	Yuill 1772		Faulds			
	T. Hamilton 1714											
	J. Somers 1714											
	J. Lang 1716			Wilson		Wilson		Langmoor		Wallace	Steven	
Clydeside												
Ricarton	J. Adie 1709	1728	J. Scott			J. Hamilton	(subdivision 1766)	Cuthbertson	A. Gray			
Bog	W. Reid 1710	1728	A. Smith		A. Wilson			Burns 1776		Hamilton	Frame	
Dykehead								Burns 1776				
Bettopyards			J. Hamilton									
Wellbog			J. Yuill			Renwick		J. Yuill				
Darngables	J. Wilson 1702	1725	J. Torrance				Torrance			Hamilton	Boyes	
Burnbrae	R. Hamilton 1685	1716				J. Mackie				Hamilton	Torrance	Reid
Airybog	J. Lawson 1714						1768		Patterson	J. Dick		
	W. Fleming 1711											
Muirhouses	J. Granger 1725	Struthers								Kirkland	Boyes	
	Fairsorbie	Meikle										

Hamilton barony (Continued)

1 Farm	2 Tacks	3 Renewals	4 1738	5 1745	6 1747–9	7 1758	8 1762–9	9 1774	10 1778	11 1795	12 1809	13 1817
Blackbeg	Renwick 1708	1725					Syme			Brownlie	Smith	
Thornhill	Dick 1709		Golder		Turnbull	Cunison				Hepburn	Mackie	
Chappell	Frain 1706		Naismith									
Simpson land	Wilson 1715 Cuthbert 1716					Corbet			Henderson			
Cornhills	Yuill 1709 Syme 1714	1733	Torrance				Robertson, Patricks	Patricks		Patricks	Hamilton Nielson?	
Dueshill	Fram 1733			Subtenant Hamilton		Arneil			1780 { Gilchrist Dick			
Over Holl-andbush	Cuthbert 1714		Paterson									McGhee
Burnblay	Hinshaw 1710		Sellars	Mackie		Cunison						
Bent	Somervell 1714		Hamilton									
Craigs	McMath 1707		Miller Mathie Smith									
Woodneuk Milns			Paterson			Corbet			Alston McGhie	Wilson		
Clydebridge			Town of Hamilton Boyd			Town of Hamilton			Gray			
Haughland Boatland			Jackson Naismith			Clark Muir	Town of Hamilton			Hamilton		
Calder Inch			Orbiston		Dalziel							

Cambuslang barony

1 Farm	2 Tacks	3 Renewals	4 1738	5 1745	6 1747–9	7 1753	8 1762–9	9 1774	10 1778–9	11 1795	12 1809
Lettrick	14 tenants 1682. E1. 32		Cooper A.						Fisher		Craig
			Hogg, John						Peddie, J.		Morse
			Cook J.				Waddles		Wipur		Hamilton
			Love						Duncan		
			Brown				Maxwell		Brown, G.		
			Turnbull				Young		Peddie, T.		
			Bouse						Barcklay		
			Miller						Jackson		
			Dick						Struthers		
			Hamilton						Subtenants 1777		
			Cowper								
			Hogg, John				Muirhead				
Flemington	12 tenants 1682 E1.32		Murray's re.					1765 →	Jackson		
			Cook, J.			Hamilton				Kerr 1797	
			Cowper, R.							Gemmell	
			Craig								
			Yuill, J.								
			Jackson								
			Cook, J.								
			Summers								
			Yuill, J.								
			Bryce								
			Anderson								

Cambuslang barony (Continued)

1 Farm	2 Tacks	3 Renewals	4 1738	5 1745	6 1747-9	7 1753	8 1762-9	9 1774	10 1778-9	11 1795	12 1809	
Hallside	12 tenants 1682 E1.32		Dunning Strang Miller Scott Bowman Turnbull, J. *Turnbull, R. Lindsay			Paterson	Gourlay		Murdochs Murdoch	Gemmell	Boyes	Patterson and Turnbull claim their fathers had tacks from 1727 and 1707 respectively
Ridloes W. Greenlees	5 tenants 1682 E1 32		Turnbull, R. Hamilton			Donald	Greig	Dick	Bowman		Hamilton	
Turnlaw	2 tenants 1662		Arbuckle Dick						Pollock	Graham	Boyes	
Clydesmiln		4 other smallholdings in 1738	Riddle			Beecham						
Westburn Newton Cathleine			Hamilton Hamilton McLae									

Bothwell Muir barony

1 Farm	2 Tacks 1681	3 Renewals	4 1738	5 1745	6 1747-9	7 1753	8 1762-9	9 1774	10 1778-9	11 1795	12 1809	
Mid Bracco	Russell & Storie Whitelaw		Russell only					Johnston/ Forrest	Storry	Brownlie		J. Nole sub-tenant 1774. Ref. to M. Johnstone – subtenant 1774? 1784–subtenants (2) Brock and Brown
Forrest	Russel Russel		Whitelaw			Russell Mack/ Marshall	/Burns	Burns/ Forrest				Subtenant Gardner 1774
Muirhead	Thomson Russell Maxwell		Marshall W. Maxwell			Hamilton Dick	Pender				Boyes	2 subtenants and cottar 1774
Dunteelan	Hamilton Fairlie Mack Meek Stuart					Ures Baillie	Marshall		Reid Meek		Boyes	

Bothwell Muir barony (Continued)

1 Farm	2 Tacks	3 Renewals	4 1738	5 1745	6 1747–9	7 1753	8 1762–9	9 1774	10 1778–9	11 1795	12 1809	
Moffathills	Walker								Jaffrey			16 subtenants 1765 – T12
Nether Braco	Waddel 1681		Cook	Storrie		Walker	Barrie		Wilson	Waddel		1 cottar 1774
	W. Russell											
	J. Russell											
	Bell/W. Russell											
Shot House	Story		Marshall	Orr		Hamilton	Barrie		Weir	Orr	Lethan	1745 Ward-rope and Allan sub-tenants
F'burn Mill	Russell		Millar			Meek	Millar					
N. Linrig			Baillie				Cleland	Lang, W.	Lang, W.	Main	Boyes	
Barblews								Main	Walker, J.		Shanks	
Annieshill								Lang, R.	Lang, R.			
Lochrig									Walker			
Dykeneuk												
Braefoot			Thomsons			Storrie	Whitelaw	Downs	Downs		Waddell	removed 1780?
Peatpots												

Lesmahagow

1 Farm	2 Tacks	3 Renewals	4 1738	5 1745	6 1747-9	7 1751-8	8 1762-9	9 1774	10 1778-9	11 1795	12 1809
Draffan	1712 Hamilton, Alex.										
	Brown, T.										
	Hamilton, And.			Watson		Torrence	Morton	J. Thompson		Cunninghams	
	Young			Brown		Hamilton, J.					
	Baird			Boyd, G.		Hamilton, W.					
	Shirrilaw										
	Weir										
	McGie										
Southfield	Hamilton, J.					Lawson		Hamilton			
	Findlay, T.										
	Findlay, T.										
O'r O'gemmell	Miller								Steel	Weir	
	Hamilton										
	Swan										
Keses A'gemmell Nether	Somervell					Stewart		Allan		Brown	
A'gemmell Barsteads	Smith			Hamilton				Stuart		Porteous	
	Sharp							Cleland	Steel		
Auchnotrick	Young's relict										
Auchenheath	Tulop			Thomson						Scott	
Bankhead	Weir, R.			Young							
Connelholm	Weir, R.			Porteous						?	
	Thomson										

Lesmahagow (Continued)

1 Farm	2 Tacks	3 Renewals	4 1738	5 1745	6 1747-9	7 1751-8	8 1762-9	9 1774	10 1778-9	11 1795	12 1809
Burnbrae	Porteous, G. & W.			Tulop		Pate				Haddows	
Bogside	Meikle			Swan				Steel			
Shaucroft	Smith, W.										
Underbank	Stewart, T.								Thomson	Stuart	
Woodside	Stewart, T.					Thomson		Burton	Thomson	Thomson	
Hillend	Hodgen			Cleland, T.					Thomson	Brown	
Righead	Hedgen			Cleland, T.				Scott			
Halhill	Cleland, T. / Cleland, J.										
Canderwatter	Sheires							Thomson	Steel	Weir	
Muirsland	Mack and Weir			Weir only							
Garselwood	Stodhart					Hamilton		Stodd(art?)		Pate	
Wellburn	Wood					Henderson				Peacock	
Whythill	Muir										
Clannochdyke	Partt										
Langlands	Tweedale										
Niveland &	Aitken &										
Knockan	Porteous							Porteous			
Milnton	Mair					Torrance	Clerkson		Burton	Steel	
Mains	Mair										
Waterside	Weir			Brown		Steel, W.	Haddow				
Auchtool	Greenshiels							Clerkson	Stevenson	Duncan	
Boreland	Leins			Smith						Swann	
Corrowmiln	Porteous / Muir and Shirrilaw			Cleland and Shearer		Watson / Burton	Morton	Watson	McGhie	Allan	
Collingair	Shearer			?		Wilson and Meikles	Wilson	McGhee		Somervell	
Watson	Mutters							McGhee		Mutters	
Abbey Green	15 houses and yards				6 houses and yards	8 houses and yards			11 houses and yards	6 houses and yards	

Avendale barony

1 Farm	2 Tacks 1719	3 Renewals	4 1738	5 1745	6 1747-9	7 1751-8	8 1762-9	9 1774	10 1778-9	11 1795	12 1809
Mains Acres	Fraser, J.										
	Currie, W.								Cochrane		
	Arkle, G.								Morton –		
	Hamilton, Agnes					Law, W. –					
	Cullen, J.					Watson, R.–	Steel, W.		Thomson		
	Wilson, T.					Semple, W.–	Scott →				
	Mack, A.					Fleming, W.	Tennant – →				
	Hamilton, Alex.					Lochore, J.					
	Marshall, A.					Scott, R.	Morton		Marshall		
	Hamilton, J.					Semple, G.					
	Park, J.					Leaper					
	Stuart, J.					Lochore – →					
	Knox, J.					Lochore – →					
Houkhead	Morison							Miller	Kirkland	Muir	
	Brownlie										
Gallowhill	Allason, W.					Steel – →	Lieper & Scott		Hamilton		
	Allason, G.				Weir	Brown – →					
	Fleming, A.										
Netherside	Thomson, A.									Paterson	
Floors	Thomson, J.						Steel, W.			Kerton	
Straven Mills	Thomson, J.			Young, J.		Struthers	Thomson, J.				
Overhouses	Allason, J.					Young, J.				Findlay	
	Morton, J.										

Avendale barony (Continued)

1 Farm	2 Tacks	3 Renewals	4 1738	5 1745	6 1747-9	7 1751-8	8 1762-9	9 1774	10 1778-9	11 1795	12 1809
Threestairs	Lawson. J.										
Newhouses	Riddle, W. / Young. J.					Fleming	Brownlie		Wilson	Semple, Anderson, Jackson	
Townhead	Archibald. J.					Thomson. M.			13 houses	13 houses	
Meadowpolls	Cochrane. J.					Lochore, A.	Tennent. A.				
Overcaldcoats	Wilson. J. / Hamilton. R.					Struthers	Fleming				
Overcaldcoats and Lockhart											With Gallow-fester 1795
Mill	Fleming, J.					Hamilton Fleming					
Syde	Willock, J.					Young. W.					
Longrighead	Morison / Stiell, A.			Loudon			Tenant, N.		Craig. J.		
Hill	1717 Miller, W.										
Overholm	Miller, W.					Young. W.	Lindsay		Brownlie	Thompson	
New Milne	Millers					Leiper			Craig. J.		
Mains	Young. W.								(waste)	Paterson	
Glengavel											
Mill	Reid								Craig. J.		
Bankend	Craig. J.						Mather	Arbuchkle. J.			
Bent	Allason, W.					Struthers, A.	Fleming				
Martinholm	Richmont, wife of Anderson			Struthers, A.		Morton, A.			Patterson		
Plewlands	Muir, A.					Craig	Nicol				
Drumclog	Muir, H. and J. / Muir, J. / Cochrane. A. / Young. J.					Granger, W.					

Avendale barony (Continued)

1 Farm	2 Tacks	3 Renewals	4 1738	5 1745	6 1747–9	7 1751–8	8 1762–9	9 1774	10 1778–9	11 1795	12 1809
Stoneyhill	Torrance, J.					Wilson, J.				Wilson	
Middle Row	Hamilton, J. Din, J.			Boyd, E. Struthers Paterson Struthers							
Nr. Creuburn	Riddel, J.							Arbuckle	Scoutar Scoutar		
Snab	Brownlie, T.						Arbuckle Meikle				
Gallowfester	Craig, W.								Fleming, J.	Young	
North Halls	Hamilton, J.									Young, W.	
South Halls	Hamilton, G.			Whyte, T.		Anderson and Morrison			Fleming, A.		
Hallmoss	Morton, J.										
Overhalkwood	Baird, J. Craig, J.			Fleming, R.							
Nether Over Halkwood	Browning, W.			Wilcox, A. Fleming and Wilson, W. Inglis, G.		Fleming, J.					
Garnerhill	Small, J.					Wilson, W.					
Nether Houses	Lochore, J.							Granger			
Kaine	Farrower, J.										
Holme	Morton, W.			Miller			Wilson, A.				
Goodsburn	Young, R.						Tennant, A.			Craig	
Netherholm	Young, J.										
Fieldhead	Robb, A.			Leiper		Dykes, A.					

Dalserf barony

1 Farm	2 Tacks / 3 Renewals	4 1740	5 1747-9	6 1758	7 1769	8 1774	9 1778-9	10 1795	11 1809
Skellyton		Bruce, R.							Boyes
		Hamilton, W.							
		Hamilton, A.							
Cornsulloch		Forrester, J.		McDowall, A.	Bell, J.				Holmes, J. / J. inc. Hamilton
		Hamilton, J			subtenant				
Dalpatrick		Brown, J.		Stewart, W.				Peter, J.	
		Frame, J.							
		Couper, R.							
		Smith, A.							
Overton		Watson, G.		Gilkerson, J.		Weir, W.	Hamiltons		Boyes
		Gouder, J.							
		Gray, J.							
		Faiket, J.							
		Morton, J.							
Westerhills		McDowall, A.		Corbet, A.			Leiper and Hamilton		
Esterhills		Bruce, J.					Hamilton, J.	Templeton	Templeton
Over Dalserf		Scott, R.		Shearer, T.	Couper, W.				Thomson
Dalbeg		Hamilton, B.		Stewart, W.	Law, J.			Templeton	
Muirhead etc.		Hamilton, G.							
Greenhill		Hamilton, W.					Smillie, T.		Boyes
Greenhill B'field		Brownlie, R			Fram, J.				
		Bell, J.							
Rayhills		Hastie, R.		Hamilton, A. with Oveton	Henderson, J.				with C'syde
Netherburn		Rennick, A.							
Clydesmiln		Gray, J.					Craig, G.	with Overtoun	
Whitehill		Thomson, J.							

Dalserf barony (Continued)

1 Farm	2 Tacks	3 Renewals	4 1740	5 1747-9	6 1758	7 1769	8 1774	9 1778-9	10 1795	11 1809
Overwood			Shearer, T. ¼		½ with Rayhill		Lawrie, R.	Hamilton, R.	Watts	Mather
Lochead			– ½ each							Kerr, J.
Doversdale			Law, A. ¼							Smellie, T.
Cannermains			Mutter, J.					Wilson, T.	Thomson, J.	Hogg, J.
Cannermiln			Hogg, R.						Purdie	
Cannasyde and Windymailer			Forrest, J.		Watt, J.		Miller, T.		Smillie, T.	

Appendix 11

References to Improvements on Hamilton Estate, 1765–85

Column 1: 'Planning' includes any farm on which enclosure/partial enclosure or major reorganisation was planned by Burrell or the estate.

Column 2: includes any farm which was 'staked out' for fencing or division by John Burrell or the surveyors.

Column 3: includes any farm on which the process of enclosing was taking place during the years indicated; refers to any examples of fencing, dyking or 'inclosing'.

Column 4: refers to any farm on which enclosure was complete by the year or years indicated.

Column 5: includes any farm on which subdivision (i.e. internal division of fields) was taking place during the years indicated.

Column 6: refers to any farm on which subdivision is known to be completed by the years indicated.

Column 7: includes any farm on which there is a reference to hedges or fences; these could be hedges and fences which were in place prior to Burrell's reorganisation. The fact that these numbers are higher in some baronies (e.g. Cambuslang and Hamilton) than those of previous columns suggests that extent of enclosure may have been greater than indicated by these previous columns. The reader should bear in mind that the tabulation is based on casual references to enclosure and not on a report or reports of progress.

Column 8: includes any farm on which enclosure is known *not* to have been completed by the date indicated, e.g. when a tenant claimed an allowance on rent for 'want of inclosing'.

TABLE A

Barony	Farm		(1) Planning	(2) Staking out	(3) Enclosing	(4) Enclosed	(5) Subdividing	(6) Subdivided	(7) References to hedges/fences	(8) Not completed by
Hamilton	Chappel	1		1765		1783			1778√	1783
	Thorniehill	1		1765		1783			1778√	1883
	Blackbog	1		1765		1783			1778√	1783
	Merryton	M	1765	1773	1774				1778√	1783
	Merryton Field		1783	1775						
	Riccarton	2		1776						
	Allanton	2	1765	1768	1768		1768		1778√	
	Cornhills	1		1768	1769	1769			1768	
				1772	1775–8				1778	1778
	Crooked stone	M		1773	1775				1770	1780 (South)
									1778 & 1783√	1795 (out field)
	Thinacres	M	1770		1775				1778√	1777
									1783√	
	Muirhouses	2								
	Boghead	1		1773	1775				1778	
	Carscallen	M	1772	1773	1774				1778	1774
									1783√	
	Darngaber	1		1773	1774				1783	
	Burnbrae	1		1773					1783	
	Browntod	1		1773						
	Killhill	1		1773					1778	
	Dykhead & Begg	1	1765		1769				1769	
					1771				1778	
	Shotlin	1	1783						1778	1777

TABLE A (Continued)

Barony	Farm		(1) Planning	(2) Staking out	(3) Enclosing	(4) Enclosed	(5) Subdividing	(6) Subdivided	(7) References to hedges/fences	(8) Not completed by
Waterside	(Parks)								1778	1776
	Quarter	M							1783	1778
Airybog		2	1768–70						1783	1770
Cambuslang	Flemington	M	1765		1765		1765	1767	1783√	1776 & 1783
	Dechmont hill	M			1767				1783√	
	Lettrick	M			1771	1769(pt) 1774 1783				
	Hallside	M	1765 1773 1776	1780					1783√	1774–1780
	Motherwell			1775						1780
	Motherwell Muir			1774						
	W. Greenlees	1	1772		1775 1779		1774		1783√ 1768 1781√ & 1783	
	Turnlaw	2								1775
Dalserf	Skellyton	M	1765 1773		1765				1778√ 1783√ 1778√	
	Broomfield	1	1765					1777		
	Netherburn	1	1765		1774					
	Cornsulloch	M	1765		1765	1783 (mostly)			1783	1774

TABLE A (Continued)

Barony	Farm	(1) Planning	(2) Staking out	(3) Enclosing	(4) Enclosed	(5) Subdividing	(6) Subdivided	(7) References to hedges/fences	(8) Not completed by
	Muirhead	1	1770						
	Burnhead		1773 1770 1773						
	Greenhill		1770 1773	1769					1779–83
	Dalpatrick	M	1773	1782	1784 (part)				1784
	Overtoun	M	1773	1781	1784 (56 acres)			1783√	1784
	Highlees	1	1773	1775				1783√	1780
	Canarmains	1		1779		1778		1778√	1780
	Whitehill			1775	1781 (half)			1778√	
	Clydesmiln	1							1780
	Over Dalserf	1768							1784
	Overwood	1783		1775				1778√	1781
	Dovesdale	1		1775				1778√	1778
	Milnton	1						1778√	
	Cannarside	1	1770			1770		1778√	1782
Arendale	Townhead	1768		1769	1770		1770		
	Goodburn	1							1769
	Meadowpots	1							1769
	Overholm	1							1769
	Creuburn	1						1769 & 1778√	1775

TABLE A (Continued)

Barony	Farm	(1) Planning	(2) Staking out	(3) Enclosing	(4) Enclosed	(5) Subdividing	(6) Subdivided	(7) References to hedges/fences	(8) Not completed by
	Hoolzhead	M						1769 & 1778√	
	Bent	1						1769	
	Drumclog	M						1769	
	Mains Acres	M 1768, 1770						1778√	1785
Townhead	Mailen	1 1770							
	Floors	1 1768							
	W. Caldcotes	2 1783			1772			1778√	1775 & 1783
	Fishes Coats	1768		1769		1774			1774
	Mid Coats	1768		1772		1774			1774
	E. Greenlees	1768	1772			1774		1783√	1774
Lesmahagow	Garrelwood	1	1770					1778√	1775
	Muirsland	1	1770						1784
	Wellburn	1	1770			1770			
	Clannoch dyke	1	1770						
	Langlands	1	1770					1778	
	Watston	1	1770			1770		1778	1775
	Draffan	M 1780	1770					1783√	
	Southfield	M	1770	1775, 1779					
	Canarmuir	1	1770	1774				1778√	1783
	Bogside	1	1770					1778√	
	Burnbrae	1	1770						

TABLE A (Continued)

Barony	Farm	(1) Planning	(2) Staking out	(3) Enclosing	(4) Enclosed	(5) Subdividing	(6) Subdivided	(7) References to hedges/fences	(8) Not completed by
	Auchty gemmel	M	1771–2					1778	1776
	Auchenheath Woods								
	Acknotrick	2 1772	1770					1778√	1772
	Bairsteads	1	1770					1778√	1776
	Hallkith	2	1770					1778√	
	Connelholm	1	1770						
	Woodside	1	1770					1778√	
	Hillend	1	1770						1774
	Underbank	1	1770						1774
	Southfield Common								
	Candowater	1	1773						
	Kniveland	1		1764				1783	1785
	Achtool	1							1776
	Righead	1		1777				1778	1778
	Peatpots	1779							
	Moffathills	2 1765	1765	1765					1774
Bothwell Muir	Muirhead	M		1769					
	N. Linrig	1		1769					
	Barblews	1			1774				
	Braco	3		1775					
	Shots	1		1775					
	Dykenook	1							1777

TABLE A (Continued)

Barony	Farm	(1) Planning	(2) Staking out	(3) Enclosing	(4) Enclosed	(5) Subdividing	(6) Subdivided	(7) References to hedges/fences	(8) Not completed by
Kilbride	Rodgerton	1		1775	1780				1785(?)
	Pielpark	1		1779	1765				
	Shielburn	2*			1769				
	Lickprevick	2			1769				
Bothwell	Woodhead								
	Haugh	1		1765					
	Raith			1769					
Kinniel	Mummerels	1769	1770	1772	1769				
	Hill Farm				1769				
	Roustead					1769			
	Bonhard	1771	1772						

TABLE B

Barony	Farm	(1) Planning out	(2) Staking out	(3) Enclosing	(4) Enclosed	(5) Subdividing	(6) Subdivided	(7) References to hedges/fences	(8) Not completed by
Summary: Hamilton (34 farms in rental)	1765–70	4	6	3				3	
	1771–5	2	10	8	1(pt.)				
	1776–80			1				13	
	1781–5				3			6	
	Total	6	16 (47%)	12	3½	1		22 (64.7%)	
Cambuslang (7 farms in rental)	1765–70	2		1	2	2		1	
	1771–5	2	2	2	1	1	1		
	1776–80	1	1	1			1		
	1781–5				1			5	
	Total	5	3 (43%)	4	4	3	2	6 (86%)	
Dalserf (22 farms in rental)	1765–70	5	4	3		1			
	1771–5		6	5					
	1776–80			1	4	1	1	8	
	1781–5	1		2				4	
	Total	6	10 (45%)	11	4	2	1	12 (55%)	
Arendale (42 farms in rental)	1765–70	5		1	1			7	
	1771–5								
	1776–80							2	
	1781–5	1				1	1		
	Total	6 (14%)		1	1		1	9 (21%)	

TABLE B

Barony	Farm	(1) Planning out	(2) Staking out	(3) Enclosing	(4) Enclosed	(5) Subdividing	(6) Subdivided	(7) References to hedges/fences	(8) Not completed by
Summary:									
Hamilton (34 farms in rental)	1765–70	4	6	3	1(pt.)	1		3	
	1771–5	2	10	8				13	
	1776–80			1	3			6	
	1781–5								
	Total	6	16 (47%)	12	3½	1		22 (64.7%)	
Cambuslang (7 farms in rental)	1765–70	2		1	2	2	1	1	
	1771–5	2	2	2	1	1			
	1776–80	1	1	1	1		1	5	
	1781–5								
	Total	5	3 (43%)	4	4	3	2	6 (86%)	
Dalserf (22 farms in rental)	1765–70	5	4	3		1		8	
	1771–5		6	5				4	
	1776–80			1		1	1		
	1781–5	1		2	4				
	Total	6	10 (45%)	11	4	2	1	12 (55%)	
Arendale (42 farms in rental)	1765–70	5		1	1		1	7	
	1771–5							2	
	1776–80	1							
	1781–5								
	Total	6 (14%)		1	1	1	1	9 (21%)	

TABLE B (Continued)

Barony	Farm	(1) Planning out	(2) Staking out	(3) Enclosing	(4) Enclosed	(5) Subdividing	(6) Subdivided	(7) References to hedges/fences	(8) Not completed by
Lesmahagow (36 farms in rental)	1765-70	1	18	1		2			
	1771-5	1	2	1					
	1776-80			2	1			11	
	1781-5							2	
	Total	2	20(56%)	4	1	2		13(36%)	
Bothwell Muir (15 farms in rental)	1765-70	1							
	1771-5		1	3	1				
	1776-80	1		2					
	1781-85								
	Total	2	1(7%)	5	1				
Kilbride (3 farms in rental)	1765-70				3				
	1771-5			1					
	1776-80			1	1				
	1781-5								
	Total			2	4				
Bothwell (5 farms in rental)	1765-70			2					
	1771-5								
	1776-80								
	1781-5			2					
	Total			2					

TABLE B (Continued)

Type of farms (included in columns above):

	M	2	1	Uncertain
Hamilton	5	4	11	
Cambuslang	4	1	1	
Dalserf	4		11	2?
Arendale	3	1	8	
Lesmahagow	3	2	17	1?
Bothwell Muir	2	1	4	
Kilbride		2	2	
Bothwell		2	2	
Total	22	11	56	

NOTES TO TABLES A AND B
√ in need of repair
M 3 or more tenants
2 2 tenants
1 single tenant
* but 10 subtenants
** i.e. allows for the assumption that farms staked out, planned or enclosing in the first 5 years would be deducted from the 170 i.e. would not be reorganised a second time.
SOURCE HPL, Burrell Journals, 1763–85.

Appendix 12

Estimated Net Out-Migration from Lanarkshire, Angus, Fife and Ayrshire Parishes

TABLE A   Estimated net out-migration from Lanarkshire parishes, 1755–1790s.

Parish	Pop. 1755	Pop. 1790s	Actual change	Estimated % of age multiplier	Estimated natural increase	Estimated net out-migration	Net out-m. as % of 1755 pop.
Avendale/Strathaven	3,551	3,343	-208	21.6	767	-975	27.5
Biggar	1,098	937	-161	21.6	237	-398	36.3
Blantyre	496	1,040	+542	21.6	107	+435	+87.7
Bothwell	1,561	2,707	+1,146	23.4	365	+781	+50.0
Cadder	2,396	1,769	-627	22.2	532	-1,159	48.4
Cambuslang	934	1,288	+354	21.6	202	+152	+16.3
Cambusnethan	1,419	1,684	+265	21.6	307	-42	3.0
Carluke	1,459	1,730	+271	22.2	324	-53	3.6
Carmichael	899	781	-118	22.8	205	-323	35.9
Carmunnock	471	570	+99	22.8	107	-8	1.7
Carnwath	2,390	3,000	+610	22.8	545	+65	+2.7
Carstairs	845	924	+79	22.8	193	-114	13.5
Covington	521	484	-37	14.4	75	-112	21.5
Crawford	2,009	1,490	-519	21.6	434	-953	47.4
Crawford-John	765	590	-175	21.0	161	-336	43.9
Culter	422	326	-96	21.6	91	-187	44.3
Dalserf	765	1,100	+335	21.6	165	+170	22.2
Dalziel	351	478	+127	22.2	78	+49	14.0
Dolphington	302	200	-102	21.6	65	-167	55.3
Douglas	2,009	1,715	-294	21.6	434	-728	36.2
Dunsyre	359	360	+1	21.6	78	-77	21.5
Glasford	559	788	+229	22.2	124	+105	+18.8
Glasgow	23,546	61,945	+38,399	21.6	5,086	+33,313	+141.5
Gorbals of Glasgow	3,000	5,000	+2,000	21.6	648	+1,352	+45.1
Barony of Glasgow	3,905	18,451	+14,546	21.6	844	+13,702	+350.9
Govan	4,389	8,318	+3,929	22.2	974	+2,955	+67.3
Hamilton	3,815	5,017	+1,202	21.6	824	+378	+9.9

TABLE A (Continued)

Parish	Pop. 1755	Pop. 1790s	Actual change	Estimated % of age multiplier	Estimated natural increase	Estimated net out-migration	Net out-m. as % of 1755 pop.
East Kilbride	2,029	2,359	+330	22.2	450	-120	5.9
Lamington	599	417	-182	22.2	133	-315	52.6
Lanark	2,294	4,751	+2,457	22.2	509	+1,948	+84.9
Lesmahagow	2,996	2,810	-186	22.2	665	-851	28.4
Liberton	708	750	+42	21.6	153	-111	15.7
New/East Monkland	2,713	3,560	+847	22.2	602	+245	+9.0
Old/West Monkland	1,813	4,000	+2,187	22.8	413	+1,774	+97.8
Pettinain	330	386	+56	22.2	73	-17	5.2
Rutherglen	988	1,860	+872	22.2	219	+653	+66.1
Shotts	2,322	2,041	-281	22.8	529	-810	34.9
Stonehouse	823	1,060	+237	21.6	178	+59	7.2
Symington	264	307	+43	22.8	60	-17	6.4
Walston	479	427	-52	22.2	106	-158	33.0
Wistoun & Roberton	1,102	740	-362	21.6	238	-600	54.5

SOURCE *OSA.*

TABLE B   Estimated net out-migration from Angus parishes, 1755–1790s.

Parish	Pop. 1755	Pop. 1790s	Actual change	Estimated % of age multiplier	Estimated natural increase	Estimated net out-migration	Net out-m. as % of 1755 pop.
Aberlemno	943	1,033	+90	21.0	198	108	11.5
Airly	1,012	865	-147	22.2	225	372	36.8
Arbirlot	865	1,055	+190	21.0	182	+8	+0.9
Arbroath	2,098	4,676	+2,578	22.2	466	+2,112	+100.7
Auchterhouse	600	600	0	22.2	137	137	22.8
Barrie	689	796	+107	21.6	149	42	6.1
Brechin	3,181	e5,000	+1,819	21.0	668	+1,151	+36.2
Careston	269	260	-9	21.0	56	65	24.2
Carmylie	730	700	-30	21.0	153	-183	25.1
Cortachy & Clova	1,233	1,020	-213	22.2	274	-487	39.5
Craig	935	1,314	+379	21.0	196	+183	+19.6
Dun	657	500	-157	21.0	138	-295	44.9
Dundee	12,477	e24,000	+11,523	22.2	2,770	+8,753	+70.2
Dunnichen	612	872	+260	21.6	132	+128	+20.9
Edzell	862	963	+101	21.0	181	-80	9.3
Essie & Nevay	500	630	+130	22.8	114	+16	+3.2
Fern	500	490	-10	21.0	105	-115	23.0
Fernell	509	620	+111	21.6	110	+1	+0.2
Forfar	2,450	4,625	+2,175	21.0	515	+1,660	+67.8
Glamis	1,780	2,040	+260	16.8	299	-39	2.2
Glenisla	1,852	1,018	-834	21.6	400	-1,234	66.6
Guthrie	584	571	-13	22.2	130	-143	24.5
Inverarity	996	929	-67	21.0	209	-276	27.7
Inverkeilor	1,286	1,747	461	21.0	270	+191	+14.9
Kettins	1,476	1,100	-376	22.8	337	-713	48.3

TABLE B (Continued)

Parish	Pop. 1755	Pop. 1790s	Actual change	Estimated % of age multiplier	Estimated natural increase	Estimated net out-migration	Net out-m. as % of 1755 pop.
Kingoldrum	780	600	-180	22.8	178	-358	45.9
Kinnell	761	830	+69	21.0	160	-91	12.0
Kinettles	616	621	+5	22.2	137	-132	21.4
Kirkden	563	727	+164	21.0	118	+46	+8.2
Kirriemuir	3,409	e4,500	+1,091	22.2	757	+334	+9.8
Lethnot	635	505	-130	21.0	133	-263	41.4
Liff & Bervie	1,311	1,790	479	22.8	299	+180	+13.7
Lintrathen	1,165	e900	-265	22.8	266	-531	45.6
Lochlee	686	608	-78	22.2	152	-230	33.5
Logie & Pert	696	999	+303	21.6	150	+153	+22.0
Lunan	208	291	+83	21.0	44	+39	+18.8
Lundie & Foulis	586	648	+62	21.0	123	-61	10.4
Mains of Fintry	709	878	+169	22.2	157	+12	+1.7
Maryton	633	529	-104	22.8	144	-248	39.2
Menmuir	743	900	+157	21.0	156	+1	+0.1
Monifeith	1,421	1,218	-203	22.8	324	-527	37.1
Monikie	1,345	1,278	-67	21.0	283	-350	26.0
Montrose	4,150	6,194	+2,044	21.0	872	+1,172	+28.2
Muirhouse	623	462	-161	22.8	142	-303	48.6
Newtyle	913	594	-319	21.6	197	-516	56.5
Oathlaw	435	430	-5	21.0	91	-96	22.1
Panbride	1,259	1,460	+201	21.0	264	-63	5.0
Rescobie	798	934	+136	22.8	182	-46	5.8
Ruthven	280	220	-60	22.2	62	-122	43.6
St Vigeans	1,592	3,336	+1,774	22.8	363	+1,411	+88.6
Strathmartin	368	340	-28	22.8	84	-112	30.4

TABLE B (Continued)

Parish	Pop. 1755	Pop. 1790s	Actual change	Estimated % of age multiplier	Estimated natural increase	Estimated net out-migration	Net out-m. as % of 1755 pop.
Strickathrow	529	672	+143	21.0	111	+32	+6.1
Tannadice	1,470	1,421	-49	21.0	309	-358	24.4
Tealing	735	802	+67	21.6	159	-92	12.5

NOTE e = estimated population figure as shown in relevant parish account.
SOURCE *OSA*.

TABLE C Estimated net out-migration from Fife parishes, 1755–1790s.

Parish	Pop. 1755	Pop. 1790s	Actual change	Estimated % of age multiplier	Estimated natural increase	Estimated net out-migration	Net out–m. as % of 1755 pop.
Abbot's Hall	1,348	2,136	+788	21.6	291	+497	+36.9
Abdie	882	e600	-222	20.4	168	-390	47.5
Aberdour	1,198	1,280	+82	21.0	252	-170	14.2
Anstruther Easter	1,100	1,000	-100	21.0	231	-331	30.1
Anstruther Wester	385	370	-15	21.0	81	-96	24.9
Auchterderran	1,194	1,200	+6	21.0	251	-245	20.5
Auchtermuchty	1,308	1,439	+131	22.2	290	-159	12.2
Auchtertool	389	334	-55	22.2	86	-141	36.3
Ballingry	464	220	-244	21.6	100	-344	74.1
Balmerino	563	703	+140	21.6	122	+18	+3.2
Beath	1,099	e450	-649	21.0	231	-880	80.1
Burntisland	1,390	1,210	-180	21.0	292	-472	34.0
Cameron	1,295	1,165	-130	22.8	295	-425	32.8
Carnbee	1,293	1,041	-252	22.8	295	-547	42.3
Carnock	583	970	+387	21.6	126	+261	+44.8
Ceres	2,540	2,320	-220	21.6	549	-769	30.3
Collessie	989	949	-40	21.6	214	-254	25.7
Crail	2,173	1,710	-463	21.0	456	-919	42.3
Creich	375	306	-69	21.6	81	-150	40.0
Cults	449	534	+85	21.6	97	-12	2.7
Cupar of Fife	2,192	3,702	+1,510	22.8	500	+1,010	+46.1
Dairsie	469	540	+71	21.0	99	-28	6.0
Dalgety	761	869	+108	22.8	174	-66	8.7
Denino	598	383	-215	22.8	136	-351	58.7
Dunbog	255	235	-20	21.0	54	-74	29.0
Dunfermline	8,552	9,550	+998	21.6	1,847	-849	9.3
Dysart	2,367	4,862	+2,495	22.2	526	+1,969	+83.2

TABLE C (Continued)

Parish	Pop. 1755	Pop. 1790s	Actual change	Estimated % of age multiplier	Estimated natural increase	Estimated net out-migration	Net out-m. as % of 1755 pop.
Elie	642	620	-22	24.0	154	-176	27.4
Falkland	1,792	2,195	+1,403	21.0	376	+1,027	+57.3
Ferry-Port-on-Craig	621	875	+254	21.0	130	+124	+20.0
Flisk	318	331	+13	21.0	67	-54	17.0
Forgan	751	875	+124	22.8	171	-47	6.3
Inverkeithing	1,694	2,210	+516	22.8	386	+130	+7.7
Kemback	420	588	+168	22.2	93	+75	+17.9
Kennoway	1,240	1,350	+110	21.0	260	-150	12.1
Kettle	1,621	1,759	+138	21.0	340	-202	12.5
Kilconquhar	2,131	2,013	-118	21.0	448	-566	26.6
Kilmany	785	869	+84	22.8	179	-95	12.1
Kilrenney	1,348	1,086	-262	21.0	283	-545	40.4
Kinghorn	2,389	1,768	-621	22.8	545	-1,166	48.8
Kinglassie	998	1,200	+202	21.0	210	-8	0.8
Kingsbarns	871	807	-64	21.6	188	-252	28.9
Kirkcaldy	2,296	2,673	+377	21.0	482	-105	4.6
Largo	1,396	1,913	+517	21.6	302	+215	+15.4
Leslie	1,130	1,212	+82	18.0	203	-121	10.7
Leuchars	1,691	1,620	-71	22.8	386	-457	27.0
Logie	413	425	+12	22.2	92	-80	19.4
Markinch	2,188	2,800	+612	22.2	486	+126	+5.8
Monimail	884	1,101	+217	21.6	191	+26	+2.9
Moonzie	249	171	-78	22.8	57	-135	54.2
Newburgh	1,347	1,664	+317	22.2	299	+18	+1.3
Newburn	438	456	+18	23.4	103	-85	19.4
Pittenweem	939	1,157	+218	21.0	197	+21	+2.2

TABLE C (Continued)

Parish	Pop. 1755	Pop. 1790s	Actual change	Estimated % of age multiplier	Estimated natural increase	Estimated net out-migration	Net out-m. as % of 1755 pop.
St Andrews & St Leonards	4,590	5,008	+418	21.0	964	-546	11.9
St Monance	780	832	+52	21.0	164	-112	14.4
Saline	1,285	950	-335	22.8	293	-628	48.9
Scoonie	1,528	1,675	+147	21.6	330	-183	12.0
Strathmiglo	*1,095	980	-115	21.0	230	-345	31.5
Torryburn	1,635	1,600	-35	21.6	353	-388	23.7
Wemyss	3,041	3,025	-16	21.6	657	-673	22.1

NOTES e = estimated population figure as shown in relevant parish account.
 * Given total (1775) = 1695. This is thought to be too high since 1754 total was c.1100.

SOURCE *OSA*.

TABLE D Estimated net out-migration from Ayrshire parishes, 1755–1790s.

Parish	Pop. 1755	Pop. 1790s	Actual change	Estimated % of age multiplier	Estimated natural increase	Estimated net out-migration	Net out-m. as % of 1755 pop.
Ardrossan	1,297	1,518	+221	21.6	280	-59	4.6
Auchinleck	887	775	-112	21.6	192	-304	34.3
Ayr	2,964	4,647	+1,683	21.6	640	+1,043	+35.2
Ballantrae	1,049	770	-279	21.0	220	-499	47.6
Barr	858	750	-108	21.6	185	-293	34.2
Beith	2,064	2,872	+808	21.6	446	+362	+17.5
Colmonell	1,814	1,100	-714	21.0	381	-1,095	60.4
Coylton	527	667	+140	21.0	111	+29	+5.5
Craigie	551	700	+149	21.0	116	+33	+6.0
New Cumnock	1,497	1,200	-297	21.6	323	-620	41.4
Old Cumnock	1,336	1,632	+296	21.6	289	+7	+0.5
Dailly	839	1,607	+768	21.6	181	+587	+70.0
Dalmellington	739	681	-58	22.2	164	-222	30.0
Dalry	1,498	2,000	+502	22.2	333	+169	+11.3
Dalrymple	439	380	-59	21.0	92	-151	34.4
Dreghorn	887	830	-57	21.0	186	-243	27.4
Dundonald	983	1,317	+334	22.2	218	+116	+11.8
Dunlop	796	779	-17	21.6	172	-189	23.7
Fenwick	1,113	1,281	+168	22.8	254	-86	7.7
Galston	1,013	1,577	+564	21.0	213	+351	+34.7
Girvan	1,103	1,725	+622	21.6	238	+384	+34.8
Irvine	4,025	4,500	+475	21.0	845	-370	9.2
Kilbirny	651	700	+49	21.6	141	-92	21.7
West Kilbride	885	698	-187	21.6	191	-378	42.7
Kilmarnock	4,405	6,776	+2,371	21.0	925	+1,446	+32.8
Kilmaurs	1,094	1,147	+53	22.2	243	-190	17.4
Kilwinning	2,541	2,360	-181	22.2	564	-745	29.3

TABLE D (Continued)

Parish	Pop. 1755	Pop. 1790s	Actual change	Estimated % of age multiplier	Estimated natural increase	Estimated net out-migration	Net out-m. as % of 1755 pop.
Kirkmichael	710	956	+246	21.6	153	+93	+13.1
Kirkoswald	1,168	1,335	+167	21.6	252	-85	7.3
Largs	1,164	1,025	-139	21.0	244	-383	32.9
Loudoun	1,494	2,308	+814	21.6	323	+491	+32.9
Mauchline	1,169	1,800	+631	21.6	253	+378	+32.3
Maybole	2,058	3,000	+942	21.0	432	+510	+24.8
Monkton & Prestwick	e582	717	+135	22.2	129	+6	+1.0
Muirkirk	745	e1,100	+355	21.6	161	+194	+26.0
Newton-upon-Ayr	e581	1,750	+1,169	21.0	122	+1,047	+180.0
Ochiltree	1,210	1,150	-60	22.2	269	-329	27.2
Ricarton	745	e1,000	+255	22.2	165	+90	+12.1
St Quivox	499	1,450	+951	22.2	111	+840	+168.3
Sorn	1,494	2,779	+1,285	25.2	377	+908	+60.8
Stair	369	518	+149	21.6	80	+69	+18.7
Stevenson	1,412	2,425	+1,013	21.6	305	+708	+50.1
Stewarton	2,819	e2,400	-419	22.2	626	-1,045	37.1
Straiton	1,123	934	-189	21.6	243	-432	38.5
Symington	359	610	+251	22.2	80	+171	+47.6
Tarbolton	1,356	e1,200	-165	24.6	336	-501	36.7

NOTE e = estimated population figure as shown in relevant parish account.
SOURCE *OSA*.

Bibliography

MANUSCRIPT SOURCES

National Register of Archives (Scotland)

874	Dr John Berry Papers
859	Sir Alexander F. Douglas-Home Papers
0094	Earl of Glasgow Papers
2177	Hamilton Papers
792	Earl of Southesk Papers
885	Earl of Strathmore Papers

Hamilton Public Library

631/1	Burrell Journals, 1763–1808, 46 volumes.

National Library of Scotland

Acc. 4322	Lockhart of Lee Papers
Acc. 5474	Lockhart of Lee Papers
Acc. 5976	Lockhart Papers
Acc. 8217	Stuart of Castlemilk Papers
Acc. 8220	Stuart of Castlemilk Papers

Session Papers: Campbell (1717–1816), Douglas (1752–71), Elphinstone (1780–1819), Hermand (1756–1820), Kames (1752–68), Kilkerran (1736–57), Meadowbank (1750–1814), and Pitfour (1740–74) Collections.

Scottish Record Office

SC20/5	Sheriff Court Processes, Cupar
SC44/22	Sheriff Court Processes, Dunblane
SC37/8	Sheriff Court Processes, Hamilton
SC38/22	Sheriff Court Processes, Lanark
SC41/6	Sheriff Court Processes, Linlithgow
SC42/5	Sheriff Court Processes, Peebles
GD16	Airlie Muniments
GD288	Balfour of Balbirnie Muniments
GD5/497	Bertram of Nisbet Papers
GD1/732	Blantyre Papers
RH2/8/75	Cunninghame of Auchinharvie Papers

GD45	Dalhousie Muniments
GD3	Eglinton Muniments
GD179/3697	Handaxwood Papers
GD26	Leven and Melville Muniments
GD150	Morton Papers
GD213/54	Oswald of Auchincruive Papers
GD86/770	Berwick Poll Tax Lists, 1693
E79/8/A	Midlothian Poll Tax Lists, 1693
GD178/2	Selkirk Poll Tax Lists, 1893
E70/13	West Lothian Poll Tax Lists, 1693
CH2/35/9	Biggar Presbytery Records
CH2/56/4	Carluke Kirk Session Records
CH2/57/2	Carmichael Kirk Session Records
CH2/60/3	Carnwath Kirk Session Records
CH2/63/2	Carstairs Kirk Session Records
CH2/72/1	Covington Kirk Session Records
CH2/522/1	Crawford Kirk Session Records
CH2/451/1	Culter Kirk Session Records
CH2/953/2	Douglas Kirk Session Records
CH2/115/1	Dunsyre Kirk Session Records
CH2/522/4	Kirkpatrick Kirk Session Records
CH2/404/1	Lamington Kirk Session Records
CH2/301/2	Pettinain Kirk Session Records
CH2/376/4	Roberton Kirk Session Records
CH2/363/2	Walston Kirk Session Records
CH2/376/3	Wiston Kirk Session Records
CH1/2/86	General Assembly Papers
CH1/187	General Assembly Papers

CONTEMPORARY PRINTED SOURCES

R. Beatson, *General View of the Agriculture of the County of Fife* (Edinburgh, 1797).
Edinburgh Evening Courant, 1750–5.
W. Fullarton, *General View of the Agriculture of the County of Ayr* (Edinburgh, 1793).
J. B. Greenshields, *Annals of the Parish of Lesmahagow* (Edinburgh, 1864).
J. Headrick, *Agriculture of Angus* (Edinburgh, 1813).
T. S. Keith, *General View of the Agriculture of the County of Aberdeenshire* (Edinburgh, 1814).
J. Naismith, *General View of the Agriculture of the County of Clydesdale* (Edinburgh, 1794).
G. Robertson, *Rural Recollections* (Irvine, 1820).
Revd Mr Roger, *General View of the Agriculture of Angus* (Edinburgh, 1794).
D. Semple, ed., *Renfrewshire Poll Tax Returns* (Glasgow, 1864).
Sir John Sinclair, ed., *The Statistical Account of Scotland, 1791–97* (Edinburgh, 1791–7), 21 vols. New edition by I. Grant and D. J. Withrington (Wakefield, 1975–9).
Sir J. Sinclair, *General Report of the Agricultural State and Political Circumstances of Scotland* (Edinburgh, 1814).
Sir J. Sinclair, *Analysis of the Statistical Account of Scotland* (Edinburgh, 1825).
John Stuart, ed., *List of Pollable Persons within the Shire of Aberdeen, 1696* (Aberdeen, 1844), 2 vols.
A. Wight, *Present State of Husbandry in Scotland* (Edinburgh, 1778).

SECONDARY SOURCES

Unpublished Theses

I. H. Adams, 'Division of Commonty in Scotland', Ph.D. Thesis, University of Edinburgh, 1967.

P. Clapham, 'Agrarian Reform on the Airlie Estate', M.Phil. Thesis, University of Strathclyde, 1990.

J. Morrison, 'Rural Society in the Lothians, 1790–1850', M.Litt. Thesis, University of Strathclyde, 1985.

D. B. Walker, 'The Agricultural Buildings of Greater Strathmore, 1770–1920', Ph.D. Thesis, University of Dundee, 1983.

Articles

I. H. Adams, 'The Land Surveyor and His Influence on the Scottish Rural Landscape', *SGM*, 84 (1968), pp. 248–55.

I. H. Adams and I. D. Whyte, 'The Agricultural Revolution in Scotland: Contributions to the Debate', *Area*, 9 (1977), pp. 198–205.

I. H. Adams, I. D. Whyte and M. L. Parry, 'The Agricultural Revolution in Scotland: Contributions to the Debate', *Area*, 10 (1978), pp. 198–205.

W. A. Armstrong, 'Labour I: Rural Population Growth, Systems of Employment and Incomes' in G. E. Mingay, ed., *The Agrarian History of England and Wales, vol. VI, 1750–1850* (Cambridge, 1989).

J. V. Beckett, 'Landownership and Estate Management' in G. E. Mingay, ed., *The Agrarian History of England and Wales, vol. VI, 1750–1850* (Cambridge, 1989).

C. G. Brown, 'Religion and Social Change' in T. M. Devine and R. Mitchison, eds, *People and Society in Scotland, I, 1760–1830* (Edinburgh, 1988).

C. G. Brown, 'Protest in the Pews. Interpreting Presbyterianism and Society in Fracture during the Scottish Economic Revolution' in T. M. Devine, ed., *Conflict and Stability in Scottish Society, 1700–1850* (Edinburgh, 1990).

R. H. Campbell, 'The Scottish Improvers and the Course of Agrarian Change in the Eighteenth Century' in L. M. Cullen and T. C. Smout, eds, *Comparative Aspects of Scottish and Irish Economic and Social History, 1600–1900* (Edinburgh, 1977).

R. H. Campbell, 'The Landed Classes' in T. M. Devine and R. Mitchison, eds, *People and Society in Scotland, I, 1760–1830* (Edinburgh, 1988).

L. M. Cullen and T. C. Smout, 'Introduction' in L. M. Cullen and T. C. Smout, eds, *Comparative Aspects of Scottish and Irish Economic and Social History, 1600–1900* (Edinburgh, 1977).

T. M. Devine, 'Glasgow Colonial Merchants and Land, 1770–1815' in J. T. Ward and R. G. Wilson, eds, *Land and Industry: The Landed Estate in the Industrial Revolution* (Newton Abbot, 1971).

T. M. Devine, 'Temporary Migration and the Scottish Highlands in the Nineteenth Century', *Econ. Hist. Rev.*, 2nd ser., XXXII (1979), pp. 344–59.

T. M. Devine, 'Social Stability in the Rural Lowlands of Scotland, 1780–1840' in T. M. Devine, ed., *Lairds and Improvement in the Scotland of the Enlightenment: The Proceedings of the Ninth Scottish Historical Conference, University of Edinburgh, 1978* (Glasgow, 1979).

T. M. Devine, 'The English Connection and Irish-Scottish Development in the Eighteenth Century' in T. M. Devine and D. Dickson, eds, *Ireland and Scotland, 1600–1850: Parallels and Contrasts in Economic and Social Development* (Edinburgh, 1983).

T. M. Devine, 'Scottish Farm Labour During the Agricultural Depression,

1870–1914' in T. M. Devine, ed., *Farm Servants and Labour in Lowland Scotland, 1770–1914* (Edinburgh, 1984).

T. M. Devine, 'Scottish Farm Service in the Agricultural Revolution, 1780–1840' in T. M. Devine, ed., *Farm Servants and Labour in Lowland Scotland, 1770–1840* (Edinburgh, 1984).

T. M. Devine, 'Women Workers, 1850–1915' in T. M. Devine, ed., *Farm Servants and Labour in Lowland Scotland, 1770–1840* (Edinburgh, 1984).

T. M. Devine, 'The Union of 1707 and Scottish Development', *Scottish Economic and Social History*, 5 (1985), pp. 23–40.

T. M. Devine, 'Introduction' in T. M. Devine and R. Mitchison, eds, *People and Society in Scotland, I, 1760–1830* (Edinburgh, 1988).

T. M. Devine, 'Scottish Society, 1760–1830' in T. M. Devine and R. Mitchison, eds, *People and Society in Scotland, I, 1760–1830* (Edinburgh, 1988).

T. M. Devine, 'Unrest and Stability in Rural Ireland and Scotland, 1760–1840' in R. Mitchison and P. Roebuck, eds, *Economy and Society in Scotland and Ireland, 1500–1939* (Edinburgh, 1988).

T. M. Devine, 'Urbanisation' in T. M. Devine and R. Mitchison, eds, *People and Society in Scotland, I, 1760–1830* (Edinburgh, 1988).

T. M. Devine, 'Social Responses to Agrarian Improvement: The Highland and Lowland Clearances in Scotland, 1500–1850' in R. A. Houston and I. D. White, *Scottish Society, 1500–1800* (Cambridge, 1989).

T. M. Devine, 'The Failure of Radical Reform in Scotland in the Late Eighteenth Century: The Social and Economic Context' in T. M. Devine, ed., *Conflict and Stability in Scottish Society, 1700–1850* (Edinburgh, 1990).

T. M. Devine, 'The Paradox of Scottish Emigration' in T. M. Devine, ed., *Scottish Emigration and Scottish Society* (Edinburgh, 1992).

R. A. Dodgshon, 'The Removal of Runrig in Roxburghshire, 1680–1766', *Scottish Studies*, 16 (1972), pp. 121–37.

R. A. Dodgshon, 'The Nature and Development of Infield–Outfield in Scotland', *TIBG*, 59 (1973), pp. 1–23.

R. A. Dodgshon, 'Runrig and the Communal Origins of Property in Land', *Juridical Review*, 20 (1975), pp. 189–208.

R. A. Dodgshon, 'Towards an Understanding and Definition of Runrig: The Evidence for Roxburghshire and Berwickshire', *TIBG*, 64 (1975), pp. 15–33.

R. A. Dodgshon, 'Farming in Roxburghshire and Berwickshire on the Eve of Improvement', *Scott. Hist. Rev.*, LIV, no. 158 (1975), pp. 140–54.

R. A. Dodgshon, 'Agricultural Change and its Social Consequences in the Southern Uplands of Scotland, 1660–1780' in T. M. Devine and D. Dickson, eds, *Ireland and Scotland, 1600–1850* (Edinburgh, 1983).

F. Dovring, 'The Transformation of European Agriculture' in *Cambridge Economic History of Europe* (Cambridge, 1965).

A. Fenton, 'The Rural Economy of East Lothian in the Seventeenth and Eighteenth Centuries', *Transactions of East Lothian Antiquarian and Field Naturalists Society*, 9 (1963), pp. 1–23.

W. Ferguson, 'The Electoral System in the Scottish Counties before 1832' in Stair Society, *Miscellany II* (Edinburgh, 1984).

M. W. Flinn, 'Trends in Real Wages, 1750–1850', *Econ. Hist. Rev.*, 2nd ser., XXVII (1974), pp. 395–413.

W. H. Fraser, 'Patterns of Protest' in T. M. Devine and R. Mitchison, eds, *People and Society in Scotland, I, 1760–1830* (Edinburgh, 1988).

A. Geddes, 'The Changing Landscape of the Lothians, 1600–1800, as Revealed in Old Estate Plans', *SGM*, 54 (1938), pp. 129–43.

A. Gibson, 'Proletarianisation? The Transition to Full-Time Labour on a Scottish

Estate, 1723–1787', *Continuity and Change*, 53 (1990), pp. 357–89.

M. Gray, 'Scottish Emigration: The Social Impact of Agrarian Change in the Rural Lowlands, 1775–1875', *Perspectives of American History*, VII (1974), pp. 95–174.

M. Gray, 'North East Agriculture and the Labour Force, 1790–1875' in A. A. MacLaren, ed., *Social Class in Scotland: Past and Present* (Edinburgh, 1976).

M. Gray, 'Migration in the Rural Lowlands of Scotland, 1750–1850' in T. M. Devine and D. Dickson, eds, *Ireland and Scotland, 1600–1850* (Edinburgh, 1983).

M. Gray, 'The Social Impact of Agrarian Change in the Rural Lowlands' in T. M. Devine and R. Mitchison, eds, *People and Society in Scotland, I, 1760–1830* (Edinburgh, 1988).

E. J. Hobsbawm, 'Scottish Reformers of the Eighteenth Century and Capitalist Agriculture' in E. J. Hobsbawm *et al*, eds, *Peasants in History* (Oxford, 1980).

B. A. Holderness, 'Prices, Productivity and Output' in G. E. Mingay, ed., *The Agrarian History of England and Wales, vol. VI, 1750–1850* (Cambridge, 1989).

R. A. Houston, 'Geographical Mobility in Scotland, 1652–1811', *Journal of Historical Geography*, 11 (1985), pp. 379–94.

E. H. Hunt and F. W. Botham, 'Wages in Britain during the Industrial Revolution', *Econ. Hist. Rev.*, 2nd ser., XL (1987), pp. 380–99.

G. Kay, 'The Landscape of Improvement: A Case Study of Agricultural Change in North-East Scotland', *SGM*, 78 (1962), pp. 100–11.

J. H. G. Lebon, 'The Face of the Countryside in Central Ayrshire During the Eighteenth and Nineteenth Centuries', *SGM*, 62 (1946), pp. 7–15.

J. H. G. Lebon, 'The Process of Enclosure in the Western Lowlands', *SGM*, 62 (1946), pp. 100–10.

D. G. Lockhart, 'Sources for Studies of Migration to Estate Villages in North East Scotland', *Local Historian*, 14 (1980), pp. 35–43.

D. G. Lockhart, 'The Planned Villages' in M. L. Parry and T. R. Slater, eds, *The Making of the Scottish Countryside* (London, 1980).

G. E. Mingay, 'Introduction' in Mingay, ed., *The Agrarian History of England and Wales, vol. VI, 1750–1850* (Cambridge, 1989).

R. Mitchison, 'The Movements of Scottish Corn Prices in the Seventeenth and Eighteenth Centuries', *Econ. Hist. Rev.*, 2nd ser., XVIII (1965), pp. 278–91.

R. Mitchison, 'The Making of the Old Scottish Poor Law', *Past and Present*, 63 (1974), pp. 58–93.

R. Mitchison, 'The Poor Law' in T. M. Devine and R. Mitchison, eds, *People and Society in Scotland, I, 1760–1830* (Edinburgh, 1988).

V. Morgan, 'Agricultural Wage Rates in Late Eighteenth Century Scotland', *Econ. Hist. Rev.*, 2nd ser., XXIV (1971), pp. 181–201.

S. Nenadic, 'The Rise of the Urban Middle Classes' in T. M. Devine and R. Mitchison, eds, *People and Society in Scotland, I, 1760–1830* (Edinburgh, 1988).

M. Overton, 'Agricultural Revolution? Development of the Agrarian Economy in Early Modern England' in A. R. H. Baker and D. J. Gregory, eds, *Explorations in Historical Geography* (Cambridge, 1984).

M. L. Parry, 'Secular Climatic Change and Marginal Agriculture', *TIBG*, 64 (1975), pp. 1–13.

M. L. Parry and D. Mill, 'A Scottish Agricultural Revolution?', *Area*, 8 (1976), pp. 237–9.

R. Perren, 'Markets and Marketing' in G. E. Mingay, ed., *The Agrarian History of England and Wales, vol. VI, 1750–1850* (Cambridge, 1989).

J. H. Porter, 'The Development of Rural Society' in G. E. Mingay, ed., *The Agrarian History of England and Wales, vol. VI, 1750–1850* (Cambridge, 1989).

E. Richards, 'Patterns of Highland Discontent, 1790–1860' in R. Quinault and R. Stevenson, eds, *Popular Protest and Public Order* (London, 1974).

W. P. Robinson, 'Richard Oswald the Peacemaker', *Ayrshire Arch. and Nat. Hist. Colls*, 2nd ser., III (1959), pp. 119–35.

T. R. Slater, 'The Mansion and Policy' in M. L. Parry and T. R. Slater, eds, *The Making of the Scottish Countryside* (London, 1980).

T. C. Smout, 'Scottish Landowners and Economic Growth, 1650–1850', *Scottish Journal of Political Economy*, 11 (1964), pp. 218–34.

T. C. Smout, 'The Landowner and the Planned Village in Scotland, 1730–1830' in N. T. Phillipson and R. Mitchison, eds, *Scotland in the Age of Improvement* (Edinburgh, 1970).

T. C. Smout and A. Fenton, 'Scottish Agriculture before the Improvers – an Exploration', *Agricultural History Review*, 13 (1965), pp. 73–93.

B. M. W. Third, 'Changing Landscape and Social Structure in the Scottish Lowlands as Revealed by Eighteenth Century Estate Plans', *SGM*, 71 (1955), pp. 83–93.

B. M. W. Third, 'The Significance of Scottish Estate Plans and Associated Documents', *Scottish Studies*, I (1957), pp. 39–64.

L. Timperley, 'The Pattern of Landholding in Eighteenth-Century Scotland' in M. L. Parry and T. R. Slater, eds, *The Making of the Scottish Countryside* (London, 1980).

J. H. Treble, 'The Standard of Living of the Working Class' in T. M. Devine and R. Mitchison, eds, *People and Society in Scotland, I, 1760–1830* (Edinburgh, 1988).

B. Walker, 'The "Great Rebuilding" on a Scottish Estate', *SGM*, 101 3 (1985), pp. 139–48.

C. A. Whatley, 'The Experience of Work', in T. M. Devine and R. Mitchison, eds, *People and Society in Scotland, In, 1760–1830* (Edinburgh, 1988).

C. A. Whatley, 'How Tame were the Scottish Lowlanders during the Eighteenth Century?' in T. M. Devine, ed., *Conflict and Stability in Scottish Society, 1760–1850* (Edinburgh, 1990).

G. Whittington, 'Was there a Scottish Agricultural Revolution?', *Area*, 7 (1975), pp. 204–6.

G. Whittington, 'Agriculture and Society in Lowland Scotland, 1750–1870' in G. Whittington and I. D. Whyte, eds, *An Historical Geography of Scotland* (London, 1983).

I. D. Whyte and K. A. Whyte, 'Some Aspects of the Structure of Rural Society in Seventeenth Century Lowland Scotland' in T. M. Devine and D. Dickson, eds, *Ireland and Scotland, 1600–1850* (Edinburgh, 1983), pp. 32–40.

I. D. Whyte and K. A. Whyte, 'Continuity and Change in a Seventeenth Century Scottish Farming Community', *Agricultural History Review*, 32 (1984), pp. 159–69.

I. D. Whyte and K. A. Whyte, 'Poverty and Prosperity in a Seventeenth Century Scottish Farming Community' in R. Mitchison and P. Roebuck, eds, *Scotland and Ireland: A Comparative Study of Development* (Edinburgh, 1987).

D. J. Withrington, 'Schooling, Literacy and Society' in T. M. Devine and R. Mitchison, eds, *People and Society in Scotland, I, 1760–1830* (Edinburgh, 1988).

J. R. Wordie, 'The Chronology of English Enclosure, 1500–1914', *Econ. Hist. Rev.*, 2nd ser., XXXVI (1983), pp. 483–505.

E. A. Wrigley, 'A Simple Model of London's Importance in Changing English Society and Economy, 1650–1750', *Past and Present*, 37 (1967), pp. 44–70.

Books

I. H. Adams, *Directory of Commonties* (Edinburgh, 1971).

I. H. Adams, ed., *Descriptive List of Plans in the Scottish Record Office*, vols 1–3 (Edinburgh, 1966, 1970, 1974).

J. R. Allan, *The North-East Lowlands of Scotland* (London, 1952).

M. Berg, *The Age of Manufactures* (London, 1985).

J. Blum, *The End of the Old Order in Rural Europe* (New Jersey, 1978).

C. G. Brown, *The Social History of Religion in Scotland Since 1700* (London, 1987).

R. A. Cage, *The Scottish Poor Law, 1745–1845* (Edinburgh, 1981).

R. Callander, *A Pattern of Landownership in Scotland* (Haughend, 1987).

R. H. Campbell and A. S. Skinner, eds, *The Origin and Nature of the Scottish Enlightenment* (Edinburgh, 1982).

I. Carter, *Farm Life in North-East Scotland* (Edinburgh, 1979).

E. Cregeen, ed., *Argyll Estate Instructions, 1771–1805* (Edinburgh, 1964).

L. M. Cullen and T. C. Smout, *Comparative Aspects of Scottish and Irish Economic and Social History, 1600–1900* (Edinburgh, 1977).

T. M. Devine, ed., *Lairds and Improvement in the Scotland of the Enlightenment* (Glasgow, 1979).

T. M. Devine, ed., *Farm Servants and Labour in Lowland Scotland, 1770–1914* (Edinburgh, 1984).

T. M. Devine, *The Great Highland Famine* (Edinburgh, 1988).

T. M. Devine, ed., *Conflict and Stability in Scottish Society, 1700–1850* (Edinburgh, 1990).

T. M. Devine, *The Tobacco Lords* (Edinburgh, 1990 edn).

T. M. Devine and D. Dickson, eds, *Ireland and Scotland, 1600–1850* (Edinburgh, 1983).

T. M. Devine and R. Mitchison, eds, *People and Society in Scotland, I, 1760–1830* (Edinburgh, 1988).

J. de Vries, *European Urbanisation, 1500–1800* (London 1987).

T. Dickson, ed., *Scottish Capitalism: Class, State and Nation from Before the Union to the Present* (London, 1980).

R. A. Dodgshon, *Land and Society in Early Scotland* (Oxford, 1981).

A. Fenton, *Scottish Country Life* (Edinburgh, 1976).

M. W. Flinn, ed., *Scottish Population History from the Seventeenth Century to the 1930s* (Cambridge, 1977).

H. Hamilton, *Life and Labour on an Aberdeenshire Estate, 1735–50* (Aberdeen, 1946).

H. Hamilton, *An Economic History of Scotland in the Eighteenth Century* (Oxford, 1963).

J. Handley, *The Irish in Scotland, 1798–1845* (Cork, 1943).

J. Handley, *Scottish Farming in the Eighteenth Century* (Edinburgh, 1953).

J. Handley, *The Agricultural Revolution in Scotland* (Glasgow, 1963).

E. J. Hobsbawm *et al.*, eds, *Peasants in History* (Oxford, 1980).

B. A. Holderness, *Pre-Industrial Britain: Economy and Society, 1500–1700* (London, 1976).

R. A. Houston, *Scottish Literacy and the Scottish Identity* (Cambridge, 1985).

R. A. Houston and I. D. Whyte, eds, *Scottish Society, 1500–1800* (Cambridge, 1989).

A. Kussmaul, *A General View of the Rural Economy of England, 1538–1840* (Cambridge, 1990).

L. Leneman, ed., *Perspectives in Scottish Social History* (Aberdeen, 1988).

K. J. Logue, *Popular Disturbances in Scotland, 1780–1815* (Edinburgh, 1980).

M. Lynch, ed., *The Early Modern Town in Scotland* (London, 1987).

M. Lynch, *Scotland: A New History* (London, 1991).

S. G. E. Lythe, *The Economy of Scotland in its European Setting, 1550–1625* (Edinburgh, 1960).

A. A. MacLaren, ed., *Social Class in Scotland, Past and Present* (Edinburgh, 1976).

G. E. Mingay, ed., *The Agrarian History of England and Wales, vol. VI. 1750–1850* (Cambridge, 1989).

R. Mitchison, *A History of Scotland* (London, 1970).

R. Mitchison and P. Roebuck, eds, *Economy and Society in Scotland and Ireland, 1500–1939* (Edinburgh, 1983).

N. Murray, *The Scottish Handloom Weavers: A Social History, 1790–1850* (Edinburgh, 1978).

M. L. Parry and T. R. Slater, eds, *The Making of the Scottish Countryside* (London, 1980).

N. T. Phillipson and R. Mitchison, eds, *Scotland in the Age of Improvement* (Edinburgh, 1970).

S. Pollard, *The Genesis of Modern Management* (London, 1965).

L. J. Saunders, *Scottish Democracy: The Social and Intellectual Background, 1815–1840* (Edinburgh, 1950).

T. Shanin, ed., *Peasants and Peasant Societies* (London, 1971).

J. S. Shaw, *The Management of Scottish Society, 1707–1764* (Edinburgh, 1983).

B. H. Slicher Van Bath, *Agrarian History of Western Europe, 1500–1850* (London, 1963).

T. C. Smout, *A History of the Scottish People* (London, 1969).

J. A. Symon, *Scottish Farming, Past and Present* (Edinburgh, 1959).

A. E. Whetstone, *Scottish County Government in the Eighteenth and Nineteenth Centuries* (Edinburgh, 1981).

G. Whittington and I. D. Whyte, eds, *An Historical Geography of Scotland* (London, 1983).

I. D. Whyte, *Agriculture and Society in Seventeenth Century Scotland* (Edinburgh, 1979).

Index

and dispossession 136–9
on the Hamilton estate, Lanarkshire 11–12, 94, 139
reduction in numbers 137–8
summonses of removal 118–19

tacks, *see* leases
Tait, John 75
Tawney, R. H. 1
Tayfield estate, Fife 141
tenant farmers 5–11, 15
    and agricultural improvements 60, 65–74
    bankruptcies 112, 115
    on the Cavens and Preston estate 81–3
    collective action by 66–7
    and commercialisation 44
    control and supervision of, on the Hamilton estate, Lanarkshire 106–9
    and dispossession 111–35
    Douglas estate, Lanarkshire 86–7
    education 68
    erosion of multiple tenancies 68
    Hamilton estate, Lanarkshire 96, 100, 104–6, 106–9
    and improving leases 70–4
    legal action against landlords 67
    local variations in reduction of 125–7
    mobility of 67–8, 115
    numbers of 28, 133–4
    obligations to landowners 63
    single and multiple tenancies 4, 9–11, 20, 24, 25–9, 111, 134, 166; and dispossession 119–22, 125, 142; on the Hamilton estate, Lanarkshire 96, 100, 104–6
    and size of holding 7–8
    turnover of 115–18; on the Hamilton estate, Lanarkshire 96–7
textile production
    growth in 36, 40
    in rural communities 14, 40

theft 158
Thomson, John 127
Tiree, island of 134
towns, development of small 133, 146, 152–3, 156–7
tradesmen, as cottars 14
transport developments 41, 50
turnip husbandry 51, 55, 144
turnpike trusts 41

Union of the Parliaments (1707) 19–20
urban population 35–6, 37
urbanisation 16, 35–6, 37–40

villages
    creation of, on the Douglas estate, Lanarkshire 87–8
    development of country 40–1, 128, 133, 146, 151–3, 156–7

wage labourers, and dispossession 112, 157
wages
    of farm labour 140, 144
    increase in 37, 144, 154
Walker, William 139
Wallace-Dunlop, Sir Thomas, of Craigie 70
Watson, William 133
weather conditions 3
    and agricultural crisis 74, 75, 107
Webster, Alexander 35
West Calder, religious dissent 159–60
West Lothian
    poll tax returns 5, 184–8
    tenant farmers 5, 10, 11
Whyte, I. D. 8, 19, 20
Wiston, Lanarkshire 143, 146
woollen manufacture 14
Wreaths farm, Cavens estate 81, 82–3

Young, James 142
Young, William 142